INDIA AND SOUTH EAST ASIA

INDIA AND SOUTH EAST ASIA

The Security Cooperation

Lieutenant General Yoginder Mohan Bammi (Retd)

United Service Institution of India
Ministry of External Affairs Chair

GYAN PUBLISHING HOUSE
NEW DELHI-110002

India and South East Asia - The Security Cooperation

Rs. 540

ISBN: 81-212-0880-7

Published in 2006 in India by
Gyan Publishing House
5, Ansari Road, Darya Ganj, New Delhi-110002
Phones : 23282060, 23261060, Fax : 011-23285914
E-mail : gyanbook@vsnl.com
Website : http://www.gyanbooks.com

Laser Typesetting at : Shiva Infosystem, Delhi
Printed at : Salasar Imaging System, Delhi

Contents

	Preface	7
	Introduction	11
1.	Concept of Security in 21st Century	13
2.	The Region	17
3.	The South China Sea	91
4.	ASEAN and Other Regional Groupings	103
5.	Countries with Interest in the Area	117
6.	Security Threats to the Region	149
7.	India and the Region-Past and Future	183
8.	Proposed "Look East" Policy for India – 2035	215
9.	Conclusion	227
	Appendices	
	A Comparative Social Data-ASEAN Countries-2002	231
	B Comparative Data of ASEAN Countries (Economic Status)	232
	C Growth Rate of ASEAN Countries 1991-98	234
	D Global Flow of FDI to ASEAN, China and India 1987 to 1998 (In Us $ Millions)	235
	E FDI to ASEAN and India From Selected Countries	236
	F Comparative Data – Armed Forces of South East Asian Countries	237

G Growth of Military Strength of South East Asian Countries-1990/91 to 2001/2002 238
H Growth of Naval Power of South East Asian Countries-1991-2001 241
J Growth of Air Power of South East Asian Countries 245
K Profile of Air Power of South East Asian Countries 246
L Direction of Trade of India-Exports (In Crores) 248
M India's Buisness Ventures and Investments in South East Asia-1994-99 and Comparative Investment Flow to Manufacturing Sector in Projects in South East Asia Through Foreign Investment, Country Wise - From 1990 to 1998 (In US $) 253
N India's Exports to Foreign Countries 254
Q India's Exports to Countries of South East Asia 255
R Scope of Enhancing Imports and Exports Between India and South East Asian Countries

Index 257

Preface

This research project was undertaken to "analyse the security threats being faced by countries of South East Asia, and the role that India can play" to mitigate them. Having served as Defence Advisor with our High Commissions in Malaysia and Singapore from 1977 to 1980, the developments in South East Asia, over a period, have been of great interest to me. Thus, I undertook the study, under the aegis of the Centre for Research of the United Service Institution of India, New Delhi.

The topic is of perpetual interest to India, as her geographical location lends her to be a bridge between West and East Asia. India has historic ties and influence in the region. The Indian Ocean is her lifeline, which dominates all sea routes between the Middle East and South East and East Asia. Thus, peace, stability and security in the region is of importance to India.

The study proposes to first comprehend the implications of security in the present day environment and then discuss the importance of South East Asia to India. Thereafter, with a brief historical perspective, an attempt has been made to identify strengths and weaknesses of each country of the region. Efforts to analyse the strategic interests of non-South East Asian powers in the region has also been made, and the importance of the South China Sea considered.

In the last two decades, India has made major gains in science and technology, medical and industrial fields. Besides a pool of skilled manpower, she has a well-trained and modern Defence Force. Her economic status and policy of non-interference in other's internal matters bestow upon her the advantage of extending assistance to developed and under-developed countries, so that they can manage their own security. Hence, an attempt has been made to examine India's relations with each country and the region as such, to identify fields for enhancing the cooperation.

In the quest to understand the subject, two prominent books, *India and the Indian Ocean*[1] by Sardar K M Panikkar and *The Indianised States of Southeast Asia*[2] by G Codes, were studied. Views of a number of India's retired ambassadors, with expertise in the region were sought, prominent among them being E Gonzalves, N Ram, S T Devare, Rajiv Sikri, G Parthasarthy, C V Ranganathan and S K Bhutani. Dr Swarn Singh and Dr B Ghoshal, both Professors in the Jawaharlal Nehru University, New Delhi spared their time to explain their perceptions. The diplomatic missions of China, Indonesia, the Philippines, Singapore, Thailand, Australia, Vietnam, Malaysia and Myanmar in India, and the foreign officers from South East Asian countries attending the National Defence College, New Delhi, were approached for their views. The East Asia Division of the Ministry of External Affairs, and the Regional Information Secretariat for South East Asia, New Delhi were able to explain India's stand on various issues.

The thrust of the study, therefore, is on what India can do in South East Asia, in the next three decades or so. It is hoped that the study will re-kindle India's interest in the region and will be beneficial to all. The study concludes with identification of areas of diplomatic, economic and military cooperation and recommends a futuristic *Vision for India's Look East Policy up to year 2035,* in phases.

References

1. Sardar K. M. Panikkar, *India and the Indian Ocean : An Essay on the Influence of Seapower* (1945).
2. G Coedes, *The Indianised States of Southeast Asia* (Honolulu: East West Center Press, 1968).

Introduction

While India may not be part of South East Asia, the security environment of the region has a direct bearing on the stability, trade and economy of India. The 1400 km land border between India and Myanmar (a member of ASEAN) now offers new challenges and opportunities for India. During World War II, this route was exploited by the Japanese to invade the Indian sub-continent right up to Kohima. Today it offers opportunities for developing land routes for trade and tourism and energy, by passing or supplementing the Strait of Malacca.

Post 11 September, the US led Operation Enduring Freedom against Taliban and subsequent operations against terrorism, including the Al Qaeda, has brought even countries like China in support of the fight against international terrorism. America being in the lead, has increased support to all countries, which are fighting against terrorism. As a result, Indonesia, Malaysia, Singapore and Thailand have stepped-up their anti-terrorist operations.

American led Operation Iraqi Freedom of March 2003 has created new fears in the minds of regimes like Iran and North Korea. The US doctrine of pre-emptive operations has created a fear in these countries, forcing them to declare their intentions of re-starting enrichment of plutonium for developing nuclear weapons.

The economies of India and most of the South East Asian countries have also shown healthy growth, which needs to be taken note of. It is in this international and regional environment that India needs to evolve her 'Look East' policy.

New Delhi **Yoginder Mohan Bammi**
September, 2004

1

Concept of Security in the 21st Century

Security of a state has always been enunciated in terms of national boundaries, external threats and internal disorder. Main reasons for conflicts and wars varied from establishing sovereignty, acquiring territories, spreading religious ideologies, imposing political systems, acquiring mineral wealth and resources, to looting riches of another country. Human security was either ignored by the states or was given a lower priority. Welfare of the people and impact of trade and commerce on socio-economic affairs of a state were considered the responsibility of the sovereign, who also controlled or guided the system of government and political aspirations of the masses. Now, besides the government, even non governmental organisations and international agencies show concern for human security. The threat to human security comes from famines, ethnic conflicts, social disintegration, terrorism, pollution and drug trafficking, which in the present global environment are not restricted or confined within na tional borders. In modern times, security encompasses every facet of human life and development. Threats to human security could arise from economic, food, health, personal, environmental, community and cultural, or political factors.[1] These may create internal instability of such magnitude that hostile external powers may be tempted to violate the laid down boundaries of a nation.

While some threats may initially dominate an area or a country, in present day scenario of global market economy and media linkage through information technology, they rapidly assume a global character, such as green house gases and drug trafficking. Similarly, economic disparities and poor job opportunities may force migration of people across borders for better life, even if they are not wanted in the receiving countries. Frustration over inequality in income and political power often builds up into serious civil conflicts between groups, whether ethnic, religious or social. This creates serious security threats to not only the country, but also its neighbours. The influx of 10 million refugees during March-May 1971 from East Pakistan into India due to the civil war in East Pakistan is a case in point.

Thus, the impact of environment—pollution, global warming etc, illegal acts of gun running, violations of human rights and socio-economic factors like poverty, hunger, lack of educational facilities, shortage of drinking water, unemployment, and an unstable economy, pose as much threat to a nation as a hostile country across the border. In today's global environment of interdependence of economies, trade - both exports and imports, legal and contraband, foreign direct investments and currency values and uplift of human resources are as important for a nation's security as is the strength of her armed forces. Thus, economic destabilisation can be as dangerous as an attack by a hostile neighbour. Among the social weapons, besides the threat from illegal drugs and narcotics, spread of AIDS can be as dangerous for a nation as was opium addiction to China in the 19th century.

Insurgency, terrorism, religious fundamentalism and cyber warfare know no boundaries. As has been proved by the 11 September 2001 attacks these devastating and potent attacks not only shook the security of a nation but also influenced the geo-political environment and potential threats, world over. Piracy on high seas has always been a threat to international trade, but the proliferation and easy availability of sophisticated arms and equipment, coupled with advancements in communication technologies have enhanced the threat of conventional and non-conventional weapons being used by state and non-state actors.

The spread of information technology (IT) interdependence of countries for energy and trade, awareness of human rights, environmental degradation, illegal trafficking in drugs and people, smuggling of arms, piracy on high seas, ethnic issues leading to migration of population, and spread of fundamentalism and terrorism across the globe have become important security ingredients. These new threats do not always remain restricted within a country, but also affect the neighbours and the society at large. Security of a nation is no longer restricted to its political system and regional boundaries, or to conventional, sub-conventional and nuclear threats, which may be posed by the adversary for destabilising it by stoking an internal conflict.

With the global interlinking of economies, modernisation and industrialisation, leading to rise in demand for energy resources and awareness of socio-economic factors impinging on human rights, the world is on its way to becoming an interdependent homogeneity. Aspects of human security including health, poverty, hunger, employment avenues and social welfare will draw even greater importance in the coming twenty five years. Security can no longer be tied to state sovereignty. In the future, instigation of insurgency, trans-border terrorism and religious fundamentalism will pose a greater threat than those posed by enemy tanks, ships and aircraft.

A country would have to give special attention to the expanded threat to national security. Well being and prosperity of the people will become the first priority of the sovereign, in which economic resilience, good governance and military power will play major roles in ensuring safety of the nation. In the coming quarter century, security of a nation cannot be viewed in isolation and would be influenced by regional and global trade and economic issues and problems. Thus, it would demand regional or global solutions.

India stood for and still advocates a non-aligned and nuclear weapon free world. By virtue of her size and location she has a right to be a regional power, but she is not in competition with any one, nor does she have extra-territorial ambitions. Wanting to establish good friendly relations with all her neighbours, she wants peace and stability in the region so vital for her economic growth, without which the well being of her people or the region cannot progress. Hence, besides strengthening co-operation between the armed forces, India has to see how she can assist in "enhancing self reliance of the individual countries and the Region, to meet the new security threats". While diplomacy, economic and regional alliances, defence and security pacts and arrangements may be able to provide temporary security against internal threats to a country, an economically weak nation would often fall against external pressures. Therefore, any future plan of India's assistance to a country should lead to enhancing the human security of the host country.[2]

References

1. *Human Development Report* of the UN,1999.
2. *Ibid.*

2

The Region

Geographically, South East Asia encompasses the countries located on the rim of South China Sea or inside this water span, extending from the Straits of Malacca to the Straits of Taiwan, and does not include either India or Myanmar. However, as events in India and South East Asia have influence over each other due to strategic domination of India over the Indian Ocean, the destinies of the two regions are interlinked. Similarly, while India is not a member of ASEAN, the member states of the grouping have a great stake in developing closer co-operation with India, as they do with other countries like China, the USA, Japan, Australia and Russia. For the purpose of the study, the region spreading from the Strait of Malacca to the Straits of Taiwan encompassing the South China Sea, a vital link between the Indian Ocean and the Pacific, has been considered.

While India's links with China date back to the Mauryan times, nearlly 2400 years ago, it was during Ashoka's rule in the third century that Buddhism spread through the land route to Myanmar and then Burma, Thailand, Laos, Cambodia, Vietnam and Korea. In the meanwhile, traders from Bengal, Gujarat, Malabar Coast and the Coromandel Coast undertook sea voyages and reached Malaya, the Indonesian archipelago and Thailand, which resulted in the spread of Hinduism in these areas. As early as the second century AD, the Chola rulers from southern India had sent maritime expeditions and traded with Burma, Malaya, Indonesia and Vietnam. Though initially the Indian influence spread mainly via the land route through the emissaries sent by Ashoka, the Brahmanic influence followed trade through the Bay of Bengal and Andaman Sea, which reached its zenith by the 11th century. In the meanwhile, establishment of a port at Malacca led to the opening up of Java and South China Sea from 350 AD, while the Kra Isthmus allowed transhipment of goods across the narrow land neck to the Gulf of Thailand, for onward transhipments.

The temples of Angkor Wat and Angkor Nam in Cambodia, Buddhist statues and sculptures in Myanmar, Laos and Vietnam, the worship of Hindu Gods in Java-Bali region of Indonesia, the depiction of Ramayana in the temples of Thailand and the many splendid statues of Buddha in Bangkok, are all proof of spread of Indian influence. Indian diaspora is well settled in these countries and enjoys a good reputation.

In this period, China had also been active in the region. Besides expanding her influence through the land routes, China had developed a strong naval armada. Numbering upto 62 ships with 20000 sailors under Admiral Cheng He (a Yunani Muslim eunuch) China had launched many expeditions between 1405 and 1433 sailing through the South China Sea to the Pacific, and the Indian Ocean.[1] Similarly, trading posts were established in the littoral states, protection was awarded and embassies established in them, at times with the backing of naval power. The courts of China's rulers established special ministries to deal with the Chinese living abroad, and maintained close links with them. The Chinese gained influence by use of military power, embassies, and by exchanging gifts and receiving "tributes" from states deemed to be "vassals".

Islam arrived in the region around the eighth century through the Arab traders in the Indian Ocean littoral region. At this stage, the Malay peninsula was known for its Hindu-Buddhist settlements, as was Kra Isthmus on the Gulf of Siam. Parameshwara, a prince of Palembang fled Java and landed in Singapore in about 1390 AD. He sailed north and realised that Melaka – now spelt Malacca – was better suited for trade, agriculture and defence. Thus, Malacca became an important port bustling with trade.

Simultaneously, the Chinese Admiral, Cheng He, commanding the great armada of Ming dynasty, visited Malacca. Realising its strategic importance, he placed Parameshwara under his protection, thus precluding the rise of any major power in Nanyang (meaning the South). In 1414, Parameshwara married a Muslim princess from Northern Sumatra and embraced Islam. Thereafter, the religion spread upwards from Malacca into the Malay peninsula through Indian Tamil and Gujarati Muslims. The people of the region freely adopted Hindu-Buddhist traditions, which greatly encouraged trade and commerce and resulted in influence of Indian culture being kept alive by the traders from Bengal, Gujarat and South India. The mingling of Hindu-Islamic traditions was peaceful, a trend which prevails even now.

The period of Mughal and British rule in India, from 13th to 18th century saw a large number of Western powers fighting for influence over South East Asia, some even using India as a base. In this the British were the most successful, taking control of Burma, Malaya, Singapore, Hong Kong and Australia. Expansion of the British Empire resulted in opening of new labour intensive vistas of agriculture, trading and industrial activity, leading to flow of Indian labour to Burma and Malaya. Chinese traders also settled in Malacca, Singapore, Indonesia, the Philippines, Thailand and North Borneo.[2] In 1511, the Portuguese took over Malacca, while in 1819 Stamford Raffles founded Singapore.

In the meanwhile, the Dutch had taken control of Indonesia and the French were well established in Vietnam. Though the Russians and the Americans who had taken the Philippines from Spain also contested for power, it was the British who ruled the waves. In the Far East, Japan was also eyeing the energy resources of China and Korea, and exerted power over them. Most nations were eyeing territories that dominated the sea-lanes passing through the South China Sea, linking the Indian and Pacific Oceans. Thus, the importance of South China Sea was well realised even in that period.

During the 18th and 19th century the Chinese business community thrived in most places, but India alone was able to leave her cultural footprint.In the 20th century, the British dominated South and South East Asia, the Indian Ocean and the South China Sea. While the Dutch had a presence in Indonesia, the French controlled Indo-China (Laos, Cambodia and Vietnam). Japan also had an ambition of dominating the region and the Indian Ocean, while China was too weak to exert her influence. During the Second World War, the region suffered great economic and social deprivation under the Japanese Forces, who overwhelmed all opposition posed by the colonial rulers and the local kings. Besides occupying the landmass, the Japanese Navy dominated the South China Sea up to Singapore. By her surprise attack on the Pearl Harbour in December 1941, Japan came close to achieving full domination of the region. However, she did not have enough resources for the

Pacific Ocean which became apparent in the battles of Coral Sea and Midway in 1942, or for the Indian Ocean as seen after their attack same year on the British Navy at Ceylon. Thus, by guarding the flanks of Burma, the Allies were able to defeat the Japanese ambition of controlling the South China Sea and the Indian Ocean.

After the end of World War II in 1945 status quo ante was restored with Britain controlling Malaya, Singapore, Burma and Hong Kong. The US re-occupied the Philippines, and France regained Indo-China. As regards Indonesia, though the Dutch re-occupied the country, a small enclave remained under the Portuguese, but Sukarno continued to struggle for independence of the country. All this while, bulk of the people of Indian community continued to remain in the country of their residence.

The rise of Communism in China started in 1920s and 1949 saw them wresting complete control of the country from KMT, forcing the Kuomintang regime to escape to Taiwan and Burma. All this while, though the South China Sea remained a vital sea way for trade between countries of the Indian and the Pacific Oceans, not much attention was given to its security.

Resurgence of Independence Movements

India's independence movement set the trend and stage for de-colonisation of South East Asia. In stages, Burma, Indonesia, Malaya, Indo-China, Singapore and Ceylon gained independence. Post-independence, these countries had to evolve a mechanism to work with each other and with India.

At the Asian Conference held in New Delhi in 1946, Prime Minister Nehru came out strongly in favour of independence for Indonesia and other countries from the colonial yoke. The Afro-Asian conference held at Jakarta in 1950 passed the resolution of Panchsheel, laying the foundation for the Non-Aligned Movement. After gaining independence in 1947, India enunciated a policy for her diaspora and advised them to identify with the country of their residence and form part of the local society. This policy has remained consistent, and has won the Indians great respect from the locals.

During the period of 1950s and 1960s, there was great admiration for India and her leaders of the freedom movement, especially in Malaya and Indonesia. Tengku Abdul Rahman,the father of modern Malaysia and President Sukarno of Indonesia were two influential leaders of the South East Asian region, who established close ties with India. However, there was soon a personality clash between Nehru and Sukarno, which resulted in cooling of relations with Indonesia. The late 1950s also saw the Sino-Indian border dispute coming in the open, leading to a full scale attack on India by China in 1962, which in reality was a Chinese attempt to degrade India's emergence as a regional leader dominating the non-aligned movement. India supported Indonesia during her confrontation with Malaya in 1960s in Borneo and endorsed Indonesia's admission to the UN, which to an extent resulted in cooling of relations between India and Malaya.

India, meanwhile, also faced an aggression by Pakistan in 1947 in Jammu and Kashmir. The 1962, Chinese aggression not only sapped India's energies but also lowered the status of her diplomacy and her Armed Forces. While India was engaged in seeking diplomatic, economic and military assistance from America and other western countries for facing the dual threat, South East Asia did not figure high on New Delhi's policy spectrum.

The Cold War Period

Soon after World War II, when the world was split into two divergent and competing blocks, in South East Asia nationalism showed strength in Vietnam, where the British, and later the French, were defeated, though pockets of western influence remained in South Vietnam. Similarly, China and the USSR increased their influence and supported North Korea's offensive southwards, against the Americans who were supporting South Korea. All this while, India stood for non-alignment and remained neutral, but she provided a medical team under the UN and later headed the Neutral Nations Repatriation Commission. At the same time, in Europe, the formation of NATO in 1949 and the Warsaw Pact resulted in a major power struggle between the western powers and the Communists, for supremacy. The cold war was to last for nearly four decades.

The cold war did cast its shadow over South East Asia. In 1948, Mr Quirino, President of the Philippines, while visiting Delhi for the conference on Indonesia, suggested the formation of an Asiatic Organisation like the Pacific Union, for creating a bulwark against Communism. Though not a military alliance, the idea was for Asianisation of the region in political, economic and cultural fields. The idea to form a non-communist bloc was again discussed during May 1950 in Australia where India, Ceylon, Pakistan, Indonesia and Thailand also participated. Pursuing a non-aligned policy, India perceived all such groupings as power blocs of the Cold War, and did not support them.

The success of Communists against the French in French Indo-China resulting in its break up into Vietnam, Laos and Cambodia, and control of mainland China by the communists in 1949, greatly alarmed America and non-communist countries of the region.

This resulted in Washington making security of South East Asia a "core issue" of her foreign policy. On 29 March 1954, John Foster Dulles, US Secretary of State, issued a policy statement calling for united action to "forestall the Communists". He stated that the "loss of mainland of China to communists was a great disaster, which will be compounded if the loss of the million people is not restored". The meeting of 13 April 1954 in the UK saw birth of collective defence arrangement for "Peace, security and freedom of South East Asia and Western Pacific", which was supported by France also.

Thus was born the South East Asian Treaty Organisation (SEATO), which was readily joined by Thailand, Singapore and the Philippines, along with Britain and America. These countries became suspect in the eyes of other regional countries including India as SEATO opened vistas for American interference in the internal affairs of Asian countries. India opposed the Manila Treaty of 1955 establishing SEATO, as it considered it against the principle of non-alignment. However, in 1957, New Delhi supported the bilateral Anglo-Malayan Defence Agreement that allowed Britain to maintain her troops and bases in Malaya. In fact, Nehru stated that as "a new independent country may not be able to stand alone, it had to have an agreement. I do realise the importance of South East Asia, the South China Sea and the Straits of Malacca".

The Korean War 1949-1951 also showed that the Western world led by America was determined to challenge communism in any region. Realising the military potential of a growing China-Soviet nexus, the Western world led by the USA decided to check the spread of communism in the world, and targeted the USSR and China as their main adversaries. In Asia, besides SEATO, the Central Treaty Organization

(CENTO) was formed. In Europe, NATO had already been organised in 1949 and was soon challenged by the Soviet Bloc's Warsaw Pact. In South East Asia, the USSR and China strengthened their influence by giving military and economic aid to North Korea, Vietnam, Laos and Cambodia.

The cold war also saw Australia and New Zealand forming a five power defence arrangement with the UK, Malaya and Singapore, which remains in force even today. Soon, Japan and South Korea became the forward bases for American troops, and continue to be so. For the security of the Pacific region, America formed a treaty with Australia, New Zealand and the UK, named ANZUK. The US military presence in the region resulted in the Soviet Union occupying bases in Vietnam, and increasing her involvement and influence over China, Laos and Cambodia.

It was after the Bandung Conference that relations between Nehru and Sukarno started cooling, which became apparent in 1961 during the first non-aligned meet at Belgrade. They reached a low ebb in 1962, as during the Chinese aggression and later during the 1965 Indo-Pak War, only Malaysia stood firmly by India. Pakistan, which had joined the western camp and CENTO, was greatly disappointed with America for not supporting her fully against India. By 1960s, CENTO, like SEATO, remained a paper treaty only.

The 1960s saw the UK deciding to pull out most of her troops East of the Suez, a vacuum that was filled by the Americans who established bases at Diego Garcia, Persian Gulf, Singapore, South Korea and Japan. The Soviet Union also increased her influence in Afghanistan and the Middle East and established bases at Vladivostok and Cam Ranh Bay. All this while the attention of Indian planners continued to be focused on Pakistan and China, while internally developing economic and industrial infrastructure.

Very little effort was made to improve relations with the countries of South East Asia.

Early Security Concerns

In 1946, Malaya faced insurgency from elements of the Communist Party of Malaya operating from the jungles along the Thai-Malaya border, and later from Indonesia in North Borneo. This forced the British to launch massive anti-insurgency operations and suppress the Indonesians in North Borneo. Thailand faced an external threat from the likely expansion and overflow of Communism from Laos and Cambodia, a fear which was also shared by Malaysia, the Philippines and Singapore.

As the Communist power consolidated its influence in China, she paid attention to the people of Chinese origin living abroad and the communist Parties in South East Asia. Inspired by Beijing, these Communist Parties sought to control local economies and influence governments resulting in widespread anti-Chinese clashes in Indonesia, Malaya, Singapore and Thailand. China's policy of claiming regions (where overseas Chinese live), as her territories, also fuelled the fear of Communist expansion, which further forced the countries of the region to strengthen their security.

Thus, besides joining various defence and security pacts and alliances, the countries of South East Asia also started modernising and expanding their armed forces, mainly with the assistance of America and the UK. The South China Sea became prone to piracy and poaching for fishery trade, and though it was considered as an area of future extension of Cold War, the countries of South East Asia generally laid emphasis on consolidating their land and sea borders.

In the midst of the Cold War, the leaders of South East Asian countries realised the significance of cooperation among themselves, and thus was formed the Association of South East Nations ASEAN in 1967. Though initially meant to foster economic development, its scope later was enhanced to discuss regional disputes.

INDONESIA

The Indonesian archipelago, the largest in the world, consists of 17,508 islands out of which only 6,000 are inhabited. It has an area of 5,193,250 sq km out of which 2,027,087 sq km is land territory. It stretches approximately 5,120 km from East to West and 2,000 km from North to South through three time zones, and is close to the Andaman Sea. It provides a link between the Indian Ocean and the Pacific, straddling the South China Sea. The only alternate way to the Straits of Malacca is via the Sunda and Lambok Straits, which are dominated by the Archipelago. This further enhances Indonesia's importance for sea trade[3].

The largest country of the region, it is also the fourth most populated in the World, with a population of 224,784,210 in 2000, which, as per UN estimates is likely to rise to 239 million by 2010 and to 337 million by 2050.

The country is grouped in islands, the five main ones being Sumatra (the largest island, with capital Jakarta), Java, Kalimantan (Indonesian Borneo), Sulavasis (Celebes) and West Papua New Guinea (formerly Irian Jaya). Except Madura and Bali (where Hindu culture is most prominent), the smaller islands are also grouped, the largest group being Maluku (the Moluccas) and Nusa Tenggara (the Larger Sundas).

The country has land borders with Brunei, East Timor and Malaysia, while her sea borders clash with the Chinese claim over the oil producing Natuna Islands, from where recently a pipeline has been laid to Singapore, for transfer of oil.

Indonesia is the largest Muslim country of South East Asia. The principal ethnic groups are Achene's, Bataks and Minangkabans in Sumatra, Javanese and Sudanese in Java, Madres in Madura, Balinese in Slaws, Dayaks in Kalimantan, Irianese in West Papua (former Irian Jaya) and Ambones in Molucas and the Timorese in *Timor Timur.*

Some of these ethnic groups have been agitating for independence from the central control of Jakarta. Amongst these, the Achene's and the Ambones are still active. The East Timorese have broken away and become an independent country in May 2002.

Historically, there are indications that during the period 3,000-500 BC, Indonesia was inhabited by sub-Mongoloid migrants of Asia, who later inter-married with the indigenous population of the archipelago. A later mixture was brought about by Indo-Aryan migrants from the sub-continent of India, during 1,000 BC. The first Indian migrants, mostly from Gujarat came to Indonesia during the first Christian era, which saw spread of Sanskrit and Hindu religion during the Caka period, under Prince Aji in 78AD. Sumatra was named Swarn Dwipa (or Island of Gold), Java as Java Dwipa or the Rice Island and the Hindu kingdom of Borneo (Kalimantan) Island, was called Kutai. Between the first and seventh century, Hinduism spread peacefully in most islands and relations with India were based on culture, religion and trade.

Though the Mongol emperor Kublai Khan had established a foothold in 1293, it was only in the 14th century that the Hindu and Buddhist kingdoms of Sumatra and Java fell to the slow advance of Islam brought by traders from India and Persia. The first European, Marco Polo, visited Java and North Sumatra in 1292 during the rule of Majapahit, under Prince Wijaya. Gradually, between 1331-1364, the Muslims subdued the most powerful Hindu kingdom of Raja Hayam Wuruk, which had dependencies even outside the present archipelago as far as Champa (North Vietnam), Cambodia and the present day Philippines. It was the Hindu king of the kingdom of Demak who converted to Islam, and later subjugated the mighty kingdom of Majapahit between 1513-1520, which saw spread of Islam throughout the country and further North, towards Malaya. The Portuguese arrived in search of spices and established a foot hold after conquering the Islamic Kingdom of Malacca, and were followed by the Spanish. Soon, the spread of Christianity started in the area of Maluku. The Dutch followed them in 1595 and ruled till 1810, when the East India Company took control from 1811 to 1816. However, the control soon reverted to the Dutch, who in their consolidation efforts were strongly opposed by Raja Udayana of Bali.

For the next 100 years or so, the country witnessed revolts in various parts. The year 1908 saw rise of a national movement against the Dutch occupation, in which leaders like Dr Sukarno and Dr Hatta played a major role. In February 1927, Dr Hatta attended the first International Congress of the League Against Imperialism held in Brussels, where he met prominent leaders from Asia and Africa, including Pandit Nehru. This meeting of the two leaders resulted in strengthening of ties between the two independence movements. While the nationalist leaders made various demands for autonomy and freedom, the Dutch rejected them all.

During World War II, from 1940 to 1945, the Japanese occupied the country. Once the Japanese surrendered in 1945, on 17 August 1945 Dr Sukarno and Dr Hatta declared their country independent and adopted a new constitution. Indonesia became a Republic on 18 August 1945. Soon the British troops landed to disarm the Japanese while the Dutch returned to re-establish their rule. The Indonesian armed volunteers tried to resist the British, but could not match them. This forced them to retreat into the mountains and fight a guerrilla war against the occupation forces, which continued from 1945 to 1949. During this period, the Communist Party of Indonesia unilaterally declared a Republic of Indonesia in East Java, which resulted in clashes between not only the British and the Dutch, but also between the two Indonesian groups. The fighting saw the question of the Indonesian independence, from the Dutch, being debated in the United Nations.

It was under these circumstances that on 20 January 1949, Nehru initiated a proposal before the nineteen-countries Asian Conference in Delhi, demanding the Dutch to surrender complete sovereignty to the Republic of Indonesia by 1 January 1950. Under pressure from the UN, the Dutch consented to grant full powers to Indonesian leaders, but did not relinquish control over Papua (West New Guinea). The country became an independent republic on 27 December 1949 when The Netherlands finally conceded unconditional sovereignty. Later, the Dutch controlled West New Guinea was incorporated into Indonesia in 1969 and named Irian Jaya. The former Portuguese colony of East Timor was incorporated in 1975, which was not accepted by the Lisbon Government.

Sukarno ruled from 1945, and became the President in 1960.He relinquished the reigns on 22 February 1967, handing over to Lieutenant General Suharto, who ruled till 21 May 1998. Sukarno's twenty two years regime was characterised by two abortive coups, for which he blamed the Communist Party of Indonesia due to which the Chinese community which controlled most of the economy, suffered. His rule also saw rise in prices, corruption and nepotism, and the Army becoming involved in running the country. Relations with Malaysia worsened due to the *Konfrantasi* (Indonesian word for confrontation), over Borneo, but improved during Suharto's time, who was the main architect of ASEAN.

Having taken part in the independence struggle, the Indonesian Army has not only been responsible for defending the territorial integrity of the country, but has also played an important role in the internal politics and governance of the country, especially during Suharto's period. In 1975, it invaded East Timor claiming this Portuguese controlled island as part of Indonesia, which was not accepted by the international community and the UN. Ultimately, a UN sponsored referendum was held on 30 August 1999, which saw large scale violent clashes between the local pro-independence militant groups and the Army sponsored pro-Indonesian groups, after which an Australian led UN Peace Keeping Force was deployed.

During his reign, Suharto consolidated the role of the armed forces in Indonesian political and the government set-up, diversified the economy from dependence on oil and built a wide manufacturing base. But it was dependent upon exports and massive foreign investments. The 1997, economic crisis (which saw inflation rise to 250 per cent coupled with charges of family corruption, created uneasiness against Suharto. Due to extreme rise of food prices, riots erupted in April 1998, which led to Suharto's ouster. Vice President Habibie took over as President on 21 May 1998.

Habibie promised referendum in East Timur, besides economic and political reforms. However, he also failed to carry out economic reforms and to initiate action against the Armed Forces, who were alleged to have carried out human rights violations during the East Timor referendum. After a short tenure of twenty-one turbulent months, on 23 July 2001 he handed over the presidency to Sukarnoputri Megawati, the daughter of the first president.

Since taking over, Sukarnoputri Megawati has tried to revive the economy and rein-in the Army, reducing their seats in the parliament from 100 to 39. Against the military's advice, she attended the Independence Day celebrations of East Timor. She has also taken an independent stance on anti-terrorism, and despite pressures from the USA and Singapore, has not banned the Islamic fundamentalists groups who had demonstrated in front of the American Embassy, to protest against the US intervention in Afghanistan. While improving relations with ASEAN, China, Japan and India, she has differed with Australia on extradition of Indonesians involved in trafficking of illegal immigrants, specially since August 2001,when a Norwegian ship had picked up 433 asylum seekers, most of them Afghans, from a sinking Indonesian boat in the Indian Ocean.

Though the situation is presently under control and the centre has agreed to give 30 per cent share of oil royalty to the provinces, since November 1999 periodic riots have taken place in Aceh between pro-Independence supporters and the Army, and in

Molucus between the Muslims and the Christians, resulting in nearly 5,000 deaths. The Armed Forces are also seeking a better and bigger share of power. Under pressure, Megwati has appointed General Suharto (not to be mixed with the earlier President), who was in charge of East Timor during the1999 rioting.

Socio-Economic Status and Trade

Bhasa Indonesia is the official language, though English, Dutch and Chinese are also in use. The literacy rate is 83.8 per cent, 81 per cent in male and 79 per cent in female population (see Appendix A). Race wise, the country has 179 million Muslims, which accounts for 88 per cent of the population and makes it the world's largest Muslim country, eight per cent Chinese, two per cent Hindus and Buddhists one per cent. The Hindus are mainly in Bali, making 76 per cent of its population. Life expectancy is 65.61 years and the GDP is US $ 2, 800 (see Appendix B).

Indonesia has the advantage of petroleum and gas reserves. The proven oil reserves in 1999 were 5.0 billion barrels. The country has reserve of 2050 billion cubic metres of natural gas, production in 1999 was 67,677 cubic metres. In 2001, a 646 km long pipeline has been laid from West Natuna gas fields to Malaysia[4] and Singapore, which could earn up to US $ 8 b in the next 20 years. Though the country has coal, copper, nickel, gold and silver deposits, the cost of production is high.

Forests covers 60.6 per cent of the landmass, out of which 43 per cent is scheduled for logging and clearance by burning, which causes environmental hazards. In agriculture rice, sugarcane, coconut (world's largest producer), cassava, maize, soybeans, potatoes, sweet potatoes and peanuts are the main produce. Main industries are manufacture of textile (batik), apparel, footwear, mining, cement,chemicals, fertiliser, rubber, food, tourism, shipyards, paper, automobile, glass, caustic soda, paper and plywood (second largest in the world). In 1997, 41.2 per cent of the labour force was engaged in agriculture, 19.8 per cent in trade,14.5 per cent in services and public sector and 12.9 per cent in manufacturing. The 1997 economic crisis saw a rise in unemployment to 17 per cent (see Appendix C).

Environment wise, she faces a major challenge from deforestation, forest fires and pollution of the seacoast. Natural resources include petroleum, tin, natural gas, nickel, timber, bauxite, copper, fertilizer, coal, gold and silver. As the population is mainly around towns, in year 2000 the number of telephones in the country was 3.291 million.

Since 1992,[5] foreigners have been allowed to hold 100 per cent of the equity of new companies of approximately $ 50 m in remote areas, majority being from Hong Kong, UK and Taiwan. Though the FDI in 1994 was $23,724 m, but by 1998 the foreign debt had risen to $ 150,875 m. During 1998, the main exports were of gas and oil, forestry products, rubber, coffee, fishery products, coal, copper, tin, pepper, palm products and tea to Japan, America, Singapore and Germany. However, since then these have declined drastically, due to the 1997 financial crisis. (Table 1.1).

Table 1.1

(in thousand US $)

	1996	*1997*	*1998*	*1999*
Imports (including oil)	42,929	41,680	27,337	17,740
Exports (including oil)	49,815	53,444	48,848	35,083

At the height of the 1997 economic crisis, only China and Japan had offered financial assistance, but it was Thailand and Singapore, which approached America to get Indonesia the much-needed aid from international financial institutions. For 2002, the IMF, which is leading a bailout package of $ 5 billion, has forecast a growth rate of 3.5 per cent and inflation at 9.3 per cent, but they are not happy at the pace of economic reforms, including dis-investment by the government and its anti-corruption measures. Though foreign investors are still cautious, only China has shown great interest in increasing trade and investment in infrastructure development. Also, unlike in 1967, Beijing maintained silence during the 1999 anti-Chinese riots.

It was reported that the oil reserves of Indonesia, currently the 17th largest producer in the world are declining rapidly; production from 1.25 million barrels per day during 2002-2003, may come down to 1.1 millions barrels per day. Competition from other gas producing countries like Australia, Malaysia, Qatar and Russia may also reduce Indonesia's market share of the world trade. In the meanwhile, Jakarta has to take a final decision on either to allow Exxon Mobil to carry out deep drilling in the oil fields straddling East and Central Java as per agreement of year 2002; or to wait till 2010 and allow the state owned Pertamina? This is especially important, as oil production from Aceh has been adversely affected, due to disturbed security situation in that province. Notwithstanding the above, the economy seems to be recovering and prospects for the future are bright.

Security Concerns

Besides the economic crisis leading to inflation and unemployment, the major internal security challenges being faced by Indonesia is the secessionist struggle in Aceh.

Situated on the Northern–most tip of the main island Sumatra, the Aceh region has rich oil and gas reserves. For the last 26 years, the local Achenese have been agitating and demanding independence from the central rule of Jakarta. This had resulted in the Army being employed to fight the insurgents of Free Aceh Movement (GAM), whose leaders have taken refuge in Sweden, while clashes between the Army and the locals have resulted in nearly 10,000 casualties. In early 2001, the unrest had forced Exxon Mobile to close down their gas production. However, by deploying nearly 2500 troops for anti-guerrilla operations, the production recommenced in end 2001, but a loss of $ 400 million had already been incurred.

After taking over, President Megawati signed a special autonomy law for provinces, allowing greater autonomy and share of oil revenues to provinces including Aceh, but it was not accepted by GAM. Though the Army felt that the Government was being too soft with the rebels and wanted to undertake military operations, they were overruled by the President, who decided to give peace another chance.

An international peace initiative was launched in Geneva on 29 December 2002 by Japan, the World Bank and the Asian Development Bank to end the deadlock between leaders of Free Aceh Movement-GAM (represented by Zaini Abdulah and Hasan di Tiro, both living in exile in Sweden) and the Indonesian Government, but it failed. Hasan declined to attend the talks and insisted that the offer of greater autonomy and economic aid was not acceptable and insisted that the GAM would settle for nothing less then independence, this was not acceptable to Jakarta. However, a cease-fire was agreed to, which showed hope of ending the fighting. It provided for a team of 50 international monitors from Thailand and the Philippines to monitor the peace. Also, though the agreement did not address the basic issue– independence or autonomy– it provided for substantial autonomy and free elections in Aceh and the willingness of Jakarta to continue the dialogue, in return to which the rebels had to give up their arms. Indonesia, and more so, Japan, were concerned about the disruption in supply of liquefied-natural gas from Aceh and the strategic position of the troubled province on the Straits of Malacca. If peace prevailed then Japan had offered to give support and aid for foreign loans, a hydro electric power plant and a flood-control project for Aceh.[6]

Thus, while an uneasy peace prevailed in Aceh, further talks between the government and the Free Aceh Movement GAM were held in Tokyo on 24 April 2003 in which General Zinni, of the US also participated, but the talks failed. Though the four month old fragile cease-fire had came under stress even earlier resulting in nine killings (including five separatists), and the Government had re-deployed 100 peace monitors due to threats to the Acehnese capital Banda Aceh, Jakarta had hoped that the GAM leadership will agree to surrender their weapons and accept the proposal of enhanced autonomy and end the dispute. The government gave the GAM two more weeks to hand over their weapons, though the Indonesian Military had been warned to be ready to move-in, if the talks failed. Thus, soon after the expiry of the deadline, approximately 50,000 Indonesian troops (with helicopters, armoured cars, naval vessels) moved in, to disarm the 3000 strong-armed guerrillas of the GAM.

Foreign observers felt that while Jakarta had allowed special autonomy to the locals in 2001,the

GAM insisted on complete independence, which was not acceptable to the government. It was reported that the uncompromising stance of the Aceh Governor Abdullah Puteh and other leaders were responsible for the breakdown of the peace talks. The GAM leadership in Sweden, who were in contact with their 18 district commanders through satellite telephones, were of the view that there was no reason to surrender their weapons, as there was no clear commitment from the Indonesian military to assume a more defensive posture, or to permit the rebel groups to have a stake in Aceh's future. However, David Gorman, coordinator of the Henry Dunant Centre in Geneva, who had earlier brokered the December 2002 peace deal, said that the door should be left open for dialogue.

After the talks failed, on 15 May 2003 President Megawati consulted members of the House of Representatives and her advisors and declared a state of emergency in the province of Nanggaro Aceh Darussalam, allowing the armed forces to restore the situation. She stated that as the series of amicable efforts made by the government, either by means of the stipulated autonomy for the Province, as an integrated approach in a comprehensive development plan or as a dialogue held overseas, had failed to stop the intention and actions by the Free Aceh Movement (GAM) to secede from the unitary state of the Republic of Indonesia and declare its independence, the government has no other option but to declare emergency, to ensure unity of the country.

World over, there was disappointment at the failure of the peace talks and most observers blamed the GAM for it. They felt that the government could not have given any further concessions, and that GAM leaders living abroad were not in touch with ground realities. The GAM, on the other hand, played on the sentiments of the locals, who were the only people who offered stiff resistance to the Dutch in 1870 as even then though their Sultan was finally defeated at Kota Aceh, he continued to lead a band of guerrillas against the Dutch.

While there are fears of the military adopting strict regime and violating human rights of the locals, the soldiers are likely to be more conscious of their acts, as this time around, special instructions for not violating human rights have been issued. General Endriartono Sutarto, the Military Commander, has instructed that "if any soldier violates orders and causes suffering to people in the field, then just shoot them in the head". The Army is also undertaking development projects, for which elements of engineers and doctors have been included in the contingent. The military suspects that the guerrillas had used the ceasefire period to procure modern weapons (like mortars and rocket launchers) from Cambodia, via Thailand. On the request of a section of Aceh citizens for self-defence, the government is also backing a proposal for creation of a civil militia.

Earlier, the military had estimated that the situation can be brought under control within six months, but in July 2003, General Sutarto stated that he was not certain how long it would take. The Army has plans to adopt the strategy of re-locating population from their villages, so as to cut their links with the GAM. The British had tried this model very successfully in the jungles of Malaya in the 1960s,where villagers from the fringes were moved to new sites. The Americans had also tried it in Vietnam, but had failed as the Viet Cong had a mass support base. In Aceh, it is likely to offer stiff resistance and create more hostility, though the Army has stated that the "re-location" will be done, selectively.

The situation continues to be fluid, and Exxon Mobil, who have the biggest oil stakes in the island, are yet to start operations. The Army has killed 80 and rounded up 60 GAM suspects. It has also been blamed for two Human Rights violations, for which trials have been held. President Megawati's government is not likely to accede to the GAM demand of independence, as it could set precedence and result in disintegration of Indonesia. Often, precedence of East Timor is given for granting independence to Aceh, but there are no similarities between the two. While East Timor was not originally part of Indonesia and was occupied by her in 1975, Aceh has been an integral part of the Republic, since her inception. Thus, grant of independence to Aceh will set in motion disintegration of Indonesia, leading to bloodshed and anarchy. This, the government is determined not to permit. While the US and the West had been critical of the human rights record of the Indonesian Army, it is likely that in the present situation where national integrity is at stake, they may not be very vocal.

Peace in Aceh is of special significance for India, as it is only 30 km from Indira Col the southern most island of the Nicobars. In 2000-2001, there were some reports of efforts being made by Pakistan's ISI to establish bases in Aceh, as have been recent reports of Al Qaida cadres and supporters seeking refuge there. Thailand is also concerned about Aceh becoming a node for cadres of Jemeah Islamiah, who have been responsible for terrorist acts in their country.

Since 2000, Jakarta has been facing pressure from Malaysia, Singapore, Thailand and the Philippines to act against Indonesian Islamic terrorist groups, which had been linked with terrorist activities in these countries. However, Indonesia had been slow to react, probably as she did not want another problem on her hand. Though after the 11 September 2001 attacks on America there were indications of Al Qaida having links with Islamic groups in South East Asia, still Jakarta was not investigating them seriously.

On 12 October 2002, Islamic radicals attacked two night clubs in Bali, resulting in the death of 202 civilians (mostly foreign tourists from Australia) and injuries to over 350. This saw the government under extreme pressure from the West as well as ASEAN countries, to initiate prompt and strict measures against the culprits. Thus, Indonesia not only drew up a new anti-terrorist law but also arrested the main three culprits. Jakarta showed a strong commitment to fight terrorism by conducting their speedy trial, giving indications of a transformed and sincere judiciary and police. The authorities also explored the likely links between the Bali culprits and Abu Bashir, the leader of Jemeah Islamiah (who had earlier propounded the idea of Pan-Islamic state consisting of Indonesia, Malaysia and Southern Philippines) and Al Qaida.

Till date all suspects of the Bali trials turned out to be Indonesian citizens, who had undertaken the blasts to protest against western influence in Indonesia. Ali Ghufar (also known as Mukhlas), age 42, was identified as the ring leader. During his trial, he did not show any remorse for his deeds. Amrozi Nurhasyin, age 40, a mechanic by profession, denied any links with Jemeah Islamiah, but "expressed happiness at the results of the blasts". As per police investigations, Amrozi had attended meetings where the plan for the bombing was hatched and given finances for purchase of material to make the explosives. Abbas, the brother-in-law of Ali Ghufar, was also tried for terrorist actions. Besides the three, thirty other suspects were arrested and are being tried. So far, while Ali Ghufar and Amrozi have been given death sentences, trials of the others are continuing.

There is every likelihood that the rest would also be awarded severe punishments.

By organising the ASEAN Summit at Bali in October 2003, President Megawati has sent a clear message that "terrorism will fail." She also invited President George W Bush to halt at Bali, on his return from Thailand, in October 2003.

The trial of Abu Bakar Bashir, (who was involved in anti-American and anti-Christian activities since 1983; his present outfit, Jemeah Islamiah was established in 1993), for continuing subversive activities and formation of a Pan-Islamic state in South East Asia (consisting of Indonesia, Malaysia and Muslim populated areas of southern Philippines), took place in 2003. While he could not be linked with the Bali blasts, the police charged him for inciting bombing of churches in December 2002, which had resulted in death of 19 and injuries to 84 people. He was also charged with plotting insurrection against the established democratic government, links with terrorist organisations planning attacks on the embassies of the USA and Singapore in Indonesia, propagating revenge killings of Catholic priests for slaughter of Muslims in Ambon and, the 2002 assassination attempt on Megawati when she was Vice President. He had also claimed links with bomb blasts in eleven cities, with the aim of "reviving the Jihad (holy war) spirit of Indonesian Muslims, as a way of undermining the government". Though Bashir was suspected of having links with Al Qaida, so far this has not been established. By September 2003, Bashir had been tried and sentenced to four years imprisonment.

According to many Western observers, this punishment is too lenient. However, as there was no evidence linking him with any terrorist attacks, he could only be tried for treason. Also, as he has a large following in the region, it is quite likely that the Government did not want to create an internal upheavel, by awarding a stiffer punishment.

The Indonesian authorities were keen to interrogate Humbali, a terrorist who was arrested in Thailand, to strengthen the case against Bashir. However, Humbali was whisked away by the US, as he is suspected of having links with the planners of 11 September terrorist attacks. Another prominent terrorist leader, Idris was arrested from Medan on 12 June 2003. He is reported to have links with Jemeah Islamiah, and has been directing their operations and logistic support. He is suspected of having links with Al Qaida, and was responsible for planning the blasts at the US Consulate in Bali.

Investigations in the case were also handicapped, as Jemeah Islamiah is not listed as an illegal group, though many of its leaders had participated in the Afghan War. They are also linked with training of Moro and Islamic liberation movements in the Philippines, where they have been running camps for upto 700 terrorists, since 1997-98. Though Bashir denied that Jemeah Islamiah even existed, the police suspect that he is the Amir—spritual leader— of the organisation. A milder sentence announced to Bashir, on charges of sedation, was viewed with concern by America and Australia. Singapore, on the other hand considers him responsible for running a network having 500 to 600 members, who are out to spread terrorism in the state.

The Police suspect that Bashir's outfit may have also been involved with the bombing attack on JW Marriott Hotel in Jakarta's business city on 5 August 2003, which left 10 dead and injured 147. His links with another terrorist leader, Amrozi, and the links with Al Qaida are also being investigated. Amrozi's trial, which commenced on 5 August 2003, may throw fresh light on the role of Bashir in terrorism in

Indonesia. In fact, Maulana Abu Bakar Bashir[7] is a leader to be watched.

There has been trouble in other areas of Indonesia also. Unlike Aceh, the Indonesian Armed Forces were able to control the situation in Moluccan Islands, which resulted in nearly 9000 deaths. The situation has also been brought under control in North Maluku. However, Ambon often witnesses communal riots between the Muslim Laskar Jihadi extremists and the Christians. As regards Central Kalimantan, the situation became critical as Jakarta decided to re-habilitate new migrants in the area, which was resisted by the indigenous Dayak tribesmen. The clashes have resulted in large-scale rioting and killing of the migrant Madurese. Though efforts have been made in parts of Borneo to resolve the economic, social and cultural grievances of the Dayaks, the situation remained tense and the army had to be deployed. In the province of Irian Jaya also, the October 2001 special autonomy bill has not fully met the aspirations of the local Papuans, though they have been given 80 per cent of the revenue accruing from fisheries and forestry and 70 per cent from oil, gas and mining.

There are few social problems being faced by the Government. Though a new human rights legislation has been passed, it is still to be fully implemented. The number of cases of corruption against the politicians and members of the armed forces continue to rise, as do detention of political prisoners. This often creates unrest amongst the masses. Jakarta again witnessed street demonstrations against rise in prices in January 2003, but the situation seems to be under control.

Besides the internal threat from secessionist tendencies of political and religious groups, the Exclusive Economics Zone (EEZ) of the country is disputed by China and Malaysia in South China Sea. Strained relations with America and Australia continue, though the US Under Secretary of Defence and the Australian Prime Minister visited the country in early 2002. While during her state visit to the USA President Megawati was well received in Washington, her reluctance to take a strong stand against Jihadi fundamentalists and reports of Al Qaida using some of the uninhabited islands of Indonesia have strained relations. The November 2002 terrorist bomb attacks in Bali has brought the fear of international terrorism finding its breeding ground in Indonesia to the fore. As Indonesia is the only Muslim country of the region where demonstrations were held against the US led operations in Afghanistan and Iraq, the likelihood of international Islamic fundamentalism taking advantage of the uninhabited islands to expand their operations, cannot be ruled out.

Often, western and Pacific security analysts cast doubts on the survival of the largest country of Southeast Asia, and fear that Indonesia may break apart.[8] They anticipate a clash between the political masters and the armed forces, especially if the economy does not recover soon. However, so far, the armed forces have shown full loyalty to the President and the elected government, and President Megawati seems to be in full control of the country.

It is fair to assume that by initiating decisive and firm action in Aceh and against the Islamic fundamentalists, President Megawati has sent clear message to foreign powers as well her countrymen, that she can take hard decisions and will not allow any break-up of the country. Besides attracting foreign trade and investments, this is likely to strengthen her position over the years. Jakarta is likely to deal firmly with the problem in Aceh, but adequate safeguards against human rights violations by the armed forces will need to be taken. Drive against anti-secessionist and Islamic fundamentalist groups will continue, and will earn grater appreciation from the West. This may result in resumption of defence aid, economic assistance and flow of FDI, which will boost the sagging economy.

Prompt action, fair trial and stiff punishments awarded to the terrorists has already resulted in an appreciable change in the American policy towards Indonesia. While President Bush has asked the Congress to approve arms aid and closer ties with Indonesian military to help them in fighting terrorism, a joint naval exercise was conducted by the two countries in May 2002. This cooperation is likely to improve. If the US arms embargo is not lifted soon then Indonesia may turn towards Russia and China for military hardware.

THAILAND

Situated at the western extremity of the South Asian region, the Thai peninsula has an area of 517,000 sq km, which runs southwards towards Malaysia and Singapore. Thailand divides the Indian Ocean, has the Gulf of Thailand leading to the South China Sea to its East, and the Bay of Bengal and the Andaman Sea to its West. The country has 1800 km long semi-mountainous and thickly forested porous borders with Myanmar in the West. It also shares borders with Laos in the North and the East, Cambodia in South East and Malaysia in the South. Besides domination of the seas, Thailand's close borders with China across a strip of Laos's territory makes it vulnerable to threat from communist neighbours.[9]

The country did not come under colonial rule in the 20th century. However, it came under the influence of western inspired democracies, which resulted in King Rama VII accepting a constitutional monarchy in 1932. The next 41 years saw military rule till 1973 when a democratic civilian government came to power. Since then, a series of military and civilian leaders have run the country. In 2000, Mr Thaksin Shinawatra, a telecom tycoon, became the Prime Minister.

Socio-Economic Status and Trade

Thailand has an area of 514,000 sq km and had a population of 61,230,874 in 1990, which is expected to touch 70,295,643 by year 2050. The country is very rich in forest and mineral resources. Thai is the official language, though due to Western (mostly American) influence and tourism, English is also spoken. Literacy rate is 93.8 per cent (96 per cent for males and 91 per cent for females). 95 per cent of the people are Buddhist, three per ceent Muslims, 5 per cent Christians and one per cent Hindus. While 94 per cent of the population follows Buddhism, six per cent practise other religions. Life expectancy is 65.29 years for males and 71.97 years for females, and the per capita GDP is US $ 6400 (see Appendices A–C).

While four per cent of the labour force is employed in agriculture, 15 per cent work in industry and 31 per cent in services. Tourism, garments, agricultural processing, cement, manufacture of light machines, jewellery and computer components are the main industries. The main agricultural produce are rice, fishery, fruits and vegetables. The country exports computer parts, textiles and rice and imports capital goods, intermediate goods and raw materials and consumer items. Natural resources include wood, tin, rubber, natural gas, tungsten, gypsum and fishery. The country faces environmental threats from air and water pollution,, poaching and deforestation. Communications are well developed in the cities, with nearly 5.4 million telephone connections.

As regards security concerns, the border with Myanmar where the Shan and Kachin rebels and drug warlords have their areas of influence, often witnesses clashes and armed intrusions by opposing groups. While Myanmar blames Thailand of supporting Shan and Karen guerillas who are fighting the military Junta of Maynmar, Thailand accusses Mayanmar of supporting the United Wa State Army (UWSA), which has been exporting drugs into Thailand. As was seen in February 2001, often troops of the two countries occupy battle locations, creating fears of an open clash. In February 2001, Thailand accused Myanmar of massing 10,000 troops just across the border, backed by 2500 soldiers of ethnic minority UWSA. Both sides moved up artillery and Thais even moved light tanks.Myanmar accused Thailand of supporting guerrillas of Shan State Army living in mountains near the border and assisting them in drug trafficking activities. Though the situation was defused by diplomatic intervention, such provocations or acts in future could spark an armed conflict between the two neighbours.[10]

The situation again reached a flashpoint in May 2002, when shells fired by the Myanmar Army landed on Thai territory. After the clashes, it was decided to establish three permanent and thirteen temporary check posts along the border, as Thailand's biggest worry is the inflow of narcotics and methamphetamine tablets from Myanmar. Though Thailand has few disputes on border marking with Cambodia, they are of minor nature.

While Thailand also has maritime conflicts with Malaysia, but here joint development has been agreed to. As regards Gulf of Thailand, there are disputes with

Cambodia and Vietnam, while there is a dispute with Mayanmar in the Andaman Sea.

Smuggling, intrusions and illegal drug trafficking from Laos and Cambodia also pose serious threats, as do the Muslim rebel groups residing in the forests of Thai-Malaysia border belt. As late as November 2002, there had been five bomb blasts in the Muslim dominated area of the South, raising concerns about Al Qaida activists.[11] In this regard, the arrest of Islamic terrorists, especially in the southern region bordering Malaysia, has raised great security concern.

In April 2003, four marine soldiers were killed while battling militants along the Thai-Malaysia border. The ambush of the military vehicle indicated work of experts, who also took away weapons and ammunition. Though the government issued strict orders to the Armed Forces to tackle the problem and decided to conduct joint operations with Malaysia, the USA was irked that Thailand was not taking adequate measures to curb militancy, and was not endorsing the American led war in Iraq. The US also pressed for permission to establish an Intelligence post in Southern Thailand, for monitoring activities of Jemeah Islamiah in the region. Washington also hinted that the aim of Exercise Cobra Gold[12] (being conducted annually since 1980s) for the year 2003, would be changed from conventional security to counter terrorism.

In June 2003, the police arrested Navang Penanan, a Thai national, with $ 240,000 and Uranium. However, it turned out to be Cassium 137,used in medical and industrial equipment. Three Thais suspected of planning bomb attacks on the embassies of the USA, Australia, Singapore, the UK and Israel in Bangkok, in 2003 when Thailand was to host Asia Pacific Economic Meet, to be attended by heads of states including President Bush, were arrested. Their links with Jemeah Islamiah and Al Qaeda were also investigated, jointly by Thailand and Singapore. The Thai Prime Minister accused foreign based militants, including those of the Middle East, for stirring chaos in his country. Same month, two Thai nationals were also arrested in Thailand for having carried out terrorist attacks in neighboring Cambodia, during elections in that country.

All these events resulted in Mr Thammamh Isarangura, the Defence Minister to state that "the world situation has changed. We are afraid terrorists will try to use Thailand as a place to launch their atrocities against international targets". He senssed that the southern part of the country, whose predominantly Wahabi Muslim population form10 per cent of Thailand's 2.8 million Muslims and are suspected of being fundamentalists, are likely to become a base for Jemeah Islamiah. He also identified Wahabism with the strict type of Islam, which is followed by terrorist leader Osma bin Laden. But till September 2003, no Thai Wahabi group has been listed as 'Terrorist', either by America or by Thailand. However, it is suspected that Jemeah Islamiah cadres have been sheltering in southern Thailand, a region where corruption is rampant, poverty is widespread and education is primarily run by madrasas. Financial aid from Middle East and Saudi Arabia is also reported to be flowing in Narathiwat region, which is dominated by Wahabis.

Thai Police achieved a major success in a joint operation with the CIA when in August 2003 they arrested Ridnan Isamuddin "Hambali", in Aynthaya. An Indonesian citizen, Humbali is suspected of being not only a senior operational commander of Jemeah Islamiah, but of having links with Al Qaeda. As he was reported to be in league with Khalid Shaikh Mohammad, accused of being the mastermind of terrorist attacks of 11 September 2001 he was whisked away by America to an undisclosed location, for further interrogation. Though Indonesia demanded his presence for the trial of Abu Bhashir and he was also required by Singapore for trials of other terrorist suspects, America refused to make him available. Hambali is also suspected of having had an active hand in the Bali bombing and the Marriott Hotel blasts, besides other terrorist attacks in Malaysia, Singapore, Indonesia and Thailand. Bangkok is also concerned about the fall-out of the situation in Aceh province.

Reports of Al Qaida supporters and Islamic fundamentalist activists of Malaysia establishing bases in the region continue to cause concern, but the main potential threat to Thailand is from an expansionist China. Thailand has a security alliance with America and though her armed forces are reasonably well equipped, gun-running, drug trafficking and piracy in the Straits of Malacca have continued unabated. Though there are territorial disputes between Thailand and few other neighbours, Bangkok hopes to resolve these issues by dialogue, adopting ASEAN philosophy of dialogue rather than armed clash. Greater cooperation in anti-terrorist operations with Malaysia, Indonesia, Singapore and the Philippines is also likely, as the threat to all these countries stems from a common adversary.

MALAYSIA

The second largest country of the region in terms of size and economic progress, it consists of two distinct wings. While peninsular Malaysia forms 40 per cent of the landmass, the eastern wing is made up of provinces of Sarawak and Sabah on the northern island of Borneo. The western wing juts out southwards from the Thai Peninsula and dominates the Straits of Malacca with Singapore, while the eastern wing dominates South China Sea, Brunei and Indonesia.

Between the western and eastern wings of the country lie islands with proven and active oil reserves, whose ownership is disputed by Indonesia and China as is her EEZ. A causeway links her southern state of Johore with Singapore. Singapore depends upon Malaysia for her drinking water supply. The country is heavily wooded and mountainous, with number of streams, rivers and offshore islands. After the financial crisis of 1997 lowered the status of Indonesia, Malaysia has emerged as the leading country in the region.[13]

Historical records show that in early Christian era, a mix of Hindu states existed along the Malay rivers. The Chinese under Admiral Cheng He arrived in Malacca in 1405, followed by Islam. European interests saw the Portuguese arriving in 1511, followed by the Dutch in 1641 and the British in 1795. During World War II, Japan occupied the country; the British returned at the end of the war. In 1957, Malaya achieved independence (*merdeka*), peacefully. However, soon the country was besieged by internal disorder in the form of riots between the ethnic Chinese (who controlled the economy) and the Malays, the Communist inspired insurgency along the Thai border and external confrontation (*Konfrontasi)* with Indonesia in Borneo. In 1963, the North Borneo states of Sabah and Sarawak, along with Singapore joined Malaya to form Malaysia, but the experiment did not succeed. Fearing domination by the Malays, Singapore broke away from Malaysia in 1965, to become an independent republic. Though inter-communal violence between the Chinese and the

Malays again erupted in 1969, since then the country has enjoyed peace. Also, the Communist insurgency in the North has been finished, resulting in very good all-round progress.

A monarchy with an elected government, the multi-religious society of Malaysia has experienced peace and progress since then, enabling the country to advance in all spheres. An important founder member of ASEAN, besides Singapore, she was the only country of the region, which came over the economic crisis of 1997, with flying colours.

Socio-Economic Status and Trade

With an area of 329,750 sq km and a population of 21,793,293 in 1990, expected to increase to 43,122,397 by 2050, it has a per capita GDP of US$ 12,900. Official language is Bhasa Malaysia, though English, Chinese, Tamil and Telugu are also spoken. Literacy rate is 93 per cent, while the life expectancy is 80 years for males and 73 years for females. As arable land is only three per cent, only 16 per cent of the labour force is involved in agriculture and fishery, 27 per cent in manufacturing, 17 per cent in trade and tourism, 15 per cent in services and 10 per cent in construction. Industrial products include rubber and palm oil (India being the major importer), light machinery, tin, logging and petroleum. Malaysia exports electricity, petroleum products and LNG, chemicals, palm oil, wood, rubber and timber, and imports food, fuel and lubricants, natural gas and heavy machinery.

The environmental threats to Malaysia arise from air pollution, deforestation and haze, as was experienced in 1998 due to uncontrolled forest fires in Indonesia. The second most advanced country of the region, it has 4.4 million telephones.

Internally, while the country has faced ethnic rioting between the Chinese and the Malays over economic issues, presently the only threat envisaged is from Islamic fundamentalists to the otherwise fast growing economy and progressive state.The gravity of the situation was highlighted by Prime Minister Mahathir in October 2002, when he declared that Islamic separatists had tried to overthrow his Government. These people believe that they can overthrow these governments and set-up what they call is a 'Muslim State'. He also cautioned that Malaysia is not an exception, but the war against terrorism must not appear as being waged against only Muslim terrorists, as not all Muslims are terrorists. Dr Mahathir was bold in condemning terrorism of all kinds, including state-sponsered violence and suicide bombings. During a debate on terrorism and on the issue of who is a terrorist, he stated that it was wrong to believe Islam advocates terrorism. He also condemned defamation of Islam by freedom fighetrs, jihadis and ummah, who subscribe to terrorism. He emphasised that the war on terrorism must not be viewed as a war on Islam. Besides cooperating actively with neighbouring countries, Malaysia has also signed an agreement with America to fight terrorism.

In the meanwhile, the arrest on 20 February 2002 of Lieutenant Colonel Abdul Manaf Kamsuri (Retired) and sixty nine others for their links with the Islamic terrorists has caused concern, though strict law enforcement has reduced illegal migrants, drug trafficking and smuggling. While minor differences over sea-lanes and islands in South China Sea also remain unsolved with Singapore and Indonesia,[14] these have been shelved under the ASEAN spirit.

Despite cooperation in anti-terrorist operations, Malaysia continues to adopt an independent policy on international affairs. Responding to Malaysia's criticisms of US led Operation 'Iraqi Freedom', Mr Najib Razah stated, "Ours is a principled foreign policy, not based on pragmatism. We should occupy the high moral ground". The Prime Minister designate, Mr Abdullah Radawi, who takes over in October 2003, is likely to follow the policy of Dr Mahathir Mohamad.

In July 2003, Malaysia agreed to the establishment of a South East Asian Anti-Terrorist Centre in her capital. Aimed to monitor and analyse activities of the militants in the region, the Centre will also impart specialised training for improving regional security. Though the establishment of the centre was initially proposed by the US, Malaysia being her critic on Iraq has not included America as a partner. However, Washington may be invited on special occasions.

The current threat being faced is from regional terrorism and fundamentalism. However, the long term external security concern is from an expansionist China through Thailand and the South China Sea, besides gunrunning and piracy in the sea-lanes. The Armed Forces follow western doctrines. In the 1960s and 1970s they had achieved very good results in tackling the communist insurgency in the jungles dominating the Malaysia-Thailand border. They are well trained and equipped with modern weapons, and are orienting to fight a conventional threat. A member of the five power Defence Arrangement, she has close defence and security co-operation with most of the ASEAN countries, Pakistan and India.

Malaysia is likely to continue to lead the region and ASEAN, and her foreign and domestic policies are not likely to see a major change under the new Prime Minister. Her efforts to cooperate in anti-terrorist operations and regional activities will further boost her status in all forums.

MYANMAR

Situated in the north east region of India, it has an area of 678,600 sq km. It has land borders with China, Thailand, Bangladesh and India. Besides the land border with the north-eastern states of Arunachal Pradesh, Nagaland, Manipur and Mizoram, Myanmar has a sea border with the Andaman and Nicobar group of islands. Though the 1400 km long international land border between India and Myanmar is well demarcated, due to historical and socio-economic background there is quite a bit of official and un-official population and trans border trade and affinity between the Burmese and the Indian population of the region. Being mostly mountainous and endowed with jungle covered low hills, insurgent groups of both countries, smugglers, drugs and arms traffickers have often used the 1400 km porous Indo-Myanmar border to their advantage.

As was witnessed during the Second World War, Myanmar provides an easy access route for a land invasion of India. The developments in south western China and enhanced involvement of Beijing in the country, including development of river and road communications running north-east to south-west, could pose a major security concern to India. These routes would provide new avenues to China to project her power not only along India's north eastern borders, but also in the Bay of Bengal.

Myanmar's position between China and the Indian Ocean makes it economically and strategically important to China. Since 1950s, both countries have shared close political relations, while relations with India have often been cool. Beijing has all along respected Yangon's independence and domestic situation, while Myanmar has lent support to Beijing's "one-China" principle on Taiwan.

Socio-Economic Status and Trade

It has a population of 41,734,853 as per 1990 census, which is likely to go up to 44,430,144 by 2050. While English is spoken in the cities, Burmese is the main language of the country, though ethnic groups use their own language. In 1995, the literacy rate was 83.3 per cent (males 88.7 per cent and females 77.7 per cent) and while 89 per cent of the people are Buddhists, four per cent each are Chinese and Muslims, Animist one per cent and others, two per cent. Life expectancy is 53.6 years for males and 56.29 years for females.

In 1999, the per capita GDP stood at $ 1200. While 65 per cent of the labour force was employed in agriculture, 10 per cent worked in industry and 25 per cent in services sector. The main industries are agricultural processing, fishery, textiles, footwear, teak wood, pharmaceuticals and fertilisers. Mining of copper, tin, tungsten and iron has also contributed to the economy. The arable area is 15 per cent of the total land mass and the main agricultural produce are paddy, rice, corn, oil seeds, sugar cane, pulses and hard wood.[15]

The country exports pulses, beans, prawns, fish, rice and teak, while it imports machines, transport equipment, construction material and food products. Natural resources include petroleum, timber, tin, antimony, zinc, copper, tungsten, lead, coal, marble, precious stones and natural gas. The main environmental problems being faced by the country are deforestation, industrial pollution, soil erosion, waterborne sanitation and treatment of drinking water. The country has only 158,000 telephones, mostly in population centres situated along the rivers.

Security Concerns

After13 years of economic stagnation and isolation, in 1989 the "Burmese Road to Socialism" advocated by General Ne Win was discarded, and the present military regime shifted towards market economy. Despite formal separation of civil and military portfolios, the State Peace and Development Council (SPDC) consists primarily of the Armed Forces, who exercise dual control. Thus, democracy continues to be muffled. General Than Shwe is Defence Minister, Chairman of the SPDC as well as the C-in-C. Since 1988, the Army (also called Tamara) has grown in size and modernisation, and is today the largest in South East Asia. As most weapons are of Chinese origin and ammunition is imported from a number of countries, the forces could face problems of logistics and maintenance.

Plagued with political and ethnic insurgencies against central rule, in recent times, the Government has started gaining control over remote and isolated border regions, by launching a series of "divide and conquer" operations. These have finally resulted in defeat of the Communist Party of Burma in 1989, and the centre has overcome most of the ethnic groups. By promising regional economic systems and step-by-step infrastructure development, most of the insurgent and political opposition has been neutralised.

The Army has seen large expansion, raised ten armoured battalions against two in 1989 (five with tanks and five with armoured fighting vehicles). The Navy has also expanded and received Chinese patrol boats fitted with anti-ship missiles, but maintenance and financial costs have posed major problems. The Air Force has also shed its anti-insurgency role and in June 2001 ordered aircraft worth US $ 130 m, from China and Russia. However, shortages of experienced pilots, maintenance personnel and supply of spares are some areas, which in future could pose problems.

Myanmar's plans to import a 10 megawatt nuclear research reactor from Russia is likely to upset the Chinese, who have been eyeing and cultivating Myanmar as a potential market and trade route for their three south-western provinces, Yunnan, Sichuan and Guizhou. Accordingly, Beijing is heavily investing in developing infrastructure in Myanmar, a road from Yunan to the river port of Bhamo on Irrawady (1500 km from Yangon) being one such project. Besides nuclear reactor, Russia has also sold ten Mig-29 aircraft to Myanmar, and considers her as a "promising partner in Asia and Pacific region". While this may sound encouraging to Vietnam and other countries in the region who have concern about Chinese presence in Myanmar, Beijing is likely to pursue vigorously export markets through Myanmar for her 130 million population of the three provinces neighbouring Myanmar. Today, besides trans-border movement of drugs and gun-running, Karen, Karenni and some Shan insurgents still operate along the border with Thailand.

The current defence strategy is based on preservation of unity, protection of sovereignty and defence of the country against an external conventional threat, while few counter insurgency and trans-border operations are also being carried out.

From international point of view, the two most serious challenges being faced by Myanmar are: supression of democracy and violation of human rights. The situation took a dramatic turn, when in

May 2003, the Military Junta decided to release twenty one political prisoners, including Aung San Suu Kyi, a move that was welcomed world over. The USA and the European Union were under the impression that the Junta had changed their policy due to their economic pressure, and hoped that this would result in improvement of relations. However, these speculations were short lived, as Suu Kyi's political rally was attacked by opposition groups supported by the Junta. She was taken into protective custody. So far the Junta has refused to release her.

In the meanwhile, there has been a change in the Junta's leadership and it appears that there was difference of opinion within the ruling party on her detention. So much so that when the issue of her detention was raised in the ASEAN Foreign Ministers meeting on 17 June 2003, Myanmar did not raise much objection, though her detention was declared as a protective step. The US and the European Union have again enforced economic sanctions on Myanmar, and also adviced International Monitory Fund to follow suit. In 2001, Myanmar's textile exports to America were just US $ 456 million, just over 19 per cent of her total trade. Even without fresh sanctions, these are likely to fall to zero, as the global treaty on Multi Fibre Agreement is likely to expire in 2004. These sanctions are not likely to have a major impct on Myanmar's exports, unless countries like China, Thailand, Indonesia and Bangladesh, who are the other major importers, also, impose similar restrictions.

It is likely that the recent changes in the Junta leadership, resulting in Lieutenant General Khin Nyunt becoming the Prime Minister, may see some relaxation of anti-democracy policies. He is on record stating that he wishes to draw a "new political road map" for the country. He also did not raise serious objections when the ASEAN member states raised the question of granting freedom to Suu Kyi, and stated that she is not under house arrest but under "protective custody", and is allowed visitors. However, Western observers feel that the policies of the new regime do not show much change, and that the military is trying to carve out an even bigger role for itself. The seven point programme announced by the Junta, envisaging resuming a national convention (which was abandoned in 1996) to draw up a new constitution and holding of "free and fair elections" thereafter, are all considered as clever deceptions by the Military Junta for drawing economic support for the country's ailing economy.

Meanwhile, amongst her neighbours Thailand is happy that Myanmar has decided to pull back her troops from the Thai-Myanmar border, as this would help in controlling the 145,000 Myanmar refugees fleeing prosecution in their country. However, reports of the Myanmar Army resorting to brutal measures to drive this minority community into Thailand, continue.

China is looking for long term ties with Myanmar, which include giving aid for dredging the Irrawadi to allow large size Chinese barges loaded with Chinese goods and road construction, in return for access to ports in the Andaman Sea and the Indian Ocean.[16] During his visit to Myanmar on 12 December 2001, President Jiang Zemin promised aid to the tune of $ 100 million, to fund twelve projects focusing on agriculture, infrastructure and human resource development. Presently, China is the third largest trading partner of Myanmar (after Singapore and Thailand), with the two-way trade amounting to $ 600 million, annually.

SINGAPORE

Located at the southern tip of the Malaysian peninsula, the city-state has an area of 647 sq km, including the main island of Singapore and 59 islets, out of which only twenty are inhabited. She straddles the Straits of Malacca and her deep harbours provide berthing facilities to ships of all size. Her excellent management in all spheres complimented by a highly trained and well disciplined population of 4, 151,264 expected to go up to 10,790,729 by 2050, has resulted in the nation becoming the richest country of the region, with a per capita GDP of US $ 27,800. This has enhanced her position as a management and financial centre, a reliable and efficient node for shipbuilding and repairs, attracting Foreign Direct Investment (FDI) from world over.

Socio-Economic Status and Trade

The official languages are Chinese, Malay, Tamil and English. Singapore has a literacy rate of 91.1 per cent; 95.9 per cent in males and 86.3 per cent in females.[17] There being full religious freedom, Buddhism, Taoism, Islam, Christianity, Hinduism and Sikhism are practiced freely. Arable area is only two per cent and is used for growing rubber, copra, fruits and rearing poultry. As regards labour force, 38 per cent work in financial and other businesses, 21.6 per cent in manufacturing, 21.4 per cent in other white colour careers, seven per cent in construction and 12 per cent in the services sector.

The country has developed a strong manufacturing and services base, and excels in electronics, financial, oil and drilling equipment, petroleum refining, rubber, ship repairs, entreport trade and bio-technology. Machinery and equipment (including electronics) make up 63 per cent of her exports, while minerals, fuel and chemicals make up the rest. She imports foodstuff, chemicals, water, soil, mineral fuels, machinery and equipment, the last two accounting for 57 per cent of imports. Singapore's natural resources are deep-sea waters and fishery. Industrial pollution, water, limited land and disposal of waste pose serious environmental challenges. The country has 54 million telephones, the highest in the region.

Singapore's controlled democracy and policy of equal opportunity for all races has resulted in the country enjoying peace and tranquillity. Thus she has been progressing at a fast pace. Though small in size, she is the economic leader of the region and will continue to be so.

Security Concerns

Though not spelt out, the potential concern seems to be from China, in the form of either blockade of the Straits of Malacca, a land threat through Malaysia, or to the outlying islands of the country. Thus, greater emphasis is being given on strengthening the Navy and the Air Force. Besides being member of the Five Power Defence Arrangement, Singapore also has bilateral arrangements with the USA and Australia.

In the immediate, the main concern is regarding the Islamic terrorists of Indonesian nationality creating chaos in the country. Twenty one suspects were arrested in September 2002, as they had plans to attack embassies of the US and other western countries in Singapore. Their interrogation also revealed their plans to disrupt daily life in the island state, by disrupting water and electricity supply.

There are differences with Malaysia over the development of the port of Johore Baru in the Straits of Malacca, which could affect sea-lanes of Singapore. Also, Singapore is dependent on Malaysia for drinking water, and there are always concerns that any rivalry or clash of personality between the top political leaders may lead to stoppage of water supply. The drinking water issue again strained relations between the two neighbours in 2002, when Malaysia decided to raise the prices, unilaterally, for which Singapore's media blamed Malaysia. Consequently, while Kaula Lumpur blamed Singapore for "tarnishing her image world over", Singapore blamed Malaysia for frequent changes in the pricing policy. The Malaysian Government also decided to take charge of all national water supply projects, and is likely to invest US$ 13.7 billion in this sphere in the next 47 years in her 14 states. However, as was evident from the joint military exercise conducted in September 2002 in the Straits of Malacca, all these problems are likely to be kept at a low key, both being members of ASEAN. As a nation, Singapore also worries if her highly educated youth will be willing to die for the country?

While Indonesia and Malaysia had criticised the American intervention in Iraq and Thailand had remained neutral, Singaore had endorsed it. She also made available her KC-135 aerial tankers, for operations from Diego Garcia, the American base in the Indian Ocean. This support was suitably rewarded by America, by agreeing to supply advanced medium range air-to-air missiles (AMRAAMs) for her F16 aircraft (similar to missiles currently held by Malaysia and Thailand). Prime Minister Goh Chok Tong was also hosted by President George W Bush and a Free Trade Agreement between the two countries followed. President Bush has described Singapore as the "beachhead for the US in Asia", and has promised all assistance for the island country to overcome the economic slowdown caused by SAR.

Singapore is likely to continue to support American actions and policies,world-over. While minor irritants between Singapore and Malaysia may crop up from time to time, the two neighbours are likely to maintain workable and friendly relations, specially for combating the common threat posed by Islamic fundamentalists and terrorism.

PHILIPPINES

It is a country of more than 7000 islands and islets (depending upon the tide) covering 307,00,00 sq km, 94 per cent on eleven main islands. Luzon is the largest island on which capital Manila is situated. Visaas are a scattered group of islands south of Luzon, with Mindanao to their South. Mindanao is the second largest island, and has a string of islands in the Sulu Archipelago, extending up to Borneo. Palawan Island is 400 km long and 40 km wide, and dominates the South China Sea and the Sulu Sea.

Though not located on the main sea route, the country dominates the South China Sea and her claimed EEZ includes a number of islands having rich oil reserves, which has resulted in a dispute with China since 1990s. A predominantly christian country, in South Mindanao islands the population is predominantly Muslim. Mindanao is also claimed by Malaysia and there is also a territorial dispute with Indonesia, but these have been put on the back-burner under the ASEAN philosophy.

Historically, the Filipinos are Malay people, akin to those of Malaysia and Indonesia. However, the 300 years rule by the Spaniards have obliterated their original identity. Ferdinand Magellan, a Portuguese who had switched sides to Spain, and sailed from Spain to discover spices, reached the Philippines in

1521. After occupying the island of Cebu, he converted the locals to Christianity. The Spanish influence gradually spread through force to other islands, and in 1571 reached Manila. During this period, other European powers, japanese and chinese also made efforts to gain a foothold, while the strong Muslim influence had entrenched in Mindanao Islands. After the defeat of Spain by England in 1588, the country was treated as a subsidiary to the new Spanish colony of Mexico, and remained in the background till 1782 when the cultivation of tobacco in Philippines gave rich contributions to the Spanish treasury.

After their victory in the 1762 War in Europe, the British took control of the country, but never extended their control beyond Manila. Internal risings led by Jose Rizal resulted in more than 100 revolts against the Spanish rule, but his peaceful movement turned violent after the Spanish rulers executed him in 1896. Soon, the American-Spanish War of 1898 spread from Cuba to Philippines, and the country came under American control. The American rule was disrupted by World War II, when it was occupied by Japan. Though promised in 1935, the country gained independence in 1945, only after Japan was defeated in the War.

The period from 1950s to 1960s saw democracy on American pattern taking roots and in 1965 Ferdinand Marcos came to power. Though he declared Martial Law to control internal anarchy, the situation continued to worsen till end 1986, specially after the 1983 assassination of the opposition leader, when the opposition united and Corazon Cory Aquino came to power. Till the recent past, the Army has played a major role in stabilising the political system, while the Roman Catholic Church continues to have great influence. American companies and economic interests have resulted in the foreign policy, economy, trade and security arrangements being influenced by Washington, and till late 1990s, the country provided bases for the U S Forces.[18]

Socio-Economic Status and Trade

In 1999, the population was 81,159,644, which by 2050 is estimated to go up to 153,913,427. Literacy rate is 94.6 per cent (95 per cent in males and 94.3 per cent in females) and though English is spoken in the cities, Philippino is the state language. The population is predominantly Christian (83 per cent being Roman Catholic and nine per cent Protestants), while Muslims and Buddhists account for four per cent and three per cent, respectively. The life expectancy is 64.65 years and the per capita GDP in 1996 was US$ 3600. The arable area is only 19 per cent, the main produce being rice, coconuts, corn, sugar canes, bananas, pineapple, mango, poultry products, fish, pork and beef. Out of the labour force, 39.8 per cent was engaged in agriculture, 19.4 per cent in government, 17.4 per cent in services sector, 5.8 per cent in construction, 9.8 per cent in marine related jobs and seven per cent in other areas.

The main industries are textiles, pharmaceuticals, chemicals, woodwork, electrical assemblies, petroleum refining and fisheries. The country imports raw material and intermediate goods, capital goods, consumer goods and fuel, while it exports electronic items, machinery, transport equipment, textiles, garments and coconut products. Her natural resources include timber, petroleum, nickel, cobalt, silver, gold and copper. The main environmental threats are caused by uncontrolled deforestation, pollution along coastal region and growing swamps. Communications are city centred.

Internally, the country often faces political uncertainties and insurgency in its southern region, which is dominated by Muslim population. While the main separatist group of the Moro National Liberation Front (MNLF), have responded to government's offer of negotiation brokered by Malaysia, a splinter group under Abu Sayyaf continues to wage insurgency in Mindanao islands. Resorting to kidnapping, ransom, use of arms and explosives, his followers continue to defy the government. There are reports that Abu Sayyaf has received aid and assistance from Al Qaida, which has forced America to undertake special training of the Philippines Army, in 2002. While the joint training and operations did inflict some casualties on Abu Sayyaf's gangs, he continues to evade arrest. However, the USA has signed an agreement in September 2002, which allows more active role by her Army to engage Abu Sayyaf, directly.

The arrest of an Iraqi businessman with nine compatriots in April 2003, exposed their plans to use the country as a base to kill Philippine and American soldiers. Two bombings in the southern city of Darao that resulted in killings of 38 civilians traced to Jemaeh Islamiah, who by now had been linked with the Bali blasts. Further bomb explosions left 15 dead and 55 wounded, while renewed bomb blasts at Darao airport resulted in 22 deaths and more than 100 being injured. Intelligence sources indicated that Islamic groups linked with Jemaeh Islamiah and Abu Sayyaf were responsible for these acts.

They also reported that Bidwai, who had been earlier arrested in 1989 for giving support to Saddam, had joined radical Islamic groups for carrying out attacks on airlines flying on trans-pacific routes. Reports indicated that these plans had been concieved by Khalid Sheikh Mohammad, who was arrested in 1995 for planning to kill Pope John Paul II and blow up the US Embassy. Later, in 1990, he formed the

Hezbul Dawah Al Islamiah, preaching radical Islam in Manila, and established links with other Islamic radical groups.

Besides others, Fathur Rohman al-Ghozi, an Indonesian bomb expert linked with the Bali blasts was considered the most important catch. He confessed to having participated in the attack on a commuter train in Manila (in which 20 persons were killed), planning atatcks on the US and western targets in Singapore and Philippines in consultation with Hambali. He was also suspected of being the operational chief of Jemaeh Islamiah and the main conduit of Al Qaeda, in the region. Awarded ten years sentence, he along with two others escaped on 14 July 2003 from a police jail, to Southern Philippines. He was reportedly being guarded by the Moro National Liberation Front, though the party has denied it. While one of his accomplices identified as Abu Sayyaf's man had been killed earlier, Ghozi was killed in an encounter with the security forces, in September 2003.

As far as the Moro insurgency is concerned, the group had shown inclination to renounce violence, and had in September 2002 signed a Landmine Treaty, to destroy their stockpile of nearly 12,500 mines. Further, in her efforts to solve the problem in Southern Philippines, in July 2003, President Arroya appealed to Malaysia to keep "cease fire observors" ready, as she planned to re-start negotiations with the Mindanao rebels. On their part, the MoroIslamic Liberation Front had expressed their readiness to depute Hashim Salamat, their leader, to start the negotiations.

On being declared a terrorist group by the USA in September 2002, Gregorio Rosal, the spokesman of the Communist Party of the Philippines declared the intention of his party to retaliate against American troops and business houses. This adds a new threat to the internal security of the country.

President Arroyo faced a national crisis, when on 27 June 2003, nearly 350 army men from Manila mutinied, occupied a shopping Mall and wired it with explosives. Though the low rank mutineers demanded resignation of Arroyo government and blamed it for corruption and mis-management of the country and the army, they finally gave up after 20 hours. Though they were arrested and sent to barracks to face trials, (charges were made by Captian Mili, one of the leaders) of corruption in the army, it gave the opposition a handle to run-down the Arroyo regime. While no senior officer supported the mutiny and no political party came out in its favour, some observers compared the situation to that in 1980 when martial law had ended. They claimed that despite 20 years of democracy, the Army still called the shots. The aspect of Arroyo being administered oath of the office of President in 2001, only after the Army had assured the judiciary of its support for her, and the role played by the military in Joseph Estrada's period,were often quoted.

While the police suspects Senator Gregorio "Grigo" Honasan for the June mutiny, four senior officers were also questioned, as was the mistress of Joseph Estrada. Mr Golez, National Security Advisor of Arroyo claimed that the mutiny was a remnant of a full blown coup plot,which was foiled a week earlier. According to him,the coup was engineered by political rivals of the President, to capture strategic buildings around Manila such as the TV station, with the ultimate aim of overthrowing Arroyo. After the mutiny, Mr Angelo Royes, Defence Secretary, tendered his resignation, which as per him was caused by "restive soldiers". Arroyo blamed the opposition, and stated that there was a "well organised and funded effort by certain forces to bring down democracy".

The country gave tacit support to American intervention in Iraq. In appreciation, the US designated Philippines as her "major non-NATO ally" equal to Australia and Israel. On 13 August 2002, the two countries also established a New Defence Policy Board under the framework of 1951 Mutual Defence Treaty, which would allow the US troops to help fight Muslim militants in southern Philippines.

Continuing unrest and militancy situation in southern Philippines, combined with the mutiny by a section of the Army, highlighted an unstable internal situation. Regional cooperation in tackling threats posed by Islamic fundamentalists and terrorists is a happy sign. Efforts in this direction are likely to continue. While the US may provide additional arms and send troops, economy of the country continues to be weak.

Externally, despite the security pact with America, the fear of China's domination of South China Sea (a number of clashes have already taken place on the islands like Mischief Reef, claimed both by Manila and Beijing), will continue to be a cause of concern.

BRUNEI (BRUNEI DARUSSALAM)

Situated in the northern seaboard of East Malaysia's Sarawak province, which surrounds it on three sides, the country has South China Sea to its north. Area wise it is comparatively a small country of 5770 sq km, with a population of 336,376, which is expected to reach 600,998 by the year 2050. Located mid-way between Malaysia and the Philippines and South of Vietnam, the country has the capability of monitoring movements in sea-lanes of South China Sea. Brunei has immense reserves of off shore oil and gas, and an excellent harbour, which allow space and facilities for ships. These factors enhance her economic relevance and importance to ASEAN.

One of Asia's most ancient kingdoms, Islam arrived here in the 13th century and then spread to Borneo and other regions, often described as the "Malay world" and reached its peak in 1473. However, rampant piracy, internal wars, corruption and encroachment by the Dutch and British resulted in the decline of the empire, which was saved when the British extended their colonial span over it in 1888. Today's Brunei is the remnant of the erstwhile Islamic kingdom.[19]

Though other countries of the region shed their imperial yokes much earlier, Sultan Sir Omar Ali Safuddin decided to delay it till 1 January 1984, as he realised the advantages of protection by the British, who had protected him from the armed revolt by anti-Malay and anti-British political parties in 1962. In 1967, Omar stepped down in favour of his son Sir Muda Hassanal Bolkiah, the 29th monarch who in 1990s was rated to be the richest man in the world, due to the wealth accumulated from oil and gas revenues.

Socio-Economic Status and Trade

The official language is Malay, but English and Chinese are also spoken. The literacy rate is 88.2 per cent (96.6 per cent in males and 83 per cent in females) and though the official religion is Islam (67 per cent of population is Muslim),13 per cent are Buddhist,10 per cent are Chinese and 10 per cent follow other religions. Life expectancy is 71 years in males and 76 years in females, and the per capita GDP is US $ 17,400 (second only to Singapore in the region). There are no taxes in the country and while 48 per cent of the labour force is employed by the government and in production of oil and natural gas, 42 per cent work in construction and services, while agriculture and fishery account for the rest 10 per cent.

The arable area being just one per cent, only rice, bananas and water buffalos are reared. The country exports crude oil, LNG and petroleum products, while it imports machinery and equipment, manufactured goods, food and chemicals. Natural resources of petroleum and gas make it a rich and attractive country, while environmental hazards of haze and smoke from seasonal fires in the neighbouring region, and floods, pose problems. The country has 68,000 telephones, which indicates her economic prosperity.

Security Concerns

Though economic prosperity prevails, the monarchy has a fear about internal stability. This which has forced it to recruit Gorkha soldiers from Nepal for two battalions of palace guards. External threats from piracy, gun-running and of Chinese expansionism in the South China Sea also guide the military expansion and modernisation plans. Being a member of ASEAN and the ARF, Brunei hopes to experience peace and stability, which would sustain the present system of governance. The armed forces of Brunei continue to train with British and ASEAN countries.[20]

Detection of a new huge oil find, off the coast of Borneo in 2003, nearly resulted in an armed clash between Malaysia and Brunei where the Economic Extended Zones of the two countries overlap. Drilling in the area of Kikeh Fish (150 km off the coast of Sabah) Petrones of Malaysia struck oil reserves estimated at 700 million barrels, or 21 per cent of her current reserves, adequate for the next 15 years. This was objected to by Brunei, as she had laid claims to these blocks as part of her Economic Extended Zone (EEZ), extending 200 nautical miles(370 kilometres) from the coastline. To establish her claim, Brunei decided to send patrol boats to drive away Malaysian rigs and exploration vassels, to which Malaysia responded by sending her naval ships to drive away Brunei's boats. However, the situation was brought under control during a meeting at Penang on 24 May 2003, between Prime Minister Mahathir and the Sultan of Brunei, both sides agreeing to carry out joint development of the shelf, resulting in a win-win situation.

Earlier also, Malaysia and Brunei had resolved their land border dispute near Limbang River by consultation. Precedence of joint exploration between Malaysia and Thailand already exist. Hence, it is likely that this and such future disputes would be solved by the neighbouring countries of South East Asia by consultations, peacefully. Finds of large reserves of oil in the shelf are likely to attract attention of China, in the Paracel and the Spratly Islands, which may revive disputes of sovereign claim lines.

VIETNAM

Situated at the end of the South China Sea, the country stretches 1600 km along the eastern coast of the Indo-Chinese Peninsula. Located at the extreme edge of South East Asia, she dominates the Gulf of Tonkin, Gulf of Thailand and influences the sea lanes of South China Sea, Vietnam has land borders with Cambodia and Laos on the west and with China in the north. Having a total land area of 329,566 sq km,

Vietnam strategically dominates not only the North China Sea, but also all the sea-lanes between the Pacific and the Indian Ocean. It also provides a land and sea challenge to China, and dominates Japan, Taiwan, and North and South Korea.

By defeating not only the French and the Americans in the 1950s and the 1970s, respectively but also giving a befitting reply to China in 1979, the Vietnamese people and their armed forces have shown their tenacity and will power to fight. Being the leading and most powerful of the three Indo-Chinese countries (Laos and Cambodia being the other), it has a major influence in the region.

As mentioned earlier, till the 14th century, the Indian influence was predominant in Champa, now the central area of Vietnam. By the end of the 15th century, Vietnam had conquered most of the kingdom of Champa (now forming central areas) and by end of the 16th century had acquired Cochin-China (now southern areas). In the 18th century, the French helped in the establishment of Gia-Long rulers, who unified Vietnam. The French control extended to Cambodia in 1863 and soon Laos was also under their control, resulting in formation of Indo-Chinese union in 1893.

From 1940 to 1945 the country was occupied by Japan. After the defeat of Japan, though the Europeans were keen to re-occupy the whole of Vietnam, the Vietminh from the north seized power and established the Republic of Vietnam in August 1945. This was opposed by the French, who promoted the southern parties in the formation of the Democratic Republic of Vietnam, as a free state within the Indo-Chinese Federation. On 19 December 1946, led by Ho Chi Minh the Vietminh launched a surprise attack and captured Hanoi, signalling eight years of hostilities. In 1954, the French were defeated at Dien Bien Phu, after which the Cold War saw its emergence in the region, with the opposing blocs supporting North and South Vietnamese. An agreement to cease hostilities was reached in Paris on 20 July 1954, envisaging division of the country into North (communist) and South Vietnam (western backed) along the 17th Parallel. However, it could only be implemented on 29 December 1959. An International Control Commission for Indo-China was formed, in which India played a major role. However, peace eluded the country and the North continued to inspire insurgency in the South. This resulted in a bitter conflict between the forces of North and South, which later enlarged into a full scale Vietnam War. While the USA and her allies supported the South, the USSR and to an extent China, supported the North.

Peace talks were again held, which resulted in the Paris Agreement of 27 January 1973 demanding an end to hostilities. However, the fighting continued till 30 April 1975, when Vietminh forces decisively defeated South Vietnam and the US forces were routed from Saigon, resulting in re-unification of Vietnam. Nearly 150,000 to 200,000 South Vietnamese people fled the country. Finally, on 2 July 1976, the unification of North and South Vietnam took place and the Socialist Republic of Vietnam was formed.

Though, during the war North Vietnam received support from both the Soviet Union and China, deterioration of relations between the two communist giants resulted in the Chinese backed Khmer Rouge from Cambodia under Pol Pot launching attacks into Vietnam. This forced Vietnam to cross the border and attack Cambodia in December 1978 and though the West denounced Vietnam and quite a few western and South East Asian countries supported the autocratic and barbaric regime of Pol Pot, India supported Vietnam's stand in the UN. While the Vietnamese forces withdrew after installing a friendly regime in Cambodia, an enraged China decided to "teach Vietnam a lesson" and invaded Vietnam in 1979. The battle tested Vietnamese fought the PLA with grit and determination, and while China was able to make some gains, her forces faced stiff opposition and suffered heavy casualties, and later vacated the areas. Being the only country in South East Asia which gave a befitting military reply to China, Vietnam is considered a leader of Indo-China states and is respected by all countries of the region.

Socio-Economic Status and Trade

In 1999, Vietnam's population was 787,773,873, literacy was 93.7 per cent and life expectancy was 66 years. Vietnamese, French, English, Chinese and Khmer are spoken here. While Buddhism is the main religion, there are some Christians and Muslims also.[21]

Rising from the ravages of wars, in 1986, Vietnam shifted to multi-sectoral market economy. Since unification, the economy of the country has progressed at the growth rate of 4 per cent to 5 per cent. Major industries include food processing, garments, shoes, machine tools, cement, chemicals, oil, coal, steel and paper. The country exports crude oil, marine products, rice, coffee, rubber, tea, garments and shoes and imports specialised machinery and equipment, petroleum products, fertilizer, cattle, steel, raw cotton and automobiles.

Total arable area is 17 per cent. Rice, corn, potatoes, rubber, soyabeans, coffee, tea, bananas,poultry, pigs and fishery are the main produce. Natural resources include phosphate, coal, manganese, and bauxite, off shore oil and gas deposits, forests and hydropower. The two main cultivated areas are the Red River Delta in the north (15,000 sq km) and the Mekong Delta (60,000 sq km) in the south, with nearly 75 per cent of the area being hilly or low mountains. In 2000, the country had a per capita GDP of US $ 1300. The country faces environmental hazards from logging, slash and burn farming and over fishing.

Years of war having greatly affected the economy of the country, in 1986, Hanoi decided to introduce free market economy. The end of the Cold War also saw the Soviets pulling out their Navy from Cam Ranh Bay where they had been based for nearly 25 years. In 1993, Hanoi re-established diplomatic ties with China and with Washington on 11 July 1995. It later signed a trade agreement with the EU. All this while, ASEAN members had been observing the developments in Vietnam. Realising the economic and strategic potential of Vietnam, though a Communist country, Vietnam was incorporated as the seventh member of the ASEAN group on 28 July 1995.

Security Concerns

While the internal problem being faced by Vietnam is to build her economy, externally she faces threat from China, both along her land and sea borders. China has laid claims and occupied few of the Paracel Islands in the oil rich fields of South China Sea and has started producing gas from them. Navies of both countries have had armed clashes over the disputed islands, but China does not seem to be in a mood for either negotiating or relinquishing control. Enraged by Vietnam's military action in Cambodia in 1978, China launched a military offensive on Vietnam in 1979. Though the PLA succeeded in advancing in the semi-hilly terrain, she faced stiff resistance from the newly formed Vietnamese Army.

Hanoi has been carrying out pro-active and flexible manoeuvres to strengthen her ties with her neighbours and engage ASEAN. In 2002, trade with South Korea increased to US $ 2.7 billion. The US, however, still describes Vietnam as a "country of concern", in which religious persecution and violation of human rights are on the increse. Hanoi is often threatened by econimc sanctions, though a bilateral trade agreement between America and Vietnam, on the lines of Myanmar, China and North Korea, was ratified in 2001. Vietnam continues to support and show solidarity with North Korea. The country is identified as "a good political partner" pursuing policy of streghthening natural defence. The economy of the country has shown signs of improvement.

Vietnam is likely to continue its progress. While the situation along the land and sea borders has remained quiet since the 1979 Sino-Vietnam conflict, in the Chinese perception the emergence of an economically strong and assertive Vietnam could pose a serious problem of leadership of Indo-China states.

LAOS (LAO)

Situated on the southern periphery of the South East Asian landmass, it has an area of 235,000 sq km, with over 70 per cent as mountains and plateaus, two third being forested. In the north it has borders with China, in the east with Thailand, in the west with Vietnam and to its south, with Cambodia. River Mekong meanders through the country and is a common link and lifeline of the region, as, besides irrigation and power generation, it is also a major water way and a cause of flooding during monsoons. Along with Cambodia and Vietnam, Laos (at times also referred as Lao) has played an important role in Indochina's affairs. After the US withdrawal from Vietnam, it had become a major source of concern of the Domino theory of communist expansion to non-communist countries of the region.

Originally occupied by migrant Thais, the first Lao muang (district) was formed in the 13th century following the invasion of south-western China by Kublai Khan's Mongol hordes. Thereafter, during the period of 14th to 17th centuries, a number of warlords ruled, and by the end of the 18th century, most of the country came under Thai suzerainty, while Vietnam continued to apply pressure for tributes. Unable to withstand the two pressures, the three warlords went to war with Thailand in 1820, with disastrous results; the country fell under Thai control.[22]

During this period, France was busy forming French Indochina in Vietnam, and with treaties with Thai, Lao came under their protection. Occupied by the Japanese during the Second World War, Lao Issara, a resistance group was formed to oppose the return of France after the war. Though the 1953 French-Laotian Treaty granted full independence, conflict erupted and continued between the royalist, neutralist and the Communist factions. Bombing of Ho Chi Minh trail in eastern Laos commenced in 1964 and continued till 1973. Besides causing internal conflicts between the royalist Vientiane and Communist Pathet Lao, it resulted in loss of many lives and large scale destruction. On per capita basis, America dropped more bombs in Laos than it did worldwide during the Second World War.

After the fall of Saigon in 1975, a Lao People's Democratic Republic was formed, and the country continued to have close ties with, both China and Vietnam.

Socio-Economic Status and Trade

In 1990, Laos had a population of 5,497,459, which is expected to go up to13, 170,000 by 2050. The literacy rate is 57 per cent males 70 per cent and females 44 per cent. While Lao is the main language, French and English are also spoken. Religion–wise 60 per cent of the population is Buddhist, while animists and others account for the balance 40 per cent. Life expectancy is 51.22 years only.

The per capita GDP is US$ 1300 and though due to the mountainous terrain and forests only three per cent of the total land is fit for cultivation, nearly 80 per cent of the labour is employed in agriculture, producing sweet potatoes, vegetables, corn, rice, coffee, sugarcane, tobacco, cotton, tea, peanuts and poultry products. In industry, tin and gypsum mining, timber, electric power generation, garments and construction projects are the main spheres of activity. Laos exports wood products, garments, electricity, coffee and tin while she imports machinery and equipment, vehicles and petroleum products and fuel.

The country has abundance of natural resources of timber, hydroelectric power generation, gypsum, tin, gold and gems stones. However unexploded ammunition and bombs, deforestation, soil erosion and lack of potable water threaten her environment. Moreover, Laos has only 20,000 telephones.

Security Concerns

Besides low economic progress, the country often faces internal political threats. Her border with Thailand remains porous resulting in illegal trade in arms and goods, which result in military tension. Being a neighbour of Vietnam and China who have a long history of rivalry for control and domination of Indo-Chinese states, also creates security vulnerabilities. However, since joining ASEAN, Laos's relations with her neighbours have improved, and there are proposals for joint economic projects in Mekong Delta.

In July 2003, rebels of the Hmang—a rag tag army of the 72 years old General Vang Pao (residing in the USA and reportedly being supported by the CIA), blew up a tourist bus in the remote hills of Northern Laos, killing innocent passengers. Hmang followers do not want trade relations between Laos and America, and are fighting for freedom of their area.

Economic and political situation in the country is likely to remain weak, which may be taken advantage of by outside powers.

CAMBODIA

Sharing borders with Thailand in the west, Vietnam in east, China and Laos in the north and north east, it has a shoreline dominating the Gulf of Thailand and the South China Sea. Providing a buffer between Vietnam and China with Thailand, any instability in Cambodia not only results in exodus of refugees, but also threatens the security of non-communist states of the region. It also provides a number of road, river (including Mekong) and rail links between Thailand and Laos,Vietnam and China, which have both security and economic implications.

One of the least developed countries of the region, during the Vietnam War, it experienced large scale aerial bombing and mine laying by the Americans. These un-exploded bombs and neutralised mines have not only resulted in many casualties, but have reduced the area available for cultivation.

During the period 1st to 6th century, the country was part of the kingdom of Funan, and being on the trade route between India and China, it developed immensely. It was during 800 AD under the ruler Jayavarman II that architecture reached its zenith and famous Angkorian temples were built and Khmer rule was established. With the establishment of French rule in the region, in 1863, Cambodia also came under the French control as an adjunct to Vietnam, which lasted for the next 90 years. Independence was declared in 1953 and King Norodom Sihanouk took over the reigns. He was overthrown by the military in 1970, and he fled to China.

The year 1969 saw Cambodia getting embroiled in the Vietnam War, as America started aerial bombing of the suspected North Vietnamese base camps, leading to a land invasion by American and South Vietnamese troops in 1970. However, these failed to achieve military objectives, nor were they able to influence the internal rivalry between the rightists and the leftists, but forced the Khmer Rouge (meaning Red Khmer in French) to the interior.

After intense infighting, Khmer Rogue captured Phnom Penh on 17 April 1975, two weeks before the fall of Saigon to North Vietnam. Soon, their leader Pol Pot attempted the transformation of Cambodia into a Maoist, peasant-dominated agrarian cooperative, and carried out large scale genocide. In the next four years, at least one million people were eliminated, on one pretext or the other. Relations with Vietnam also deteriorated, leading to Vietnam's offensive in 1978. Though defeated and driven out, the 980s saw the Khmer Rogue conducting a guerrilla war against the Vietnamese backed regime in Phnom Penh.

In 1993, elections were held under the UN, and Norodom Sihanouk was made the king and the prime minister. Though Khmer Rogue was to join the government, they continue to remain outside the political process, and pose a threat to the stability of the country. Presently, Cambodia is being ruled by a liberal multi-party communist system and has good relations with both China and Vietnam.[23]

Socio-Economic Status and Trade

With an area of 181,035 sq. km., the mostly mountainous country has two main water sources, Mekong River and the Tonle Sap (Great Lake), which is connected to Mekong by a 100 km long water channel. These two water sources are important, not only for agriculture but also for transportation and hydroelectric developments. There are three main mountain ranges, in south-west the Elephant and Cardamom mountains, along the Thai border in north the Dangkerk mountains and along north–east, the Eastern Highlands.

In 1990, the population was 12,212,306, which is likely to go up to 27,420,040 by 2050. Life expectancy was 54 years for males and 58 for females. The spread of AIDS continues to cause great concern. Literacy rate is 95 per cent and approximately 95 per cent of the population is Buddhist. The per capita GDP is US$ 710, the lowest in South East Asia. While Khmer is the most used language, French and English are also spoken.

There are few industries, like garments, rice milling, fishery, wood carving, cement and gems. Exports include timber, garments, rubber, rice and fish, while imports include cigarettes, gold, construction material, petroleum products, machinery and motor vehicles. Natural resources of timber, gemstones, iron ore, manganese, and phosphate are available in plenty, and there is a vast potential of hydropower. Illegal logging and strip mining along the border with Thailand pose serious environmental hazards.

Security Concerns

The country underwent a major political turmoil under the Pol Pot regime, which also saw strained relations with Vietnam, leading to a punitive invasion by the latter. Though hemmed-in between China and Vietnam and being politically and ideologically closer to Beijing, there is no external threat to Cambodia for now. Internally, while the recent elections have resulted in a stable government, there are some disgruntled groups who indulge in bombing and other explosions. With Laos having joined ASEAN, Cambodia also hopes to develop her economy and strengthen her resilience. The large scale aerial carpet bombing by the Americans has left a number of unexploded bombs and mines undetected and buried. This has not only resulted in a number of casualties but has also reduced the area available for cultivation.

The country held its national elections on 27 July 2003. Prior to the elections, a number of Western critics had blamed Prime Minister Hun Sen of human rights violations like censoring radio broadcasts, limiting opposition's voice, curtailing pro-democracy voices and even of murdering monks. They had alleged that the country was becoming a refuge of terrorists and criminal groups, and held Hun Sen directly responsible for it. However, though 15 people were killed in the election related violence, the elections were seen as the real test of democracy and a step towards bonafide democracy. The Combodian

Peoples Party of Hun Sen won 73 seats, but was short of nine seats for a 2/3rd majority, while Funcinoep (led by Ranariddh- son of the former King Norodom Sihanouk) won 26 and Sam Rainsay's (considered pro-West) party won 24 seats. Though efforts of Hun Sen to co-opt smaller parties for forming the Government failed (he was accused of intimidating them by placing their leaders under house arrest), the elections have been hailed as clean, by Senator McCain of the USA. Political stalemate continues, as the two smaller parties having joined hands to form the Alliance of Democrats, are willing to join the Government, but want their share in power. Rainsay has also requested western powers for support, to overthrow Hun Sen.

The conduct of free and fair elections are likely to accord greater legitimacy to Prime Minister Hun Sen, and strengthen his position.

EAST TIMOR

As mentioned earlier, the Indonesian Army had moved into the province in 1975 resulting in internal strife and clashes between followers of the pro-Indonesia and pro-Independence movements, as well as denunciation of Indonesia in international community. Bowing to international pressures and internal political changes, on 24 July 1998, Jakarta announced withdrawal of her 12,000 troops and declared amnesty for political prisoners. On 5 August, the Government also signed an agreement with Portugal to hold a referendum to decide the future of East Timor. [24]

Conducted under the UN supervision on 30 August 1999, it saw a turnout of nearly 450,000, approximately 99 per cent of the population, out of which 78.5 per cent voted for Independence. This resulted in pro-Indonesia groups accusing the UN of rigging the elections, leading to violence. Thousands of people took refuge in the hills while much of the capital, Dili, was burnt to the ground by the pro-Indonesian protesters.

After one year under the UN supervision team led by Australia, an independent country was born on 31 May 2002. Though the Indonesian Army was not in favour of President Megawati attending the ceremony, she decided to attend it. On their part, the leaders of East Timor are making efforts to maintain cordial relations with all countries of the region, including Indonesia.

The country dominates the sea lanes between Indonesia and Australia, and is rich in oil and gas. She has good harbours and under guidance of Australia, is seeking aid from Western countries.

Security Concerns

Presently, the country does not face any external or internal threats. However, a clash between the Australian and pro-West interests with those of Indonesia or China, especially if large reserves of oil are detected, could draw-in this newly independent country into rival camps. The country's entry into the ASEAN fold, was blocked by Myanmar, as the pro-democracy elements of Myanmar had had links with the Timorese resistance groups.

The reduction in strength of Australian-led UN peacekeeping force is likely to be slowed. Earlier, it was envisaged that the 2785 strong force will be reduced to 1750 by June 2003, and will wind-up by December 2003. However, East Timor is likely to ask for the Force to stay back, till her own security forces are adequately trained by Australia.

The other area, which dominates security of the region, is the South China Sea, not only due to sea lanes but also because of its reserves of oil.

References

1. These voyages and domination of sea are sited as one of the basis of the claim of China over the South China Sea.
2. Chapter 1, Silk Roads and Spice Routes, Pages 9 to 24, Reorienting India, by B C Verghese.
3. Indonesia 2002, an Official Handbook, issued by the Embassy of Indonesia, New Delhi.
4. News from Indonesia, Vol. III, No. 8, August 02, issued by the Embassy of Indonesia, New Delhi.
5. The Statesmen Year Book 2001.
6. Far Eastern Economic Review, 2 December 2002.
7. His group was also suspected of having been behind the Bali Explosion. Far Eastern Economic Review, 24 October 2002.
8. Article by Harold Crouch, an Australian expert of the region, Far Eastern Economic Review, 24 October 2002.
9. Country web site, Govt. of Thailand.
10. Far Eastern Economic Review, 14 November 2002.
11. Initially, these US sponsored exercise was aimed to deter a Vietnam aggression against Thailand, via Laos and Cambodia. Initially it was aimed to cover traditional security threats, like border disputes, overlapping territorial claims and inter-state tensions critical to security of a country. Later, it's aim was changed to "improve interoperability between the armed forces of the region with America, and to conduct peacekeeping operations." In year 2002, nearly 10,000 troops from Thailand, Singapore and America participated in the exercise, in which thrust was laid on combating terrorists and separatist groups. 25 Observers were also invited, including from Malaysia, Vietnam, China, Mongolia. Post 9/11, besides conventional warfare,

search and rescue missions and formation of security communities between friendly countries, its scope has been expanded to cover "anti-terrorist operations".

12. Country web site, Govt. of Malaysia.
13. In December 2002, the International Court has upheld Malaysia's claim to the Islands. Far Eastern Economic Review, December 2002/January 2003.
14. Burma Net News and web site, Govt of Myanmar.
15. Asian Defence Journal, Vol. II, 7 of 1999 and Burma Net News and web site, Govt of Myanmar.
16. Web site Strait Times of Singapore, October 2002.
17. Lonely Planet-South East Asia on a shoestring, 1998.
18. Lonely Planet-South East Asia on a shoestring, 1998.
19. Asia Year Book 2002 of Far Eastern Economic Review. Naval exercises were held with Indonesian Navy in Java Sea on 27 August 2002. News from Indonesia, Vol. III, No 8, August 02, issued by Embassy of Indonesia, New Delhi.
20. Statesmen Year Book, 2002 and Lonely Planet – South East Asia on a shoe string-1998.
21. Statesmen Year Book, 2002 and Lonely Planet – South East Asia on a shoe string-1998.
22. Statesmen Year Book, 2002 and Lonely Planet – South East Asia on a shoe string-1998
23. Asia Year Book 2002 of Far Eastern Economic Review, June 2002.
24. Website of eou.com.

3

The South China Sea

As South China Sea is an important area of concern and plays a vital role in economic and security environment of South East Asia, it is essential to know some details of this water body, so that its relevance as the most likely flashpoint in the region can be appreciated in the correct perspective. Stretching 1600 km from the Straits of Malacca to the Straits of Taiwan, from Singapore to Taiwan, it embraces the Philippines, Malaysia and Indonesia.[1]

Having an area of approximately 648,000 sq nautical miles (nm), this long pond has about 200 small islands, rocks and reefs, majority being grouped into Spratly and Paracel Island chains. Most of these islands remain partially submerged, are a shipping hazard and are not fit for inhabitation. Out of the two chains of islands, Spratly is more important as it dominates the main sea-lanes.

Nearly half the sea tonnage of the world going from the Indian Ocean to the Pacific transits through South China Sea, through three choke points of Straits of Malacca, Sunda and Lambok (the last two in Indonesian waters). Heavy oil tankers follow Lombok and Makassar Straits, while others clear Malacca Straits, leaving one metre clearance from keel to

WORLD CRUDE OIL FLOWS

34.8 million barrels per day

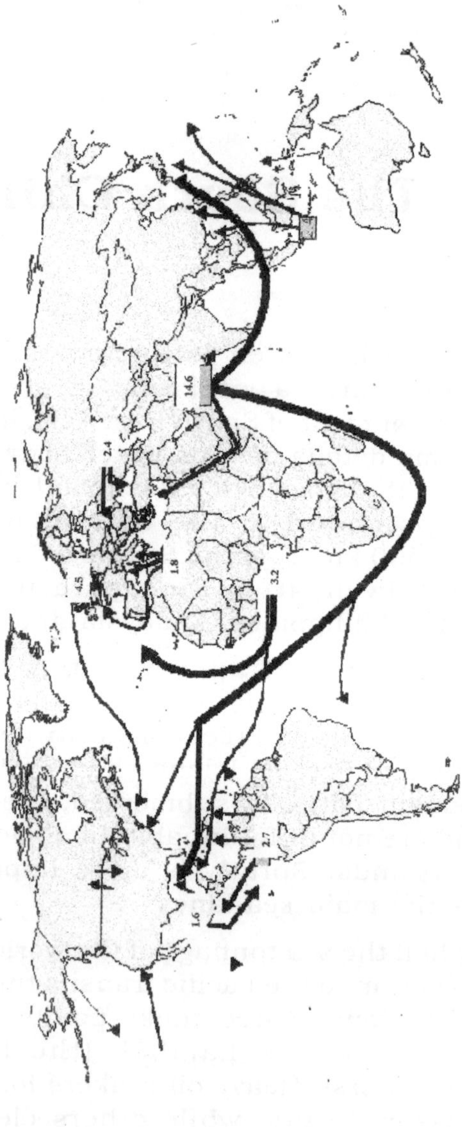

Energy Information Administration

http://www.eia.doe.gov/emeu/security/oilflow2.gif

seabed. The oil passing through South China Sea is nearly three times that of Suez Canal and fifteen times that through Panama Canal, mainly for East-Australian countries. As far as Japan is concerned, nearly 80 per cent of her trade and majority of her oil imports pass through this "long pond" (Refer Map).

South China Sea is reported to be full of mineral wealth of hydrocarbons like oil, natural gas and liquid natural gas (LNG). Though estimates vary, out of the proven oil reserves of 6.9 billion barrels per day (bbl), currently 2.0 bbl are being extracted; 50 per cent by Malaysia, the balance by China, Vietnam and Indonesia. As regards LNG, Indonesia, Brunei and Malaysia are currently producing nearly 1/4th of the world's requirement, which is mainly being exported to Japan. Natural gas is the most abundant hydrocarbon reserve, being nearly 60 per cent to 70 per cent of the total resource, and is being produced by Malaysia, Vietnam, China and Indonesia (in Natuna Islands). The likely demand of the region by 2020 is likely to be 20 trillion cubic feet, four times the present consumption.

As per Chinese estimates, the oil potential of Spratly and Paracel Islands is between 105 to 213 bbl, while estimates of the USA are 28 bbl. Even giving 10 per cent economic productivity, as per Chinese estimates, the Spratly could provide 1.4 to 1.9 million barrels per day, while the US estimates would come to 137,000 to 183,000 bbl.

Besides the importance of South China Sea from the point of shipping and mineral wealth, Article 3 of the UN Law of the Sea has laid down territorial zone of 12 nautical miles (nm) as the sea breadth from the shore of a country (including uninhabited islands), while Articles 55 to 75 have defined the Exclusive Economic Zone (EEZ) of 200 nm for sovereign rights for exploration, conserving and managing natural

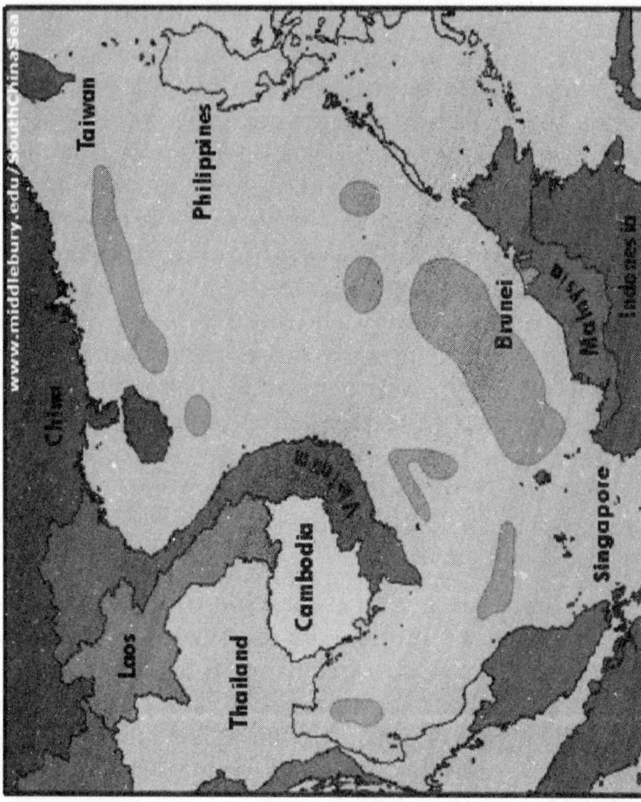

Source: Daniel Y. Coulter, South China Sea Fisheries: Countdown to Calamity. Contemporary Southeast Asia, March 1996.

resources. This has led to conflicting claims and a rush by countries on the seaboard of South China Sea to occupy the atolls and islands in Spratly and Paracel Islands, often resulting in armed clashes.

Implications of the Law of the Sea Conference (SLOC)

Before proceeding further, it would not be out of place to mention some implications of the third Law of the Sea Convention of the UN, voted on 30 April 1982. It was adopted by 130 states, while USA, Israel, Turkey and Venezuela opposed it; 17 countries abstained.

This convention comprising of 320 articles and nine annexures, provides guidelines for international maritime behaviour. The salient features, which effect countries of South East Asia are :-

(a) The drawing of baselines.

(b) A 12 nm territorial sea.

(c) Unimpeded transit through international straits.

(d) An Extended Economic Zone of up to 200 nm.

(e) A continental shelf regime and rights to manage living and non-living resources of the continental shelf to a minimum of 200 nm.

The Convention also lays down the concept of archipelago waters and regulatory power over the ocean for archipelago states.[2] As per this convention, new claim lines have been drawn by countries of the region in the South China Sea, which often overlap.

Claim Lines (Refer Map)

While China, Taiwan and Vietnam lay claim to the Paracel Islands, the Spratlys are claimed by Malaysia, Philippines, Indonesia, Vietnam, Brunei and China.

COMPETING CLAIMS IN THE SOUTH CHINA SEA

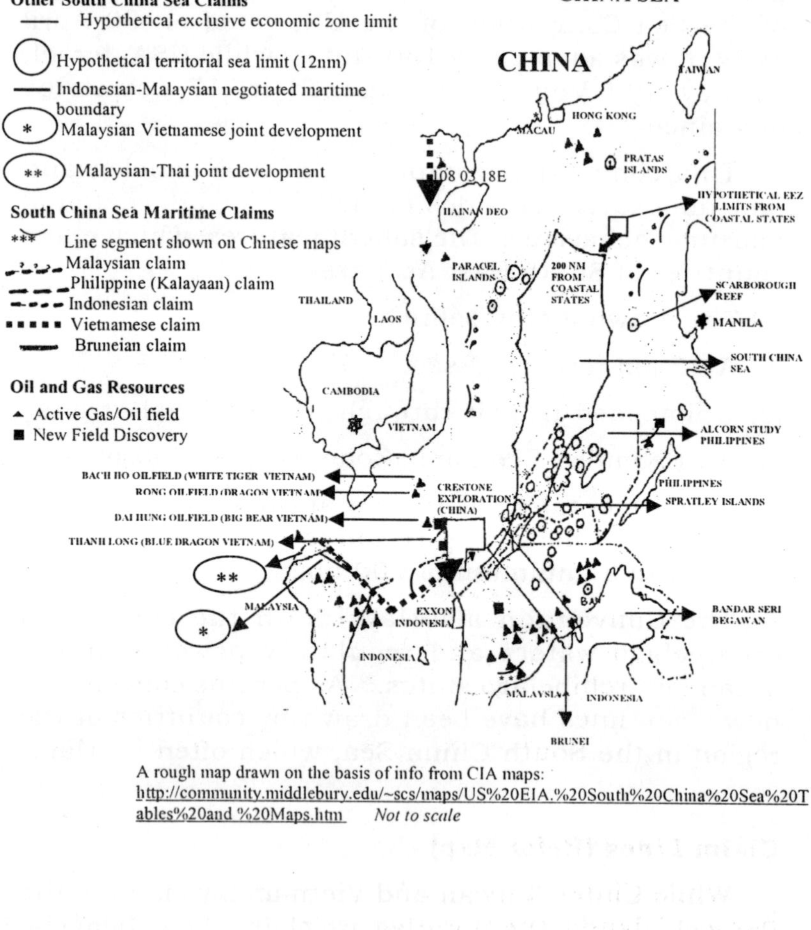

A rough map drawn on the basis of info from CIA maps: http://community.middlebury.edu/~scs/maps/US%20EIA.%20South%20China%20Sea%20Tables%20and %20Maps.htm *Not to scale*

In their efforts to lay claims on these islands, except for Brunei, all other countries have made efforts to occupy and establish fishing villages and military posts on them. By 2001, few reefs of Spratly Islands were occupied by claimant countries, which often resulted in armed clashes

The Claim Lines are as under-

(a) Brunei does not occupy any of the islands, but claims them as per her EEZ shelf, which includes Louisa Reef.

(b) China lays claims over Spratlys, named Nansha and over most of South China Sea, on the basis of the naval expeditions of Han Dynasty in 110 AD and the Ming Dynasty in 1433 AD. She had also claimed them during 19th and 20 century, till the Japanese occupied them during the Second World War. In 1947 China produced a map with nine undefined dotted lines, and claimed all islands within those lines. In 1992, a Chinese law restated her claims in the region. Today, Beijing occupies eight islands in Spratly to enforce her claim, while she seized Paracels from Vietnam in 1974.

(c) Indonesia does not claim any islands, but Taiwanese and Chinese claims clash with her EEZ and continental shelf, including those of Natuna gas fields.

(d) Malaysia's claim is based upon the continental shelf principle, and she occupies three islands within her continental shelf. She has tried to build one atoll by bringing soil from the mainland and has built a hotel also.

(e) Philippines' claims are based on proximity and activities of her explorers of 1956. In 1971, Manila claimed eight islands called Kalayaan

and re-designated them as Palawan Province in 1972.

(f) Taiwan's claims are based on the same principle as that of China, and are not clearly defined. She occupies Paratas Island in Spratlys.

(g) Vietnamese claims are also based on historical and continental shelf principle. Hanoi claims entire Spratly (Truong Sa) as an off shore district of her Khanh Hoa province and large areas of South China Sea. They also claim Paracels (Hoang Sa), which were seized by China in 1974. Hanoi's claims are also based on Beijing's pattern, using archaeological evidence to support sovereignty, as in 1930s France had claimed Spratly and Paracels on behalf of its then colony of Vietnam. Presently, Hanoi occupies twenty reefs in Spratlys to enforce her claim.

Thus, it would be seen that both Spratlys and Paracels have unresolved claims, which could lead to future confrontation between the countries of South East Asia. Some of the important clashes since 1970s are outlined below:-[3]

(a) *Between China and Vietnam.* Even before North Vietnam had fully defeated South Vietnam, in 1974 China took advantage and occupied a few atolls, in which 18 soldiers were killed. They again clashed in 1988 on Johnson Reef in the Spratly, where several Vietnamese boats were sunk and 70 sailors were killed. In 1992 Vietnam accused China of occupying Da Lac Reef. In retaliation between June and September, the Chinese seized 20 Vietnamese cargo ships transporting goods from Hong Kong. The next clash between the two took place in 1994 over the internationally recognised territorial waters of Vietnam's Tu Chinh oil exploration blocks 133, 134 and 135, which China claims as part of her Wan' Bei-21(WAB-21) block. In 1999 the two countries have signed an agreement over Paracel Islands, and today the Chinese have full control over the oil exploration projects. However, differences over Spratly continue to exist.

(b) *Between China and Philippines.* The dispute refers to Spratly's Mischief Reef. The first clash took place when the Philippine Navy detected Chinese occupation of the atoll in 1995, and evicted them in March 1995 and destroyed the markers put up by the Chinese. Beijing claimed it as fishermen's facilities, while on ground they had constructed a barrack for housing troops. January 1996 saw another clash between the two sides near Capones Islands, resulting in 90 minutes gun battle between the Philippines Navy and the Chinese boats. The third incident occurred in April 1997, when the Philippines Navy ordered a Chinese speedboat and two fishing craft out from Scarborough Shoal, removed Chinese markers and raised their own flag. The PLA sent three of her warships to survey Panata and Kota Islands occupied by Philippines. In May and June 1999, Chinese fishing boats again intruded in areas claimed by Manila, and on their refusal to withdraw, were sunk by the Philippines warship. May 1999 also saw Manila accusing Beijing of harassing one of her naval vessels in the Spratlys, which had run aground.

(c) *Between Philippines and Vietnam.* January 1998 saw Vietnamese soldiers firing on a Philippine fishing boat near Tennent (Pigeon Reef). The Vietnamese also fired on Philippines reconnaissance aircraft in October 1999.

(d) *Between Taiwan and Vietnam.* In 1995, Taiwanese artillery shelled a Vietnamese supply ship.

(e) *Between Malaysia and Philippines.* In October 1999, Manila reported that her two reconnaissance aircraft nearly clashed with two fighter planes of the Malaysian Air Force over a reef occupied by the Malaysian troops.

Piracy in South China Sea

While the area has always been prone to piracy and highjacking, the 1999 attack by Indonesian pirates branding knives resulting in capture of Japanese ship Alondra Rainbow carrying $ 20 million cargo of aluminium ingots, off the coast of Indonesia has raised the issue afresh. Though in a bold action on high seas the ship was recaptured by the Indian Navy, its crew had been adrift for ten days in the Andaman Sea and were rescued by Thai fishermen.[4]

The attempted piracy cases in Indonesian waters had also doubled in 1999 to 113, from 60 in 1998. Indonesian pirates were also blamed for acts in Malaysian and Singapore waters. As Japan's oil cargo and sea trade was most affected, for the first time since World War II, the South East Asian countries reacted favourably to Japan's proposal to collaborate in joint patrolling of the sea-lanes. Though some nations still linger on memories of Japanese wartime atrocities and colonial rule, the anti-piracy co-operation is likely to give Japan an opportunity to expand her military role in South East Asia.

Besides claims on natural resources, the issue of sovereignty over the islands is likely to be contested strongly in the years to come. While efforts have been made by the Asean Regional Forum (ARF) to resolve the issue, there are differences in approaches being recommended by China and the remaining ASEAN members, who want to deal with the issue as a group. The USA considers this a regional issue and is not likely to interfere, as long as the Sea Lanes continue to be available for international use. In 2000, China circulated a draft code of conduct for countries having territorial claims in the area, which differed with the 1995 draft of ASEAN countries, as it did not call for a freeze on construction on islands or atolls and excluded Paracel Islands from its purview.[5] China's signing of the Treaty of Amity and Co-operation with ASEAN has raised hopes of the possibility of a peaceful resolution, which needs to be watched.

Before studying strategic interests of other countries in the region, it will be pertinent to study the mechanisms of economic and conflict resolution existing in the region.

References

1. Website of eou.com.
2. Commander Vijay Sakhuja, *Confidence Building from the Sea : An Indian Initiative* (New Delhi: Knowledge World, 2001).
3. CIA Maps and Publications for the Public. Update on South China Sea of March 2002. Website wmaster@cia.doe.gov.
4. Report of International Maritime Association, UK, 2002.
5. *Far Eastern Economic Review*, 10 February 2000.

4

ASEAN and Other Regional Groupings

ASEAN

The 1955 Afro-Asian conference was a trend-setter in regional peace and co-operation, and proposed the ideology of non-alignment at Bandung. Though most countries of the region attended the deliberations, initially the Philippines hesitated to attend, while China and others turned it into a forum for anti-US tirade. Philippines on the other hand spoke against communism, supported America and denounced neutralism. In the 1950s, Pandit Nehru enjoyed great diplomatic stature. At the conference he denounced military organisations like SEATO. However, China maintained a conciliatory approach and saw no reason why relations between China, Thailand, Philippines and other neighbouring countries could not develop on the principles of Panchsheel.

Soon after the Bandung Conference, Malaya, Singapore and Philippines floated the idea of an Asian confederation primarily to counter Communist expansion, and invited India to join. As at the same time the West was also mooting security pacts like SEATO and CENTO for which some of these countries had opted, India looked at any such grouping with suspicion. Also, as India was keen to develop good neighbourly relations with China and all countries of South East Asia, she declined the offer of joining any of them.

In 1963, Malaya tried a confederation with Singapore and formed Malaysia, but it did not last long and Singapore broke away in 1966. Malaysia's relations with Indonesia under Sukarno deteriorated due to the conflicting claims over Sabah and Sarawak in East Malaysia, as also with the Philippines over Mindanao Islands, leading to armed conflicts.

The August 1967 Initiative

The initiative taken by Indonesia under Suharto to form the ASEAN was welcomed by Singapore, Malaysia, Thailand and Philippines . While there were socio-cultural, ethnic, political and economic diversities among the countries, their leaders were pragmatic enough to realise that their future lay in co-operation, rather than in confrontation. Thus, their foreign ministers signed the Bangkok Declaration on 8 August 1967, forming ASEAN with five founder members — Indonesia, Malaysia, the Philippines, Singapore and Thailand. The primary objectives of the Association were to accelerate economic growth, social progress, cultural development and promotion of peace. They appreciated that "reduction of tension between South East Asia's non-communist states would free their weak post-colonial governments to tackle internal communist challenges, and to address development priorities".

The Bangkok Declaration also stated that ASEAN's primary responsibility was that of strengthening "the economy and social stability of member countries and the region, and ensuring their peaceful and progressive national development." The members were determined to ensure their stability and security from external aggression. Thus, while ASEAN was formed with no rigid political or economic agenda, the threat of armed communist insurgencies, presence of extra regional powers and the fear of Domino theory after fall of the US in Vietnam, created a new security paradigm. Hence, member countries sought protection and assistance from the USA to counter the threat of communism, giving impetus to the Treaty of Amity and Cooperation (TAC). Meanwhile, in 1971, ASEAN had passed a declaration proclaiming the region as a Zone of Peace, Freedom and Neutrality (ZOPFAN), which was incorporated in the February 1976 Declaration.

The Treaty of Amity and Cooperation (TAC) was signed at Bali on 24 February 1976 after the first summit, which aimed to enhance cooperation between the member countries in economic, social, cultural, technical, scientific and administrative spheres. The member countries decided to bury their bilateral differences and work for promoting peace and stability, based on the cardinal principles of mutual respect, non-interference, consensus, dialogue and consultation for the economic unity and growth of the region. It was hoped that this would substantially enhance the social development and economic growth of the people, leading to all round prosperity. They formed a number of committees to guide the grouping and Brunei was admitted in 1984. Appreciating the strategic importance of Vietnam as a potential market as well as a bulwark against China, though there were initial reservations on admitting a communist country, by 1990s seeing the improvement in Hanoi's relations with Washington and Beijing, she was admitted in the grouping in 1995. Laos and Cambodia became ASEAN members in 1997. As for Myanmar, while America and the West had declared economic sanctions due to the anti-democracy policies of the military regime, China's military and economic influence and trade in the country had increased since 1990s. Thus, despite reservations from the West, Malaysia and Indonesia spearheaded the move to invite Myanmar into the grouping, in 2000.

ASEAN Regional Forum (ARF)

While the end of the Cold War signalled closing down of military bases and reduction in tension in the region, the potential threat from China, especially in the South China Sea was viewed with alarm. Thus, in its post Ministerial Meeting at Bangkok in July 1994 it was felt that the security concerns of South East Asia and North East Asia could not be separated, and there was a need to have a forum for discussing these. To co-opt China in a security dialogue, ARF was formed with ASEAN, USA, UK, China, Russia, Japan, Australia and Canada. Based on Article 2 of the Treaty of Amity and Cooperation signed at the first ASEAN summit at Bali, it incorporated the following as its basic tenants:-

(a) Mutual respect for independence, sovereignty, equality, territorial integrity and national identity of all nations;

(b) The right of every state to lead its national existence free from external interference, subversion, or coercion;

(c) Non-interference in internal affairs of one another;

(d) Settlement of disputes and differences by peaceful means;

(e) Renunciation of the threat or use of force; and

(f) Effective cooperation among themselves.[1]

Being the most important non-military security forum, its members had decided to follow a three-stage policy for resolving regional disputes. First, the confidence building measures, the next preventive diplomacy and the last, conflict resolution. As of now, the only conflict facing the region is the Chinese claims on Spratly and Paracel Islands. India also became a member in 1996, and by August 2002 the strength of the Forum had increased to twenty two.[2] Though all ASEAN members and China are signatories to the 1982 UN Convention on Law of the Sea, and ASEAN in 1992 declared her intention to resolve all her disputes in the South China Sea peacefully, the dispute is nowhere near a solution. In fact, few western analysts feel that with the growing Chinese demand for oil, the dispute is the future flashpoint in the region.[3] India going nuclear in May 1998, to an extent did affect the invitation extended to India to join the ARF.

ASEAN Free Trade Agreement (AFTA)

ASEAN has proved its success as a regional and supra-regional grouping, and at the global level compares favourably with European Union as the economic integration of North America and South America into NAFTA and MERCURSOR, respectively. AFTA is designed to integrate member countries into the global economy. With a motto of agree first and negotiate later, it is not a very rigid arrangement, but aims to enhance attractiveness of ASEAN as an investment region. ASEAN plans to establish Free Trade Zones within her six developed economies by 2003 and with the balance four, by 2010 (Myanmar, Laos, Cambodia and Vietnam).

Besides developing regional economic cooperation within ASEAN, they want to enlarge the scope by organising meetings like ASEAN + 3 held in 1998 (between ASEAN, Japan, China and South Korea), and ASEAN + 1(with India) in 2002. Such meetings aim to increase the leverage capacity of ASEAN while dealing with APEC and other forums. Keeping the economic standards of the countries in mind within ASEAN three economic zones have been created:-

(a) Indonesia-Malaysia-Singapore economic growth triangle-(IMS-GT), popularly known as Southern Growth Triangle.

(b) Indonesia-Malaysia-Thailand economic growth triangle-(IMT-GT), also known as Northern Growth Triangle.

(c) The East ASEAN growth triangle, comprising Indonesia, Malaysia, Philippines and Brunei, (EAGA), also known as Eastern Growth Triangle.

(d) The remaining countries, Vietnam, Myanmar, Laos and Cambodia are grouped as Economically Developing Countries.

The concept of South Asian Growth Quadrangle (SAGQ) was explored in December 1996, with four geographically contiguous countries like India, Bangladesh, Bhutan and Nepal, transcending political legacies for economic benefits. The Greater Mekong sub-regional grouping is one such project being examined. SAGQ proposes to expand trade in textiles, leather, rubber, jute, fisheries, tea, gas, tourism, hydro power, mineral based industries, coal, oil and gas, to name a few. It is estimated that with a middle class of approximately 250 million people, even an increase of US dollars four in their income will result in increase of purchasing power to US $ one billion, which has immense potential for boosting the economic growth of these countries. However, the proposal of SAGQ is still at the conceptual stage, and its impact on SAARC and other economic-political aspects are yet to be fully analysed.[4]

When compared with China joining WTO, there are concerns amongst the weaker four of being neglected till 2020. To avoid being surprised by another economic crisis, in 1998, ASEAN formed a Surveillance Process. To enhance economic and trade relations, two proposals, an ASEAN Industrial Co-operation Scheme (AICS) and an ASEAN Investment Area (AIA) were also floated.

Realising the threat of terrorism in the region, on 1 August 2002, America signed an agreement for curbing terrorism in the region, with ASEAN countries. This covers increase in aid to fight terrorism, sharing of intelligence and in bolstering of ties between the law enforcement agencies of member countries. The dialogue partners also agreed to block finances of such groups, and for creating special financial intelligence units. Malaysia, Indonesia and Philippines also signed a similar pact, to fight terrorism. Later, ASEAN also signed a code of conduct, to govern territorial disputes in the South China Sea.

In view of the new threat posed by terrorism, the Security and Intelligence Chiefs of the original member countries have also been holding regular meetings. Initially, Indonesia was not very active in this regard, but since the 12 October 2002 Bali bombings, her participation has shown positive signs. Besides sharing intelligence and coordinating operations, the six countries have also agreed to assist each other in interrogation and trial of suspects.

Selective Grouping within ASEAN[5]

The 8 October 2003 meeting at Bali saw a new bilateral approach being advocated by Singapore and Thailand to resolve issues. These two members suggested that instead of seeking consensus on every issue which has slowed down economic integration between the developed rich countries and the less developed four (Vietnam, Myanmar, Laos and Cambodia), there is a need to adopt the European Union model. They pointed out that though AFTA's goal is to remove tarrifs by the year 2021, these have already been reduced to 90 per cent, but the trade within ASEAN has been static at 22 per cent over past five years, as countries like Myanmar, Vietnam, Laos and Cambodia cannot compete with bigger and developed countries. They argued that there is an acute realisation that for trade liberalisation and speedy progress, the process of consensus based decision-making is not workable. Prime Minister Goh of Singapore gave two option-either we hang together and be overtaken by competition from China and later India, or decide selectively to form smaller groupings. In his view, if two countries have an idea they can present it to the other ASEAN leaders to join, or they can carry on alone also. However, it must be open for others to sign on a reciprocal basis. Hence, the 2 + 10 idea should be accepted. Singapore and Thailand have already implemented it in the field of air travel, and Philippines has joined in, for cargo flights only. While the less developed countries are not likely to join, Malaysia and Indonesia, being more populated may not join either.

Achievements of the Forum

While ASEAN as a grouping has resulted in easing of bilateral tension and spreading peace and tranquility in the region, it has as yet not achieved its main objective of economic equality. Though there has also been progress on cultural and socio-economic fronts, the large disparities between the economic status of its ten member countries and commonality of produce have slowed the ambition of an open market. Specifically, the following observations may be pertinent:-

(a) Despite differences in their forms of Governments, style of functioning and human rights records, ASEAN countries have mostly acted in concert on international issues, generally along the lines of the western countries. In 1979, they voted against the Vietnamese invasion of Cambodia in support of Pol Pot regime, supported America's developing relations with China and they also have trade relations with Taiwan. After the 11 September 2001 attacks on the US, they denounced international terrorism. Though in Indonesia there were demonstrations against the US led offensive on Taliban in Afghanistan, generally they supported the western moves.

(b) The responses of member countries to the financial crisis of 1997, comments by Indonesia on the trial of Deputy Prime Minister of Malaysia, differences between Indonesia and Malaysia and between Singapore and Philippines over the Islamic fundamentalists operating from her soil, and intervention of the Australian led UN force in East Timor are few instances which show that despite professed unity, there are inherent weaknesses in the system.

(c) Though ARF is only to be chaired by an ASEAN member country in rotation, China has virtually a veto right. So far it has provided a forum for discussion on the claims in the South China Sea, but in the last seven years no progress has been made even to Stage One. Thus, the Track II (or 1.5

level) contacts have failed to achieve any worthwhile results. While China has stated that she would respect international use of sea lanes in the South China Sea and is willing to discuss sovereignty disputes over Spratlys with individual countries, ASEAN wants to discuss the issue as a group. As regards Paracel, the Chinese do not accept any claims of Vietnam, and hence the impasse continues.

ASIA PACIFIC ECONOMIC COOPERATION (APEC)

The concept of the grouping was initiated by Mr Bob Hawke, Prime Minister of Australia, on 31 January 1989, in Seoul. He stated that with the end of the Cold War and disintegration of the Soviet Union, the centre of economic gravity of the world was shifting from the mid-Atlantic to the mid-Pacific. China was getting integrated into the global business chain and the technical revolution was gathering steam. Thus, it was time to co-opt economies of the Pacific Rim countries with those of developing countries of ASEAN, namely Thailand, Malaysia, Philippines, Singapore, Brunei and Indonesia.

Initially, the grouping had eighteen countries, six from ASEAN and selected countries of the Pacific Rim, prominent being the USA, China, Australia, Japan, Canada, Chile, Mexico, New Zealand, Russia, Venezuela, South Korea and Taiwan. Later, Papua New Guinea, Peru and Hong Kong also joined the grouping. Though this was a forum for economic co-operation among countries of the Asia-Pacific region and the EU, India was not co-opted, as it is not located on the Pacific Rim.

Its leaders have pledged to work towards free trade and investment between the present members by year

2010 for the developed economies, and then by year 2020 for all other countries which qualify for the grouping. However, so far only 31 per cent of the product lines in the US tariff schedule have been made duty free, as compared to 21.4 per cent in 1996, though China has cut her average tariff rate from 23 per cent in 1996 to just 12 per cent by 2002. Liberalisation in transport and food has taken place, being two items out of the fifteen identified. The ratio of small and medium scale industries continues to be lop sided, being 1:20 in the US to 1: 120 in developing countries. However, developed countries are offering more credit for entrepreneural projects.

Since its chairmanship is not mandatory with one of the ASEAN country and it is driven by the EU, it allows the members to follow their own pace. While the trade between member South East Asian countries and the EU has grown, a preferential trade agreement is yet to be fully implemented. APEC is also committed to free trade in the Pacific, by 2020. Seen with WTO, the three economic groupings have three common facets, namely they support open regionalism, are instruments of preventive diplomacy and, can complement multilateral efforts.

During its yearly meeting at Shanghai in October 2001, it did adopt an American sponsored resolution denouncing terrorism. However, during the 2003 meeting in Bangkok, America was able to restrict the agenda to "countering international terrorism" and seeking support for her Operation "Iraqi Freedom." A few observers feel that while America seems to be driving APEC for obtaining support for her global political and diplomatic agenda, like ASEAN, economic co-operation continues to be lagging behind.

While ASEAN and APEC were formed for developing economic co-operation between the countries of South East Asia and other developed countries, these forums are yet to achieve their desired objectives. A feeling is growing amongst the more developed and economically advanced countries that the process of consensus on each issue is delaying economic progress, and needs a change. If agreed to, this policy is likely to be applied in other fields also, like security matters and membership, which is likely to weaken the organisation.

The ARF was formed for conflict resolution, but it is yet to produce any tangible results. While ASEAN and regional countries including India and Japan are directly concerned with the security environment of the region, the western countries led by the USA play a major role in formulation of policies of the forum. While economic relations between China and the region have improved since 1980s and are cordial at present, the region continues to be concerned with China's growing economic and military power. The threat of Islamic fundamentalism and international terrorism also looms large over the region, tackling of which calls for a combined and co-ordinated effort. While China is keen to sign the Treaty of Amity and Co-operation (TAC), it is to be seen whether she will abide by it and resolve her differences in the South China Sea, by peaceful negotiations. As regards the US, she already has strong military and economic interests in the region. She will continue to develop these and provide a counter to Chinese threats.

So far, ASEAN has drawn strength from the policy of consensus and non-interference in each other's affairs, and the will to resolve all issues among member countries peacefully, with the aim of achieving equality in economy. There is every likelyhood that the Singapore-Thailand proposal of 2 + 10 of AESAN may lead to weakening of the economic up-lift process. Also, while by signing the TAC China will become obliged to resolve her disputes in the South China

Sea peacefully, her growing military might and economic power will continue to cause concern in the region and otherwise.

After the financial crisis of 1997, the economy of most countries has shown recovery. An ASIA Bond has also been floated in the region, which in future will assist in facing similar financial crisis. However, as per World Bank's report of 2003, the four new members of ASEAN (Cambodia, Laos, Vietnam and Myanmar) continue to be in the "very poor" category (GDP of below US $745 per year). The disparities amongst the countries remain with Singapore having 60 times the income of Vietnam, 80 times that of Laos and 93 times that of Cambodia. There is a wide gap even among the rich members. Figures from *Military Balance* of 2003 indicate that while in 2001 the per capita income of Singapore was US $ 20,900, Brunei US$ 15, 452, Malaysia US $ 3874, Thailand at US $1760, Philippines US$ 940 and of Indonesia, only US$ 672. With countries favourably disposed towards America reaping financial and trade benefits (like Singapore) and the concept of selective grouping taking shape (2 + 10), it is likely that the economic disparity between the developed and developing members would increase.

Some analysts feel that while the professed aim of ASEAN is to "integrate all economies and uplift the quality of life of all member states", it is not likely to be achieved even in the next decade. However, lately ASEAN members have started taking security initiatives (like co-operation in fighting terrorism), which could lead to greater understanding and co-operation. With the threat of terrorism looming large in few of its member countries, the focus may shift to military matters, rather than economic integration. However, Vietnam, Laos, Cambodia and Myanmar are likely to remain in the background in any military co-operation.

The importance of the South East Asian region has been realised by countries outside the region also, as their economic, political and security interests often coincide, and at times clash with those of the regional countries.

References

1. *Asian Defence Journal*, December 1999.
2. Ten ASEAN members and twelve dialogue partners (Australia, Canada, China, EU, India, Japan, Mangolia, Papua New Guinea, South Korea, New Zealand, Russia, and the USA).
3. www.icsea.or.id/ The web site of SEA-SPAN-I, Southeast Asian Science Policy Advisory Network, Thailand.
4. "Expansion of Southeast Asian Regionalism: Lessons for South Asia", IPCS Paper by Aisha Sultanat, 2002, www.ipcs.org.
5. *Far Eastern Economic Review*, 8 October 2003.

5

Countries with Interest in the Area

CHINA

The largest country in Asia, she dominates Japan, South Korea, Taiwan, North Korea, Australia and the Pacific Ocean through her eastern sea board of East China Sea. She also dominates South China Sea where her claims to Spratly and Paracel Islands and her self-declared EEZ is contested by a number of countries of South East Asia. She has land borders with Russia, Mongolia, India, Myanmar, Laos and Vietnam, out of which she has settled the border with all, except India.

Till 1980s, her communist philosophy, expansionist policies, support to insurgencies and internal uprisings through overseas Chinese, national and military power had been a constant cause of concern to the countries of the region. However, since 1990s she has adopted a policy of peaceful dialogue and avoidance of conflict, while concentrating on economic development and modernisation of her armed forces. Today, she is the only competitor of America. Though she has developed trade and economic ties with America specially in the field of high technology machinery and equipment, she still has differences over Taiwan. A major regional power, after the demise of the Soviet Union, she is all set to become a super economic and military power in the near future.

Not to scale

Source : http://geography.about.com/library/blank/blxchina.htm

Socio-Economic Status and Trade

Having an area of 9,596,960 sq km, in 1990 she had a population of 1,261,832,482, which by 2050 is likely to reach 1,47,0408,924. The literacy rate is 81.5 per cent (89 per cent in males and 72 per cent in females), Chinese is the main language and the per capita GDP is US$ 5600. Nearly 50 per cent of the labour force is employed in agriculture, 24 per cent in industry and balance 26 per cent in services. The main industries are iron and steel, coal, machinery, garments, textiles, petroleum, cement, chemicals and fertilisers, foot-ware, toys, food processing, automobiles and electronics. Agriculture produce includes rice, wheat, potatoes, peanuts, tea, millet, fishery and poultry. While she exports machinery and equipment, textiles and clothing, footwear and toys, sports gear, mineral fuels and chemicals, she imports specialised high technology machine and equipment, plastics, chemicals, iron and steel, petroleum and fuel.

The country has natural resources of coal, iron ore, petroleum and natural gas, mercury, tin, tungsten, antimony, manganese, molybdenum, vanadium, magnetite, aluminium, lead, zinc, uranium, and a large potential for hydropower generation. The main environmental concerns arise from pollution, flood waters and deforestation, which has resulted in loss of 1/5th of soil. The country has 110 million telephones and is expanding the network. The year 2002 saw China becoming the third largest oil consumer in the world, importing 15 million barrels of crude in the first two months of 2003, up 62 per cent from 2002. Her efforts to construct a pipeline from Russia may be dashed by Japan, who has offered better terms. Thus, oil and energy are two areas of concern for Beijing.

In 2002-03, the economy is expected to grow at nine per cent. Though America has placed a two year ban on a few Chinese companies (like NORINCO), for exporting missiles to Iran, in real terms the trade between the two countries continues to grow.

Security Concerns

Presently, China has no external threats and her Armed Forces are strong enough to tackle any internal or external concerns. Till mid 1980s, China's armed forces were organised to fight the People'a War, by adopting the strategy of a "protected war of attrition" against an invading enemy. In this, the quantity rather than quality of conventional forces was perceived as a battle-winning factor. However, the demise of the Cold War has had a major impact on her strategic defence policy. Although few Chinese strategists feel that now the world is a safer place, they also predict emergence of a multi-polar world. Their analysis is that such a world will present challenges of its own, in which growing economic and military strength will have a major role. This could also increase the incidence of local wars. At the same time, advancements in science and technology have heralded a Revolution in Military Affairs (RMA), which was demonstrated by America in the Gulf War, in Afghanistan, and more recently, in the Iraq War. This has made China fully aware of the need to acquire capabilities to counter and respond accurately to such threats, even on, or just beyond, her borders. Thus, greater emphasis on information warfare and accurate ballistic missile technology is being laid.

The Peoples Liberation Army (PLA—a term which also includes Navy, Air and Missile Forces) is currently shifting her development thrust from land borders towards missiles and maritime frontiers, due to her interest in Taiwan and South East Asia. Eventually, Beijing may be aspiring to fill the vacuum in South East Asia and replace America as a major power. Besides modernising her armed force, Beijing has also resolved her border disputes with all her neighbours except Vietnam and India, with whom she is in dialogue.

Her strategic partnership with Russia, joining ASEAN and ARF, the successful return of Hongkong in 1997 and Macao in 1999, have given her additional economic and political boost. Though China's sovereignty claims in the South China Sea clash with a number of countries of the region, since joining ARF and becoming a dialogue partner of ASEAN+ 3, she is laying greater stress on increasing economic ties with these countries.

Relations with the USA

Relations with America had reached a low ebb in 1996, during the Taiwanese Presidential election. While China fired a few missiles across the Straits of Taiwan to threaten the pro-democracy party, America deployed two carrier battle groups, off the island. The relations worsened in April 2001, when an American surveillance aircraft collided with a Chinese fighter plane off Hainan Island, resulting in death of the Chinese pilot. Other areas which impact on China-US relations are human rights violations, disregard for nuclear and missile regimes, religion and espionage.

Beijing also denounced a Pentagon report stating China had deployed 450 short range missiles opposite Taiwan, which is likely to be increased to 750. China stated this was an excuse for America to sell advance weapons and create tension in the region.

In July 2003, President Hu Jintao announced further reduction in the 42,000 troops from the present strength of 2.5 billion. This lay-off, which includes 200 Generals, and is spread over next two years, is part of the ten year lay-offs, for allocating more funds for modernisation.

While the Chinese Army and missile forces are being modernised to fight in a "high technology environment", her Navy continues to lack capability of projecting power as a Blue Water Navy. According to analysts, while China has the capacity to build merchant vessels, when compared with Russian or Western standards, she lacks the design skills and electronic technology of warships. The USA and Japan are considered to be decades ahead of China, in this field. This has forced China to import modern ships, submarines and weapons, mainly from Russia.

Relations with South Korea

Relations between the two countries have seen positive convergence, especially over North Korea's nuclearisation. Though in 1999 China had threatened to "veto" a UN resolution on North Korea and stated that North Korea was a sovereign state that could develop a missile or research and develop a nuclear weapon, China now feels that a nuclear armed North Korea is unacceptable, and has expressed optimism for talks to resolve the crisis.

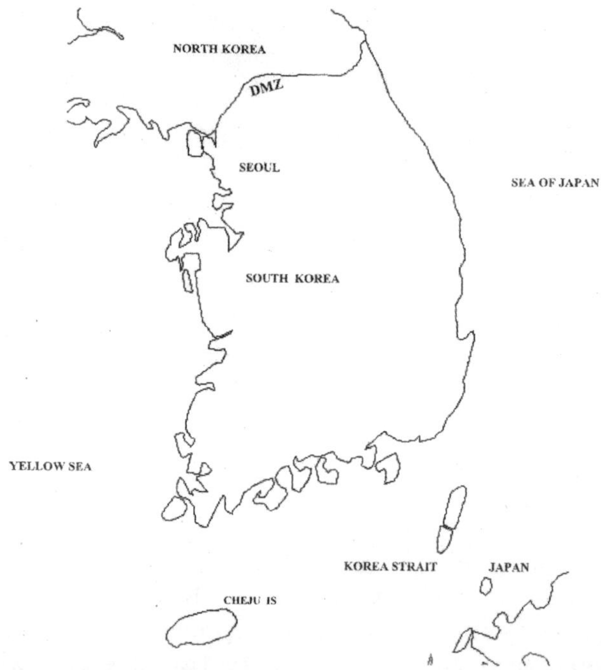

Not to scale

Source : http://geography.about.com/library/blank/blxsouthkorea.htm

It is clear that in the North Korean nuclear issue, not only is China happy to play a dominating and important role which will enhance her status in the region and internationally, Beijing's interests also seem to be converging with those of South Korea,

Japan and America. As Beijing has economic leaverage over Pyongyong and has described her relations with North Korea as between "lip and teeth", she agrees with South Korea, Japan and America, that the "Korean Peninsula must be free of nuclear weapons". This may be due to increase in trade between Beijing and Seoul, which has grown to US$ 42 billion over the last eleven years since they established diplomatic ties.

Relations with ASEAN

Since long, Beijing has been trying to establish closer political and economic relations with member countries of ASEAN. During the summit at Bali in October 2003, she signed the Treaty of Amity and Cooperation. The Treaty, initiated by the fiive founding members of ASEAN in 1976, had till now been signed by ten ASEAN members plus Papua New Guinea, and calls on its signatories to foster political and economic cooperation and not to interfere in each other's domestic affairs. It also includes provision for a high council, composed of member states that can be called to resolve disputes.

Beijing has also offered Free Trade Agreement to ASEAN members, which would do away with barriers to trade and investment, within a decade, while some hurdles could be removed as early as 2004. If agreed to, this will result in opening of markets, well ahead of the WTO. However, this move could be overshadowed by the interest of stronger countries, which may not like China to use economic diplomacy to gain primacy in the region. As it is, China leads in exports to the ASEAN countries, and is willing to finance projects in them.

Notwithstanding improvement in trade and diplomatic relations, Beijing's growing military power, acts of "Teaching Vietnam a Lesson" in 1979 and construction of facilities on Mischief Reef in the Spratlys Islands, are likely to impact on her long term ties with the region.

In future Beijing would like to create a Blue water navy, capable of projecting power over a larger distance. She would also like to exercise more control over vital sea lanes and disputed territory in regional oceans. The threat will only arise if the USA and its allies attempt to contain China's maritime ambitions. So far, China has been behaving responsibly, cooperating in international efforts to protect fishing and the maritime environment. Analysts feel that in China's perception, her major strategic challenge will be from America, while Japan and India could be her economic competitors. She believes that as shown by Kosovo, Afghanistan and Iraq, America's unipolarity and unilateralism needs to be countered, hence multi-polarity is inevitable. Notwithstanding this, Beijing is cooperating with the US led war on international terrorism as it also affects her Xinjiang province, where nearly 17 million Chinese Muslim separatists (being supported by ten groups from Afghanistan) are fighting to end China's rule over the region.[1]

Her biggest challenge is to compete with the American influence, globally and in South East Asia, both in economic and military terms. This, she is striving to achieve by first enhancing her economy and simultaneously modernising her Armed Forces to fight a "limited war under modern conditions". Though her major difference with the USA is on reunification of Taiwan, Beijing is laying stress on improving trade and economic ties, with both countries.

TAIWAN

Living under the shadow of Beijing, increasing her missile capability of adding twenty five ballistic missiles per year and American pressure to improve self-reliance, in 1999, Taiwan had embarked on a US$ 14.6 billion five-year upgradation and procurement plan. Also, as part of the theatre missile defence shield proposed by the USA, Taiwan is likely to acquire three Patriot advance capability missile systems (PAC-3). Her shopping list includes four Kidd class missile destroyers, eight diesel submarines, twelve submarine-hunting P3C Orion aircrafts, besides C^4I system.

As America may not be willing to deploy her carrier groups again to counter a Chinese threat, Taiwan is preparing to counter China's "coercive strategy", on her own.

NORTH KOREA

Having been labelled as an Axis of Evil, the country, already suffering economic strains, has been facing further fears, more so after American led Operation on Iraq in February 2003. To demonstrate her defiance and strength, she fired three short range missiles into the Sea of Japan, which in February 2003 forced America to deploy twenty four long-range bombers in Guam, to maintain a vigil on North Korea.

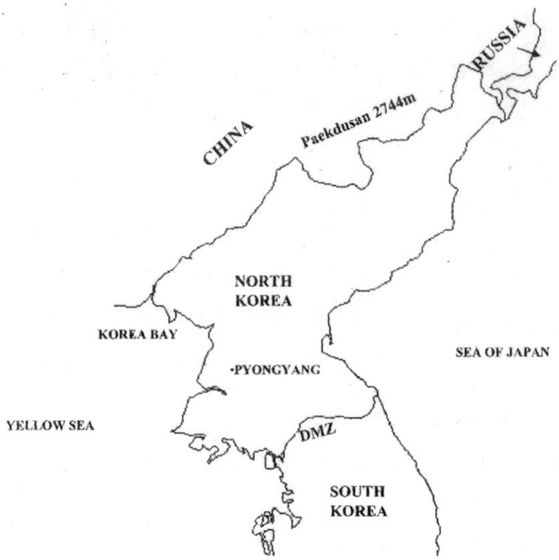

Not to scale
Source : http://geography.about.com/library/blank/blxnorthkorea.htm

As Pongyang considered herself to be the next target of the American attack after Iraq, she threatened to re-commence processing weapons grade plutonium and develop a deterrent, with nuclear weapons and argued that "no one can vouch that the US will not spark the second Iraq crisis on the Korean Peninsula". She also suspended peace talks with South Korea, and in quick succession test fired two short and medium range missiles, one close to Japan.

Alarmed at the threat of recommencement of production of nuclear material, the US sought assistance from China and Russia, re-opened dialogue and offered to re-start economic aid. As a bargain to suspending her nuclear quest, North Korea has asked

America to confirm that Washington will not attack her, and is demanding resumption of economic and developmental aid (which Washington had suspended in April 2002, as North Korea had sold six ballistic missiles to Pakistan) to overcome her economic crisis. She also stated that the "Iraqi War shows that to allow disarming through inspections does not avert a war, but rather sparks it". North Korea could guarantee its security by arming itself with a "tremendous military deterrent". Soon thereafter, on 8 April 2003, she test fired an anti-ship missile into the Yellow Sea.

Concerned at the spread of proliferation in the region, as early as February 2003, China had asked North Korea to "stop causing provocation to its neighbours, else face economic sanctions". In fact, to drive her point home, China even stopped the flow of oil for three days, though it was reported to be "due to technical reasons".

Historically, China and Russia have exercised great influence over North Korea and have always come to her rescue. Hence, America sought Beijing's help in having a multilateral dialogue with North Korea, to include Japan and South Korea. The USA is also concerned that North Korea's weapons and weapon grade uranium may find its way to terrorists. Beijing played host to the April 'six nation talks' (North Korea, South Korea, China, Japan, Russia, and America), but North Korea showed no intention of softening her stance. Her representative even claimed that they already had nuclear weapons, and had started producing weapons grade plutonium. Though the talks failed, China, Japan and South Korea stated that North Korea had offered to dismantle her nuclear programme if the West abandoned its hostile attitude towards the country. However, America rejected North Korea's terms. The fact that North Korea acknowledges possession of nuclear weapons has created grater consensus among the nations to deal with her nuclear proliferation.

The situation continues to be grim, as it has been established that North Korea has nuclear weapons and missiles capable of reaching Japan and West Coast of the USA, which provide her an excuse to intimidate and dictate terms to others. Though China is assisting America in persuading North Korea to give up nuclear weapons, she is not likely to allow America to play the brinkmanship game, or take all the credit. South Korea has adopted a conciliatory approach and President Roh had advocated engaging North Korea in dialogue and economic ties, so that the country can overcome her economic problems. Mr Roh is also worried at the proposed reduction of the US troops based in South Korea, as they provide a security shield to his country. Japan is also worried about a nuclear North Korea, as she falls within range of her missiles.

The USA has stated her desire for a peaceful elimination of the nuclear programme, in place of a nuclear North Korea. Though Washington has stated that she is looking for a peace formula to achieve the objectives, the use of military force can not be ruled out if these fail.

JAPAN

By virtue of her location at the north-western edge of the Pacific Ocean facing China and North Korea, along with South Korea she provides a launch pad for the USA and the West to counter China. Bulk of her trade and nearly all her fuel requirements sail through the South China Sea. Thus, she has great interest in ensuring peace in the South Asian Region.

Socio-Economic Status

One of the most technologically advanced countries of the world, it has an area of 177,853 sq km. In 1999, her population was 126,549,976, which is likely to go down to 101, 228,471 in the next 30 years. Life expectancy of males is 77.5 years while that of females is 84 years. Religionwise, 84 per cent of the population is Buddhist while 16 per cent follow other religions. The per capita GDP is US $ 23,400 and while 65 per cent of the labour is employed in trade and industry, 30 per cent are involved in agriculture and 5 per cent in fishery and forestry. The country has negligible natural resources of minerals and fishery and the main environmental threats arise from air pollution from power plants and acidification of lakes, which affects the quality of drinking water.

The main industries are advanced technologies relating to telecommunication, television, transportation, electronic, machine tools, non - ferrous metals, shipbuilding and chemicals. They produce rice, sugar beet, poultry, dairy and fishery products. The exports include motor vehicles, semi conductors, office machines and chemicals, while imports include fuel, foodstuff, chemicals and textiles.

Security Concerns

Japan has a defence treaty with America which provides her with a security umbrella. Her main concern is the growing economic and military power

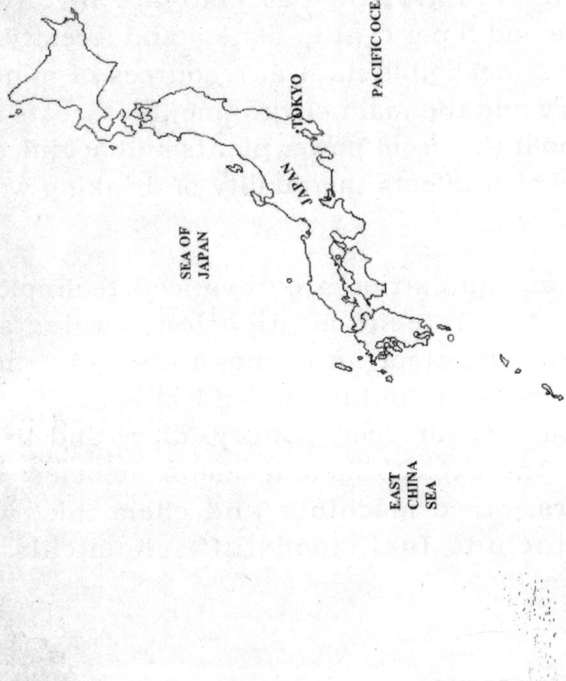

Not to scale

Source : http://geography.about.com/library/blank/blxjapan.htm

of China, disputes with Russia over islands and security of her sea lanes in South China Sea for trade. The fear of a China-Taiwan clash or a conflict between North and South Korea spilling over to Japan, are also major areas of concern. While the constitution debars sending of any military contingents overseas for combat, during Operation Enduring Freedom, Japan did send a few ships to logistically support the US forces in Afghanistan, which was adversely viewed by Beijing. Security of the fishing region and clashes with North Korean naval vassals also creates ripples in the otherwise peaceful environment.

In March 2003, the threat of North Korea's missiles and nuclear thundering rang alarm bells. While the Government supported American intervention in Iraq and was sure that Washington will come to her aid if the situation so demanded, the opposition felt that Japan's Self Defence Forces should have an inherent capability to face such challenges. Discussions in the parliament on "How should Japan combat North Korea's missiles" led to support for amending the constitution, which presently does not allow the Armed Forces to have offensive weapons. Mr Okada of the Democratic Party felt that the "argument that Japan should have the capability to hit back at North Korea's missiles should be raised".

A public debate was also held on whether Japan should purchase Tomahawk cruise missiles. The Government was able to assure the people that it was aware of the threat posed by neighbour North Korea and was concerned about the instability which would result from a Chinese attack on Taiwan. Also, the present US priorities in the region were different from those during the Cold War, and America does not need Japan as much as it did earlier. The Defence Minister felt that there would be no constitutional dilemma in launching a "pre-emptive strike" against any plans of North Korea to fire missiles at Japan, and that a "pacifist" constitution should not be viewed as a sucide note. Supporting the Minister, Mr Fukada, Chief Cabinet Secretary opined that "circumstances and public opinion could require Japan to possess nuclear weapons". Japanese Self Defence Forces would accept even a larger role abroad, if they are not involved in security of the homeland islands. Japan has sent a contingent of 1000 soldiers to Iraq, which required a constitutional modification.

Japan's major concern is oil imports. She had offered US $ 2.5 billion to Iran for developing her oil fields in Azadegam but is likely to pull out of the deal, due to advice from America. In order to reduce dependency on the Middle East, Tokyo was negotiating with Russia to invest US $ 5 billion in exploration of an oil field in Eastern Siberia, and then pump oil through a 4000 kilometre pipeline to the Russian city of Nakhodka on the Sea of Japan. Earlier, China had also offered Russia a 25 year deal worth US $ 150 billion for the same region, but the pipeline was to terminate in China's north-eastern city of Daqing. However, Japan's offer is likely to materialise as it would allow Russia to sell oil to international customers from her own port facing the Pacific Ocean. It is estimated that Siberia has the capacity of producing 10 billion barrels per day, compared with 26 billion barrels per day of Iran. Japan currently imports 88 per cent of her oil from the Middle East, a dependency which will be greatly reduced if the deal with Russia comes through.

While the American assurance to safeguard her security will continue to form the basis of Japan's security policy, faced with a potential nuclear threat from North Korea, gradually her Defence

Forces are likely to acquire an offensive capability also. However, this is likely to be based on conventional missiles, for some time to come. Search for alternate oil sources are likely to continue, as will be Japan's efforts to ensure security of her sea lanes through the Straits of Malacca. Japan is likely to continue to be guided by America's foreign policy, in future also.

Despite a very high GDP and standard of living, there are a few internal cults, which resort to terrorist attacks, but these do not pose any major security problems. Lately, Japan has also shown keen interest in patrolling of the South China Sea, right upto the Straits of Malacca.

AUSTRALIA

She has provided diplomatic and military support to the American operations in Afghanistan and Iraq. Australia has been of the opinion that a US-Australia Free Trade Zone would be of mutual benefit, but identified Australia as an Asian state. With the GDP at US$ 30,700, Prime Minister John Howard stated Australia should be identified as an Asian country and the region should take advantage of his country's strong, sophisticated and medium size economy. He was of the opinion that Asia should become their first destination for trade and investment and identified China, Singapore and Thailand as good markets for Australian goods.

In July 2003, a decision to upgrade air defence against an attack from the North was taken. Four advance radars are to be deployed at Bathurst Island. Similarly, old radars from Strateson Island are being replaced, creating a capacity to look up to 80 kilometres into Timor Sea, north-west of Darwin.

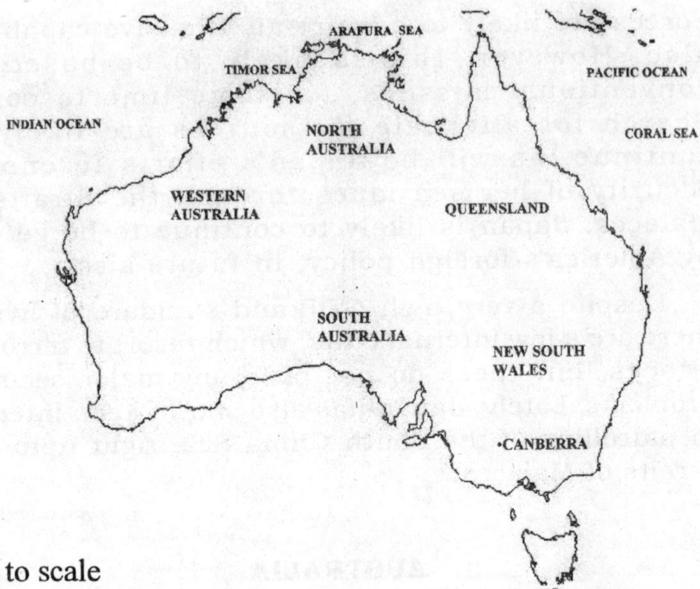

Not to scale
Source : http://geography.about.com/library/blank/blxaustralia.htm

Nearly 200 sailors from the navies of Australia, New Zealand, France, Singapore and Papua New Guinea conducted a joint exercise in July 2003. Code named Kakadu, the aim of the exercise was "to test naval defence against air, surface and submarine threats". India, South Korea, Japan, Malaysia, Thailand and the Philippines had sent observers for the exercise.

Australia has also signed a bilateral agreement with Malaysia, to coordinate efforts of their customs, immigration and defence agencies, on the lines of her agreements with Indonesia.[2]

Since 1966, Australia has been following policies of the USA, about two steps behind. Thus, she has had an uneasy relationship with some countries of Asia, specially Malaysia and Indonesia. Her desire to get close to Asia is primarily driven by the economic recovery of Asian countries. Hence, her two way trade and Foreign Direct Investment in South East Asia are likely to increase.

FRANCE

France has had historic ties since 1940s with the region, especially with Vietnam, Laos and Cambodia. Paris has also been involved in peace negotiations of their conflicts, and French is still spoken in these countries.[3]

Considering the modernisation programmes and economic resurgence of the countries of the region, Paris has once again focused her attention towards the region. Though France provided a contingent in East Timor under the UN, she is not likely to get involved in any security alliance.

UNITED STATES OF AMERICA

The United States has been historically committed to protect her political and economic interests in the Asia-Pacific region and South East Asia. To America, the region of South East Asia and Asia-Pacific offers the opportunity to demonstrate her determination to defend friendly countries, by economic and military power, which Washington proved by her full-scale involvement in the Second World War. During the Cold War, the region became an arena for contesting, containing and defeating communism, and the influence of the Soviet Union and China. Though Western Europe remained the priority area, just like her full-scale involvement during World War II, America also got involved in the Korean and the Vietnam Wars, and participated in a number of UN peacekeeping missions in the region, like East Timor. The end of the Cold War, break-up of the Soviet Union and signing of the NPT considerably lowered tension in Europe resulting in withdrawal of troops from Germany, which allowed America to re-focus her strategy for the Asia-Pacific region. While the US did reduce her forces in South East Asia and closed down few bases in the Philippines, she continues to maintain sufficient troops in Japan and South Korea, and has close defence ties with Thailand, the Philippines, Singapore, Australia and Taiwan. Prior to 11 September 2001, the US policy could be considered as driven by economic interests and a desire to rule the world as the most powerful super power in a uni-polar world, close to being hegemonic. The region is also of vital economic interest to America, as it offers her the largest consumer market of the world, with great scope of sales, especially of military hardware, besides nearly US $ 65 billion in direct investment. Today, five of America's top ten trading partners are from Asia, Japan itself buying three times more than Germany, France and Italy combined. Besides increase in trade with China, in 1993 the region accounted for US 374 billion of US trade, directly employing 2.8 million Americans.

The current US policy towards South East Asia can be inferred from a set of speeches delivered by President George W Bush in September 2002. Spelling out the National Security Strategy on 17 September 2002, he stated that the great struggle of the 20th century between liberty and totalitarianism ended with a decisive victory for the forces of freedom—and a single sustainable model for national success: freedom, democracy, and free enterprise. In the 21st century, only nations that share a commitment to protecting basic human rights and guaranteeing political and economic freedom will be able to unleash the potential of their people and assure their future prosperity. The policy paper stated that today the US enjoys a position of unparalleled military strength and great economic and political influence, which will be used to create a balance of power that favours human freedom: conditions in which all nations and all societies can choose for themselves the rewards and challenges of political and economic liberty. America will defend the peace by fighting terrorists and tyrants, preserve the peace by building good relations among the great powers and, extend it by encouraging free and open societies on every continent.

Addressing the joint session of the Congress on 20 September 2002, Bush stated that to ensure security of the homeland and to meet America's foreign obligations, it was necessary to build and maintain defences beyond challenges, so as to dissuade future military competition and to decisively defeat any adversary if deterrence fails. The United States, he stated, must maintain the capability to defeat any attempt by an enemy—whether a state or a non-state actor—to impose its will on the United States, allies, or friends. He spoke of the strong and dependable ties of America with the Republic of Korea, Japan, Australia, Taiwan, New Zealand and the Philippines, and the role being played by Association of Asia Pacific Economic Cooperation (APEC) towards globalisation of economies. He emphasised that the war on terrorism is not a clash of civilisations. It does, however, reveal the clash inside a civilisation, a battle for the future of the Muslim world. This is a struggle of ideas and this is an area where America must excel.

The major implications of US's policy statements on the South East Asian region would be—

(a) Continued military and economic support to Thailand, Singapore and the Philippines.

(b) Support to Australia, Japan, Taiwan and South Korea.

(c) Support to Indonesia to be linked with her anti-terrorist operations and record of human rights violations.

(d) With China, continued trade ties, cooperation in fighting terrorism, but keeping an eye to maintain American supremacy as world's number one military power. To ward off threat of missiles, develop an anti missile defence shield.

(e) Keep an eye on North Korea's proliferation programmes, and export of missile technology.

(f) While encouraging Japan, South Korea and Taiwan to spend more on defence, maintain a strong presence of US forces in the region.

(g) Relations with Vietnam, Laos and Cambodia will be influenced by development of democracies and improved human rights records of these countries.

(h) Myanmar will continue to face sanctions, till democracy is restored and human rights violations are stopped.

On the economic front, besides bilateral ties, economic ties through APEC will be further strengthened.

President Bush has stated that, in his assessment, after the military campaign in Afghanistan, South East Asia is the second front of the war on terrorism. Initially, America was disturbed that despite warnings about Indonesia becoming a hot-bed of terrorism and early warnings of the Bali blasts, Indonesia was not very active or responsive against terrorist suspects. This feeling was shared by a number of Jakarta's neighbours. Besides her war on terrorism, America is also seeking influence and support for her Operation Iraqi Freedom and trying to enhance her economic and trade ties, to counter the growing influence of China. Already, Thailand, the Philippines, and Singapore are considered important allies, while Australia, Japan, South Korea and Taiwan are closely linked with security ties. Washington is keen to have greater cooperation with Islamic countries of the region like Malaysia, Indonesia and the Philippines, which have been waging a war against terrorism and separatism.[4]

After the end of the Cold War and more so since the September strikes on the US, America has emerged as the sole economic and military power in the world. Facing a new challenge of militancy, her strategists feel that now they are less menaced by fleets and armies but more by catastrophic technologies in the hands the of embittered few.[5]

As far as Asia-Pacific region is concerned, American policy states Washington's desire to transform bilateral relations with India based on a conviction that US interests require a "strong relationship with India". President Bush also stated that America and India have common interest in the free flow of commerce, including through the vital sea lanes of the Indian Ocean, in fighting terrorism and in creating a strategically stable Asia. He stated that emergence of a economically strong, peaceful and prosperous China was crucial for promoting stability in Asia-Pacific region, and felt that by pursuing advanced military capabilities that can threaten its neighbours in the Asia-Pacific region, China was following an outdated path, that in the end will hamper its own pursuit of national greatness. He opinioned that in time, China would find social and political freedoms as the only source of greatness. He stated that Beijing and Washington were already cooperating in the current war on terrorism, Afghanistan and the Korean peninsula. As regards Taiwan, American commitment to the self-defence of Taiwan under the Taiwan Relations Act will remain the cornerstone of her policy. America strives to develop active agendas of cooperation with her long-standing allies in Europe, and Asia, and with Russia, India and China, lest these relationships become routine and unproductive.

The above strategy was further amplified by Admiral Thomas Fargo,[6] C-in-C, US Pacific Command, on taking over his post in 2002. He stated that America was keen to build and promote the concept of "security communities" and treaty alliance signatories. He stated that to advance peaceful developments, America is committed to a policy of coordination, including active military cooperation on specific regional security issues. In his views, the security communities will derive their adherence to principles of mutual cooperation, and the willingness and capabilities to work together. Military dialogue and rudimentary exercises on common tasks will be expanded, as was being done in Exercise Cobra Gold.

Considering that at present the US enjoys unparalleled military and economic power and political influence, she feels that she also has greater responsibilities to ensure peace and stability in the Asia -Pacific region. This is apparent by the presence of her approximately 100,00 troops based at six military hubs in the region, with Command Headquarters at Hawaii. Her six out of ten treaty partners are also located in the Asia-Pacific region. South Korea, Taiwan, Philippines, Singapore, Australia and Japan. After closure of Clark Air Force base in 1992 and Subic Bay Base, the US has no permanent bases left in South East Asia. Though Singapore provides a logistic hub for ships sailing from the Pacific to the Persian Gulf, the proposal of having "floating docks" has often been mooted. Having described North Korea as one of the "Axis of Evil" countries, the present attention of the US seems to be focused on North Korea. Simultaneously, Indonesia, Malaysia, Thailand, Philippines and Singapore – affected by terrorism and insertions, are also drawing adequate attention.

Regional Responses

There was mixed reaction and support for the US unilateral intervention in Iraq. While Japan, Australia, South Korea, the Philippines and Singapore supported it, Thailand was neutral. Indonesia and Malaysia, the two most populous Muslim states, opposed it as an act against Islam. Initially, despite US pressure, Malaysia, Indonesia and even the Philippines were reluctant to expel diplomats of the Saddam regime. Later, Thailand and Philippine agreed to do so, as they have only a small Muslim community. Concerned at the lack of UN mandate for Operation Iraqi Freedom, Prime Minister Dr Mahathir Mohammad of Malaysia even labelled America as a "cowardly and imperialist bully", emphasising that the UN and international law are meaningless. Indonesia also strongly criticised America, labelling her intervention as "violation of international law", but not in as strong terms as Dr Mahathir. Human rights activists of Malaysia echoed sentiments of a large number of Muslim population, when they stated that "despite claims to the contrary it is the Muslim world and the Muslim governments which are being targeted. The US has lost all moral credibility." However, Singapore gave whole-hearted support to America. Prime Minister Goh Chok Tong stated in America that "not every country will say so publicly, but we all know that America has been indispensable to East Asian peace, stability and prosperity". This consciousness tempered East Asian attitudes towards the war in Iraq.[7]

Military Implications of Operation Iraqi Freedom for South East Asia

The 1999 Gulf War had indicated that a Revolution in Military Affairs was under way and the 2003 Iraqi War has shown its capabilities. In the present conflict, the US has shown not only an ability of superior planning, but also improved capacity of employing forces with flexibility, effectively. Also, improved doctrine of integrated air-land battle, advances in C^4I (command, control, communication, computer and intelligence), improvements in logistic support and better battlefield management have become apparent. The application of precision munitions through missiles and air power has also proved the cost effectiveness and lethality of these weapon systems.

On the diplomatic front, it would be clear that America would go to any extent to save her democratic ally, at a relatively low cost.

From the above, China and North Korea would analyse that America could adopt the doctrine of "pre-emptive strike and intervention-on-the-cheap" together, if need be. While Washington would seek support of her allies and the UN, she would be prepared to go alone, if the situation so demands. Thus, while China would try to integrate military lessons in her modernisation programme, North Korea would realise that her blackmail may not work against President Bush. Through economic and diplomatic alliances. Beijing would ensure that the vacuum created by the demise of the Cold War is not easily filled by America in her backyard, an area which China has traditionally considered under her influence, especially the rim countries of the South China Sea.

Islamic Fundamentalism, Terrorism and Militancy

The American efforts to trace and wipe out international terrorism has received serious but reserved response from the region. By deciding to fight terrorism by co-operating within the region, Malaysia and Indonesia have been joined by Thailand, Singapore and the Philippines. While the Philippines did allow American troops to train her Army for fighting Abu Sayyaf's gangs in her southern region, it is only Singapore which sought and gave unqualified support and assistance to America, for which she was rewarded with the Free Trade Pact. Though Washington has not as yet openly appreciated Indonesia's efforts in rounding-up and speedily trying the Bali suspects and has not resumed economic and military aid, there are signs that relations between the two countries could improve, soon.

Non-Proliferation Security Initiative

Concerned at movement and transfer of missiles and nuclear material, in August 2003, America formed a grouping of like-minded eleven nations, to carry out selective interdiction of ships and aircrafts to and from "rouge countries". This is to be restricted to only those carriers suspected of carrying material or technology used for manufacture of either weapons or delivery systems, for weapons of mass destruction.

The grouping aims to avoid incidents like that of December 2002, when a North Korean ship 'Susan' was found carrying Scud missiles, to Yemen. Though the vessel was released reluctantly (Yemen being a supporter of America), this provision is likely to be applied against Iran, Syria, Libya and North Korea. India has not joined the grouping.

In future, there is no likelihood of a major change in America's policy towards the region. America would continue to have close diplomatic and military relations with Japan, South Korea and Australia, and strengthen her economic and trade ties with China. Relations with other countries of the region will continue to grow, though cautiously with the existing regimes of Myanmar, Laos and Cambodia. The USA will also continue to play a major role in ensuring stability in the region, and continue to engage, rather than confront China especially in her dialogue with North Korea. Washington is also likely to resume aid to Indonesia and reward countries that have supported her actions in Iraq and Afghanistan, and those involved in the fight against terrorism.

America is likely to continue to maintain her present force levels in Japan and South Korea, and remain committed to honour her security obligations to Taiwan, Japan and Australia. She is likely to take a tough stand on North Korea's nuclear proliferation while seeking the assistance and cooperation of other countries like China amd Russia. However, Washington will be prepared to go alone. As regards China, America's economic relations will grow, but latent strategic competition could lead to confrontation.

Washington's thrust on defeating international terrorism is likely to bring Washington closer to Indonesia, Thailand, Philippines and even Malaysia. America's strong ties with Singapore and cold vibes with Vietnam and Laos would continue, while the new regime in Cambodia may benefit, being more democratic. Having described South East Asia as the "second front" in the battle against terrorism, America has a self interest in bringing pressure and assisting regional powers to tackle this threat. Besides other countries, Washington has specially praised Beijing for the help extended to counter Osama bin Laden's Al Qaeda network.

Though America has rewarded allies like Singapore (with Free Trade Agreement) and Philippines (with nearly US $ 4.6 billion defence related aid to fight Abu Sayaff) and Indonesia (with US$ 50 million for police modernisation), the doctrine of pre-emptive strike has caused concern to many. Hence, despite all her efforts to woo partners, quite a few South East Asian countries (especially Muslim countries) fear that under the pretext of her global war against terrorism, America may initiate pre-emptive action against Muslim countries[8], or any other nation which does not toe her line. This was amply brought out by Dr Mahathir, when he reflected views of many of his South East Asian partners while addressing a rally against Operation Iraqi Freedom. He stated that if the US did succeed in Iraq, they would shift their focus to Iran and after Iran, to North Korea. He wondered who would be next. Amplifying the wider implications of the pre-emption, he stated that "The US-led war on Iraq has great implications for small countries such as Malaysia. Many countries can be accused of not having good government or not practicing democracy or abusing human rights. Such an accusation may lead to invasion of our country or other countries. So, this is very frightening prospect".[9]

Similar views were also expressed by President Megawati who felt that the American definition of terrorists was selective, and she wanted to see Free Aceh Movement also included in their list of international terrorist groups. She felt that America will only classify a group as "terrorist" if it directly threatens US interests.[10]

Though not spelt out openly, a number of South East Asian countries feel that the US is being hegemonic and her doctrine of "pre-emption and pre-emptive strike" poses a threat to them and the region. In future, the likelyhood of such an American policy and her military presence in the region resulting in greater pressure from China cannot be ruled out.

While this area is not likely to become an arena for great power rivaly in military or diplomatic sense, it is likely to see clash of economic interests, as some of the countries continue to remain under-developed. Presently, there is convergence of interests between America and China on terrorism and North Korea, but the basic differences over a multi-polar world verses a uni-polar world are likely to remain and could convert the area into a possible future Cold War theatre.

References

1. Damon Bristow, "Defence Spending and Defence Procurement: Military Restructuring and Deployment", *Asian Defence Review* (July and August 2002).
2. "Australia and Malaysia Sign MOU", *Asian Defence Journal* (September 2002). See also in the same journal, "ASEAN-US Battle Against Terrorism".
3. Baladas Ghoshal, French Strategic and Security Interests in Southern Asia", *Asian Defence Journal* (September 2002), pp. 8-10.
4. Micool Brooke, "US Defence Posture in Asia", *Asian Defence Journal* (December 2002), pp. 4-5."The National Security Strategy of the United States of America", speech by President George W Bush on 17 September 2002, on the net.
5. Keynote speeches by PM, of Singapore and Thailand at the ASEAN Business and Investment Summit, 6 October 2003, Bali, Indonesia. www.aseansec.org.
6. "ASEAN's Strategic Value Tends to Grow as US Competition with China and Russia for Influence Intensifies, *Asian Defence Journal* (December 2002), pp. 4-5.

7. Commander Franz-Josef Birkel, Mr Warrne Karle and Colonel David Welch, "The Effect of Bush Doctrine on Commitments and Alliances in South East Asia". *Australian Defence Force Journal*, No. 161 (July/August 2003).

   http://www.defence.gov.au/publications/dfj/adfj161.pdf

   Also refer to the keynote address by Prime Minister of Singapore Goh Chok Tong at the Asia Society Gala Dinner, Washington DC, on 07 May 2003.

   http://app.mfa.gov.sg/pr/read_content.asp? View, 1899 in Ministry of Foreign Affairs, Singapore website.

   http://app.mfa.gov.sg/generator/asppages/washington/Speechs.asp?View=Theme%201&1d=Washington.

8. Gay Christoffersen, "The War on Terrorism in Southeast Asia: Searching for Partners. Delimiting Targets", *Strategic Insights,* Volume I, Issue 1 (March 2002).

   http://www.ccc.nps.navy.mil/si/mar02/eastAsia.asp

9. *Malaysia Star,* 4 May 2003. website-mahathirmohamad.newstrove.com

10. The Effects of the Bush Doctrine on Commitments and Alliances in South East Asia, n. 7.

6

Security Threats to the Region

Prior to the Second World War, most of the region was occupied by western powers as colonies. During the War, it came under the Japanese control, which greatly disturbed socio-economic growth yet it could kindle the desire for independence in most of these colonies. After the defeat of Japan, the western powers re-occupied their colonies. Initially, they opposed the local freedom movements, resulting in insurgencies in Indonesia and a full-fledged war in Vietnam. The Cold War went on to engulf the region, resulting in wars in Indo-China (between the Vietnamese and the French), Korea (between the Chinese and Soviet backed North Korea with America and West backed South Korea) and finally between North Vietnam (backed by the Soviets) and South Vietnam, (supported by America and her allies).

The years between 1945 to 1975 saw Malaysia, Singapore, the Philippines and Thailand joining security pacts and forming defence alliances for their security against the expansion of Communism. In this they were mainly supported by America. While political institutions were taking root, few countries (like

Malaysia-Indonesia, Malaysia-Singapore, Malaya-Philippines) also faced bilateral territorial disputes, which threatened their fragile economic and security apparatus. Thus, an urgent need was felt by these countries to resolve their internal differences and strengthen their external security.

Security Arrangements

There are few arrangements and events, which merit mention-

(a) Formation of South East Asian Treaty Organization-SEATO, in 1959 (with Thailand, Malaysia, Singapore, the Philippines, the UK and USA). It has since been dissolved.

(b) Formation of ASEAN in 1967.

(c) The Five-Power Defence Arrangement-FPDA (between Malaysia, Singapore, the UK, Australia and New Zealand).

(d) Defence arrangement between Australia, New Zealand, the UK and the USA-ANZUK (still in force, though New Zealand was dropped in 1990 when she refused port facilities to US nuclear powered ships).

(e) Permitting military bases and enhancing defence co-operation between the USA-Philippines-Thailand-Singapore, UK-Malaysia, and between Soviet Union-Vietnam-Laos.

(f) The UK also maintained her military presence in Hong Kong, Singapore and Brunei.

The fall of Hanoi leading to the rout of the American troops created a sense of fear, and the 1970s saw Singapore, Malaysia, Thailand, Philippines and Indonesia arming against the likely Communist expansion. Further, the situation was viewed with greater alarm when Vietnam invaded Cambodia in 1978 and later, when Vietnam was herself invaded by China in 1979. The fear of a clash between Communist states as well as the threat from an expansionist China created serious military concerns in the region.

Besides China's expansionism and hegemony and her implied claim over territories where people of Chinese origin lived overseas, the implications of Sino-Soviet clash of the 1960s created an alarming situation in the region. In the meanwhile, after their defeat in Vietnam in the 1950s, first the French, then in1980s the Americans and finally the British in the 1990s, pulled out their bases from South East Asia. Thus, while Malaysia, Thailand and Indonesia were mainly concerned about the Chinese, the others feared Vietnam. After the fall of Saigon, a large number of South Vietnamese fled the country, mostly in boats, to the neighbouring countries, which created a serious security issue for the non-communist states of the region.

With a decline in regional differences, generally the economies of the member countries showed improvement. The ASEAN grouping (initially of five members, Indonesia, Malaysia, Singapore, Thailand and the Philippines; Brunei joined in 1967), helped them improve their economies, thereby enabling modernisation of their armed forces, with the help of western powers.

The 1990s saw a change in the leadership and the policy of the Chinese, with greater emphasis on economic build-up. After the Gulf War, the focus was more on modernisation of the PLA (the term covers armed forces of China). Though in the last ten years China has expanded her economic ties with the region, she continues to exert her claim on Taiwan and over the South China Sea.

Beginning 1970s, the relations between America and China have also improved specially in trade and commerce, though differences over Taiwan and human rights still persist. The 1990s also saw trade and economic ties growing between Beijing and the West, especially with America. Thus, China's economic build-up and the demise of the Soviet Union have further reduced the chances of any immediate major security threat to South East Asian countries.

THE PREVAILING SECURITY SCENARIO

External Threats

Following the lead of the USA to engage China in a constructive dialogue, ASEAN countries co-opted Beijing into the ARF. In 2001, China also participated in a Summit of ASEAN +3 (China, Japan and South Korea). The ASEAN members hope that this would result in change in China's attitude towards resolving regional disputes, but it has not happened as yet. China's desire to sign the TAC of ASEAN is seen as a step in this direction. Thus, while there is no major external threat to the region, the conflicting territorial claims and sovereignty rights in the South China Sea is a matter of concern.

While the likelihood of a clash between the two Koreas has receeded, it is quite likely that if the present deadlock over nuclear issue is not resolved and North Korea continues to insist on going nuclear, then America may take pre-emptive action against North Korea. This could spark a new clash not only between North and South Korea, but also threaten Japan and envelop China, Taiwan and Australia.

The possibility of Islamic fundamentalists and terrorists making South East Asia a base for terrorist and insurgency activities, is also likely to draw-in American forces. The un-occupied islands of Indonesia and those with fundamentalist sympathisers are likely to draw such elements. The likelihood of America demanding stricter action against such groups and even undertaking unilateral military action against a country of South East Asia perceived to be providing refuge to such fundamentalist groups, can not be ruled out. Such an intervention would severely strain relations between ASEAN and the West.

Regional Differences

There are a few regional conflicts too that are currently dormant under the ASEAN spirit of non-interference in each other's internal matters, but have the potential of blowing up. Few of the important ones are-

(a) Between Myanmar and Thailand. Nearly 80,000 to 100,000 Burmese refugees have been driven to the Thai-Myanmar border along the province of Changmai. Besides opposing factions being supported by Myanmar (Democratic Keren Buddhist Army and United Wan State Army, which is cultivating opium and drugs and running eight refineries across the border) and Shan State Army by Thailand, the refugees on Thai side of the border often come under attacks, of machine gun and mortar fire from the Myanmar side. Though Thai Army is concerned at the inflow of drugs (methamphetamine tablets into Thailand and heroin and opium to third countries through Thailand) and has been eager to initiate military action against the Keran and Wan Armies, the present civilian regime in Thailand has not approved the military option.[1]

(b) Between Malaysia and Singapore. Both countries suspect each other's military build-up and express opinions and comment on it. Often, Singapore blames Malaysia of improving watercourse and channels of Johore Baru port, which would adversely affect Singapore's water channels. At times, personality clashes also sour the otherwise good neighbourly relations. However, there is no likelihood of any military clash between the two neighbours, who realise that as far as security is concerned, their destinies are closely interlinked.[2]

(c) Post 11 September Scenario. After the 11 September attacks on the USA, a few Indonesian nationals supporting fundamentalists were arrested in Singapore, and their plans to attack the American consulate was neutralised. Interrogations revealed their links with a few terrorist elements in Malaysia and the Philippines. Though initially Indonesia did not co-operate in the investigations, the policy of Jakarta has undergone a change after the Bali bombings. In the future, greater cooperation in fighting terrorism is likely to take place.

In the meanwhile, the Indonesian organisation having pro Al Qaida views on Islamic fundamentalism has emerged; the Jemaah Islamia (JI), under Abubakar Bashir, the spiritual leader of the group has announced plans to form a Pan-Islamic state in South East Asia, incorporating Indonesia, the Philippines, Malaysia and Singapore. Though his hand was also suspected in the 12 October 2002 Bali bombings, Indonesia has not taken any firm action against this organisation.[3] While he has been sentenced to four years imprisonment and the problem seems to be at the nascent stage, the USA and other countries including Malaysia, Philippines and Singapore, view this as a serious matter, which could even affect relations between the ASEAN neighbours.

Non-Military Security Threats

Economic prosperity of Malaysia and Singapore often attracts illegal migration from Indonesia and the Philippines to these two countries. In the recent past, while a few such people have been sent away in ships and few Afghans who were deported from Indonesia even landed on Australian territories resulting in serious differences between Jakarta and Canberra, often Malaysia deports the illegal immigrants back, causing irritants in friendly relations.

Threat of cyber warfare, spread of diseases like AIDS, casualties due to haphazard mines laid in Laos and Cambodia, non-planned logging and felling of forests, poaching of fishery items and large scale migration of population are other aspects which cause security imbalance to the countries of the region.

Prevailing Economic Strengths of the Region

For appreciating the economic strengths, and weaknesses of these countries, a look at their economic indicators is essential. (See Appendices A and C).[4]

From the economic indicators, it can be concluded that the countries could be divided into three broad groups, the advanced countries (Brunei, Malaysia, Singapore), the developed countries (Thailand, Philippines), and the developing countries (Laos and Cambodia). Myanmar, Vietnam and Indonesia could come in the category between the developed and the developing countries. From the point of foriegn direct investment (FDI), the region attracts much more FDI than India. Similarly, it would be seen that the flow of Indian FDI to the region is also very limited. In the year 2000, the economies of India and most of the South East Asian countries have posted healthy growth, which opened new vistas of co-operation.

Being in the same geographical sphere as South India, there is commonality between the agricultural and horticultural produce of these countries with India. However, each country has special export and import needs, which can be favourably traded with India. Being closer than the Middle East and Africa, even the freight charges would be comparatively less. (See Appendices D and E).

With regard to life expectancy and literacy, Laos, Cambodia, Vietnam, Indonesia and Myanmar need special attention. However, Singapore, Malaysia, Brunei and Philippines are well advanced and may need India's assistance only in the field of higher education and in specialised technical fields

Military Strength

After analysing the security challenges being faced by the countries of South East Asia, a look at their military build-up and procurement plans is essential, as it reflects their future threat perceptions. The following tables would be relevant-

(a) Comparative Data of Armed Forces- Appendix F.

(b) Growth of Military Power -Appendix G.

(c) Growth of Naval Power- Appendix H.

(d) Growth of Air Power-Appendix J.

(e) Profile of Air Forces of the Region-Appendix K.[5]

It would be seen that military power wise, after the Middle East, the non Indo-China states of the region remain the second top importer of arms in the world. Mostly procured from the western sources, most of their aircraft, naval ships and military hardware is of 1970s vintage.

So far, the military concepts had been oriented towards countering insurgency, defence of outlying island territories, protecting the sea lanes and aerial cover to own and friendly forces. Thus, tactical doctrines and weapons procurement were oriented towards jungle warfare and security of outlying islands. Some effort was also diverted towards air defence of the country and coastal shores, but greater reliance was placed on defence and military alliances. Though these countries carry out periodic training and exercises within the pacts, they do not have adequate potential or an integrated mechanism, to take on an external threat of even medium level, what to talk of China.

Since the end of the cold war, there has been a change in the strategy being followed, on the pattern of US-China relations. While the non-communist countries hope that dialogue at various forums of ASEAN, economic links, trade and diplomacy will succeed in persuading China to see their point of view and lead to reduction of threat, simultaneously they drew-up ambitious plans to modernise their military, to face conventional threats.

The doctrine being adopted by Malaysia, Singapore, Thailand, Philippines and even Myanmar seems to be shifting towards engaging the adversary in the sky and the high seas, well away from the land borders. Besides deterring occupation of far-flung islands or the main land mass, acquisition of light and medium tanks, long range guns and anti-tank missiles and communication equipment has also been planned, which indicate a will to offer stiff resistance to a conventional threat.

While the economic boom and concerns for security had resulted in drawing- up of ambitious modernisation plans in the 1990s by the original five ASEAN members, these were upset due to the economic slow down after the 1997 financial crisis. However, with the economic revival, since 2001, these plans have been revived by Malaysia and Singapore, and to an extent by Thailand. Myanmar was the only country, which despite an economic slow down, continued to build her armed forces mainly with assistance from China, and has now turned to Russia too.

Though no country of the region has identified any external threat, each one has concerns over China's potential motives and moves, especially in the South China Sea, and Beijing's future expansionist policies over the next quarter century. Thus, Malaysia and Singapore seem to be building up strong submarine based Naval forces and are modernising their Air Forces. Indonesia has been most adversely affected by the 1997 economic crisis and the US ban on supply of spares, which will further degrade the potential of her armed forces.

While the thrust of their Air Forces is on acquiring long range and high speed interceptors like MiG 29s, F 18s and Sukhois, their Navies are creating interception and strike capabilities with submarines. Though a few acquisitions are also from China, bulk of the armaments are being imported from the West and some from Russia and the CAS, a trend which is likely to be accelerated. As there are signs of improvement in the economy of a few countries, the "feel good factor" could lead to increased defence spending.

The US led Operation Enduring Freedom against Taliban and subsequent operations against terrorism, have seen Indonesia, Malaysia, Singapore and Thailand stepping-up their anti-terrorist operations.

The US doctrine of "Pre-emptive Operations" has resulted in Iran and North Korea, initiating projects for re-starting enrichment of plutonium for developing nuclear weapons. Any US action against North Korea will destablise the region.

Modernisation Trends

Indonesia. Though the country has a large sea coast, the Army is the predominant force. The weapons and equipment are a mix of Soviet and American origin of the mid 1970s vintage. The economic crisis of 1997 and the American embargo have resulted in deferment of modernisation plans, resulting in nearly 50 per cent of the Air Force and the Navy becoming non-operational. While some observers feel that the Security Forces are ill equipped to handle terrorist attacks, others feel that the Government lacks the will to crack down against fundamentalists, due to the expected political backlash. Whatever be the reason or compulsion, such internal instability is likely to affect the flow of FDI and trade and commerce, leading to persistent slow growth of annual rate of recovery, at two to three per cent — not only of Indonesia but also of the region.

There is military conscription of two years, and in 1999 Indonesia spent US$ 1502 m on her defence, a mere 1.1 per cent of the GDP. The strength of the Army is 230,000, including a Strategic Reserve of 30,000 (Custard). The reserve potential is of 400,000 and the Para Military Forces total 194,000. The Navy has a strength of 47,000 (including 12000 Commandos,1000 Naval Aviation) with two diesel submarines and seventeen frigates. The Air Force has 21,000 all ranks, 91 combat aircraft including US built F16, F5s and British Hawk. The sanctions imposed by the US on military assistance due to violation of human rights by the Indonesian Armed

Forces in East Timor in 1999, have greatly affected the operational readiness of military hardware. However, to assuage Indonesia, Mr Colin Powell visited Jakarta on 2 August 2002, to approach them in a non-aggressive way. Washington also announced allocation of US$ 50 m for Indonesian Army and the Police, to fight terrorism.[6] Due to her weak economy, Indonesia is likely to be hard pressed to carry out any modernisation in the years to come. Coupled with the US sanctions on defence co-operation, weapons and equipment of American origin will be further degraded as spares are hard to come by. On 2 June 2002, despite differences over Islamic fundamentalists, Singapore has transferred six old trainer aircrafts to Jakarta. When affordable, efforts are likely to be made to acquire missile boats and patrol craft, so that the prevailing ethnic violence and secessionist movements spread over the archipelago can be tackled effectively and quickly, by swiftly moving troops. Though the country has elite counter-terror units designated as Kopassus (Special Forces) and the Navy and the Air Force have the expertise and skills, these are not being tasked to handle the situation. Instead, the Police is preferred, as it is more acceptable to the US Congress, which has long criticised the armed forces for human rights violations.[7]

The country is likely to continue to face dissensions, sectarian violence and secessionist movements, which may see a greater reliance by the government on the armed forces for ensuring unity of the country. Unless the present regime ensures improvement in economy and adopts tough anti-fundamentalist and anti-terrorist policies even if they are unpopular to a section of the society, it would remain unstable, volatile and dangerous, as was proved by the Bali blast.

Haunted by the memory of separation of East Timor only few years ago, the country will make all efforts to institutionalise differences between the provinces and the centre, to avoid further split or Balkanisation of the archipelago. In this regard, the present peace talks being held to resolve the issues in Aceh provide a ray of hope. Thus, unlike perceptions made by foreign analysts, Indonesia is not likely to break up. However, her internal problems would certainly slow down the economic growth, which may result in her losing her power status, despite having the fourth largest population in the world.[8]

While the representation for the armed forces in the parliament has already been reduced from 100 to 39, and there is a proposal to abolish it by the year 2005, the armed forces are likely to continue to play a major role in governance of the country. Though the Services would seek extra funds for expansion and modernisation, these are not likely to come. The combat potential of the Armed Forces would be gradually eroded, even if America was to lift the embargo on spares and training facilities. Thus, at best the armed forces would be able to maintain law and order and ensure the territorial integrity of the country.

The US continues to impose sanctions on aid for training and spares, which has most adversely affected the air force fleet, leaving only 40 per cent of its fleet air worthy. On 28 April 2003, Indonesia signed a US $ 193 million deal with Russia for import of two Su-27SK interceptors, two Su-30MK ground attack jets and two Mi-35 attack helicopters.

Earlier, there was reliance on US F16 strike aircrafts. Serviceability of the fleet has been adversely affected since 1991, when the US stopped supply of spares as a result of killings of hundreds of protestors in Dili, capital of East Timor, then under Indonesia, by the Indonesian soldiers. The embargo has continued since 1999, after the troops again killed pro-independence supporters in East Timor. Though the steps initiated by Indonesia to round-up the Bali terrorists and assist in the fight against terrorism world over have been appreciated in America and the West, Washington still waits for Jakarta to assist in tracing the killers of the two American tourists in Jakarta in 1999.

In 1997, the Government had approved procurement of 12 Su-27s, 8 Mi-17 Helicopters and up-gradation of C-130 aircraft, which were deferred due to the economic crisis of 1997. The Defence White Paper of 2002 (revised in February 2003), has stated that Indonesia did not face any external threat for next ten years. Thus, it is felt that instead of acquiring patrol crafts and upgrading her C 130 transport fleet (likely to cost US $ 500 million) for quicker response to the troubled parts of the archipelago, the decision to import high speed and technology aircraft is likely to be counter-productive.

The sudden decision of the Government to induct sophisticated aircraft despite the defence paper highlighting that the country does not face an external threat for next ten years, has given rise to opposition parties demanding an inquiry. Also, the choice of Soviet Su-27s and 30s is being questioned, as these aircraft require special periodic maintenance, for which Indonesia does not have infrastructure. Few observers also suspect "bribes" have played a role in the decision.

The internal dynamics of religious fundamentalism could result in strain on Indonesia's relations with ASEAN, but the grouping is likely to survive. However, this may see America and world's financial institutions applying greater pressure on Indonesia's already weak economy. As mentioned earlier, the 12 October 2002 terrorist attacks in Bali, followed soon thereafter by bomb explosions in Thailand, have highlighted the vulnerability of the region to terrorism. Unless checked soon and eradicated effectively, this threat has the potential of spreading and engulfing the region, and straining Indonesia's relations with her ASEAN neighbours.

Thailand. In September 2002, a new doctrine for Thailand's Armed Forces[9] and their downsizing plan was given out by General Chavalit Yongchaiyud, the Deputy Prime Minister (who was earlier Defence Minister). Emphasising ASEAN's quest for boosting regional security during troubled times and the war against terrorism, he announced that the focus of warfare will shift from internal security and counter insurgency, to conventional warfare. Due to shortage of funds, he also announced that the downsizing plan of the Armed Forces (by 30,000 between 1999-2002, including ten generals) was progressing well, and by 2006, another 30,000 all ranks will be reduced. Thus, the strength of the Armed Forces will be reduced from 220,000 in 1999 to 1,99,000.

Thailand is making efforts to improve her military power, by acquiring latest F 18 aircraft, armoured fighting vehicles and naval crafts mostly from the West, though twelve naval crafts have also been imported from China The armed forces will continue to adopt American doctrines for anti-terrorist, counter insurgency, anti piracy, anti smuggling and conventional warfare in jungle and mountainous terrain, as well as on her sea coast. Land threat from Myanmar would dictate high state of capability to fight a conventional war in semi-mountainous jungle terrain, with support of air force and artillery. Besides the small aircraft carrier already with the fleet, there is likelihood of few small or medium sized submarines being acquired. Her armed forces would continue to conduct joint annual exercises with American troops, of Cobra series.[10]

The new Supreme Commander has reduced the order of Black Hawk Sikorsky helicopters from the USA, from 33 to eight out of which three have already been delivered. Priced at US$ 14 to 15 million each, these helicopters are likely to enhance the mobility of the Army, for quick response operations.

The anti terrorist operations conducted by the Government are likely to succeed, as they are being undertaken in conjunction with other countries of the region. Assistance to the USA in Iraq will earn more status, leading to increased assistance and cooperation in economic and military fields.

Malaysia. While retaining their expertise of counter insurgency and jungle warfare, the Malaysian Armed Forces would continue to modernise, to face a "major conventional" threat of the World War II pattern, either by land or by sea. For this, modern tanks like T 90s, mechanised infantry vehicles, 155 mm guns, bridging equipment, modern small arms, mortars, shoulder fired surface to air and anti tank guided missiles (last two from Pakistan) are being acquired.

In 1990, Malaysia gave the following role to her Air Force:—

(a) Aerospace control, ensuring friendly use of air environment while denying the same to the enemy. This involves offensive counter-air, defensive counter-air and defensive-suppression operations.

(b) Force application, involving bringing down air power directly against surface targets, strategic targets and maritime air operations.

(c) Force enhancement, including air-to-air refuelling.

(d) Force sustenance, including logistic support, to own and friendly forces.

To achieve the above objectives, Kaula Lumpur decided to procure 28 Hawks Mk 108 advanced jet trainers and Mk 208 light multi-role combat aircraft from the UK, 18 Mig-29 from Russia and eight F/A-18 D combat aircraft from America. However, since their induction the Force has been facing problems of spares and maintenance, which she is likely to overcome. Her present fleet of 29 Sikorsky helicopters is being augmented with ten new Mi-17 armed utility helicopters from Russia, which would give her adequate short haul lift capability. The Malaysian Air Force is planning to modify three of its C-130 aircraft for air-to-air refuelling, acquire modern unmanned aerial vehicles, replace the aging Alouette helicopter and induct aircraft of F 18, Sukhoi 30 and Mig-29 type. The Navy has already acquired one submarine for training, and is likely to induct two more. Efforts are on to acquire new fast troop vessels, patrol vessels, Agosta Westland Super Lynx helicopter and two frigates. Besides these weapon systems, new radio equipment and satellite imagery may be procured and in the coming years Malaysia may also launch her own satellite, with the help of friendly countries.

Apart from the induction of additional modern air defence aircraft, tanks and submarines, next on list could be two small sized aircraft carriers (of the pattern of Thailand), to meet the requirements of South China Sea and of eastern and western wings of the country. Thus, by the year 2020, Malaysia could acquire adequate offensive punch as well as a credible defensive force to safeguard her two wings and off shore oil interests, ensure safety of her sea lanes and, capability to protect her outlying island territories.

The threat of piracy and militancy may result in joint patrolling in the Straits of Malacca, though differences with other ASEAN neighbours over the command and control, resource allocation and operational responsibilities are likely to continue. As regards internal security, the growth of Islamic extremism and racial polarisation of the nation's youth, have been identified as the likely destabilising factors. Steps have already been initiated to overcome this potential threat, and are likely to succeed.[11] Thus, despite internal irritants from Islamic fundamentalist parties, the present regime is likely to continue to guide the country towards greater stability, strong economy and regional cooperation. Economic prosperity would further enhance the "feel good factor", enabling greater allocation of defence funds for modernisation of the armed forces. It is likely that a small size aircraft carrier (of the Thai type) may also join the fleet. Probably, by the year 2025, Malaysia, Thailand and Singapore may also acquire short and medium range surface to surface missiles.

Gradually, Malaysia could take over the lead in the ASEAN from Indonesia, and the modernisation of armed forces would give the country strength to face minor regional challenges and contest major threats, to an extent.

Myanmar. Myanmar has porous land borders with China, India, Laos, Thailand and Bangladesh, and a sea border with India, but there are no outstanding disputes over any issue with any country. Thus, the military planners of Myanmar do not envisage any external threat. Their military doctrine revolves around internal security requirements for quelling civilian dissent in population centres and to conduct counter insurgency operations against economic, ideological and ethnic insurgents in rural districts.[12] For these, the Army (Tatmadaw) has been depending upon imports of weapons mainly from China, though Pakistan has supplied some man-portable surface to air missiles and anti tank missiles. Singapore, Israel and India have also supplied some defence items. Besides naval crafts, medium mortars, small arms, radio equipment and satellite imagery, MiG- 29 aircraft and helicopters may also be procured in the coming years.

Relations with other ASEAN members and India would improve and few items of military equipment may be procured from sources other than China. However, Beijing would continue to dominate in economic, infrastructure development and military fields. While drug trafficking may decrease under international pressure, the various factions of rebels and insurgents are not likely to give up their lucrative hold.

The military is likely to remain a dominant power in any government set-up, inviting sanctions from the western world. Naval bases along the western coast facing Andaman Sea and the Bay of Bengal would become a source of concern to India. While under the present military regime Myanmar is likely to remain close to China and try to play a neutral card, change to a democratic regime may see re-alignment of the region.

Singapore has made "diplomacy and deterrence" the twin pillars of her defence policy. While friendly co-operation for mutual benefit is sought, the role of Armed Forces is to "make it costly for any aggressor to move against the country". A concept of total defence based on five components (military, civil, economic, social and psychological), each strengthened at national and individual levels, has been adopted and the defence expenditure of minimum of six per cent of GDP has been assured. Besides upgrading and seeking aircraft like F 18, Euro fighter, F 16 Hornet, F 15 Eagle and Sukhois for replacing the existing F5E, A-4, F 16 Fighting Falcon are also being considered. Four submarines, fast patrol craft capable of carrying an infantry platoon each, modern landing ship tankers, logistic support craft and other modernisation projects are being undertaken. Emphasis is also on improving the C^4I systems, so that effective security of the sea lanes can be ensured.[13]

Internally, the country has very effective mechanism for detection and prevention of terrorism and fundamentalism, and would continue to explore new ways and means to maintain internal peace in her multi-ethnic society.

The country would continue to gain economic and military strength, and while bilateral relations with Malaysia may often come under strain, diplomatic ties under ASEAN would continue. The armed forces, specially the Air Force and the Navy would be armed with modern weapon systems, and next on the shopping list could be a small size aircraft carrier, enabling not only protection of the Straits of Malacca and domination of the seacoast, but also effective projection of power. The country may also launch a satellite and acquire short and medium range missiles, capable of launching conventional warheads. Reliance for weapons and equipment would continue on western powers, mainly the USA.

Domestic issues, like motivating the youth for service in the armed forces, population control, educational policies and the nation as a welfare state, will continue to be debated. While trade with China may increase, America would continue to exercise diplomatic and military influence over the country. Greater co-operation with non-communist regional powers and Japan is likely, in economic and security spheres. By virtue of her economic strength, Singapore is likely to exercise more clout in all forums affecting the region.

The Philippines is likely to continue to depend upon the US for her internal and external security threats. While clashes with China in the South China Sea may re-occur, her armed forces would not be strong enough to face the challenge of the PLA, alone. Thus, greater reliance on the ARF and the USA would continue. Depending upon the economic growth and availability of funds, the Navy may acquire at least one second generation(electrical or diesel) submarine, enhance capabilities for protection of off-shore assets, and amphibious capability of about a brigade group. The Army would be especially trained to fight the insurgents operating in the outlying islands.

Though modernisation plans have been temporarily put on hold, the Armed Forces would continue to get American assistance, of arms and training. Main thrust is likely to be "to quell Islamic insurgency in Southern Philippines and to safeguard territorial waters in South China Sea". Thus, enhancement of naval power, air lift capability and infantry's combat power are likely to be attended to. So far America has only provided military instructors and support, but if insurgency and Islamic fundamentalism continue to grow, then the likelihood of the US Armed Forces taking part in combat, alongside the Philippine Army, cannot be ruled out.

While the economy would improve, the problem of Muslim separatist groups operating in Mindanao Islands is likely to continue for some more time. Islamic fundamentalist groups may attempt to incite insurgency, but Manila would be able to weather them through negotiations and, if need be, the use of force.

As regards *Brunei*, she does not envisage any external or internal threat, but would continue to modernise her Armed Forces, especially her Navy. For facing internal threats, the likelihood of Gorkha troops being recruited directly from Nepal, would continue.

Compared with economic development, military modernisation would continue to be given a lower priority by *Vietnam.* Assistance from Russia, India and other friendly Central Asian States (CAS) may be sought to enhance the combat potential of her Navy, the Air Force and the Army, in that order. The economy would improve, allowing modernisation of the armed forces with weapons mostly from Russia. Emphasis would be on enhancing naval and air power, for domination of island territories and off shore establishments. The Army would be strengthened to face any external threat from the North. Influence of Hanoi on Laos and Cambodia would increase, through trade. America has shown keenness to develop economic and trade ties with Hanoi, as was apparent from the visits of President Clinton in 2000 and of Colin Powell in July 2001.

Washington may work towards including Vietnam in her regional security arrangements on the Korean peninsula and the South China Sea, including the missile defence umbrella, ultimately creating a counter balance to China. However, Hanoi is not likely to respond to these proposals, in a hurry.

Laos and *Cambodia* are likely to enhance their naval and military power, but would mainly face internal challenges. Modernisation would be restricted to supply of weapons and equipment by China, primarily to enhance Army's combat power and operations by patrol craft. Both countries would strive to improve their economies to present ASEAN standards. Thus, they would not be able to allocate large funds for modernisation of their armed forces.

Cambodia has adequate oil reserves in the Gulf of Thailand, some of which are claimed by Thailand. Currently she has to import all her needs. If explored, they could meet 50 per cent of her national budget, but at present no solution is in sight. This issue is likely to be resolved, under the ASEAN spirit.

In the coming years, while America would try to exert pressure on Cambodia on issues relating to human rights, China would attempt to strengthen her influence. It is likely that the critical economic situation may sway Phnom Penh to accept aid from America and other Western allies. China is also offering ship repair facilities at Ream (on the Gulf of Thailand), which would enable the Chinese Navy to show her presence in the area and enable greater security of the sea lanes required for oil transportation. Though Cambodia may try to get close to China to counter Vietnam and America, they also understand that "China is like fire, if you get too close you get burnt, but if you are too far you feel the chill."[14]

Likely Strategic Trends for the Next Twenty Five Years

While it is difficult to identify the potential threat to the region over the next 25 years, the current trends and their likely impact on the region are enumerated in the succeeding paragraphs.

US Policy towards South East Asia. "The security vision of America envisages her to remain engaged in world affairs, to influence the actions of others—friends and foes—who can affect her national well-being".[15] Washington views its policy towards the region as one of continuity and reaffirmation of security forces, while increasingly sharing security responsibilities with friends and allies, by broadening bilateral and multilateral engagement. This is considered necessary to allow safety of nearly US$ 500 billion trade with the region.

In this regard, by keeping nearly 100,000 troops under the Pacific Command[16] in the region, America feels that areas of uncertainty will be reduced and regional stability will be increased, besides enhancing their economic prosperity and political cooperation. By expanding security cooperation and military access with individual countries and working with ASEAN in ARF, confidence-building measures have been initiated, while dialogue with China and North Korea is expected to reduce proliferation of nuclear weapons and missiles. Since 11 September, the threat of Islamic fundamentalists and terrorists of Al Qaida or other groups has also resulted in the US urging support and firm action by South East Asian countries to eradicate the menace, especially emanating from Indonesia.

Japan and South Korea continue to be advanced bases for American troops, while Taiwan and Australia endorse all security concerns of America. Even Hongkong continues to allow visits by American warships, which further facilitates projection of military presence in the region.

Since closure of bases in Philippines in 1992, America has a "Visiting Forces Agreement" with Manila, which permits regular combined exercises and training, as was witnessed in 2002, against Abu Sayyaf. Thailand remains an important ally, with which regular Exercise Cobra Gold are conducted. Singapore has already offered special berthing facilities at Changi Naval Station, while Malaysia has shown keen interest in joint exercises and in procuring F18 aircraft.

Due to economic crisis, the modernisation of Indonesian Armed Forces has suffered. While the US has stopped all military aid due to human rights violations committed by the Armed Forces in East Timor, she cannot ignore the strategic importance of the largest Muslim state in the region. Thus, if adequate steps are initiated by Indonesia to counter terrorism, then security co-operation between the two countries could start again. Though at present Indonesia's prominence in South East Asia may be on a lower ebb, her strategic importance is immense.

America has serious concerns about the repressive regime in Myanmar and officially, economic sanctions are in place. However, Washington has allowed private companies to carry out trade and other economic activities. America also has long-term interests in Laos and Cambodia, and has been providing non-lethal economic aid to these countries, like for instance the de-mining operation. Brunei has expressed support to America, and provides transit facilities to her forces.

Following the establishment of diplomatic relations with Vietnam in July 1995, while some cooperation in "tracing and accounting missing in action" American troops of the Indochina war has been extended, the emphasis would be to develop mutual confidence. As regards security concerns, America would seem to be adopting a policy of transparency as also a cautious and gradual approach.

Considering that the US is the only super power in the world and her Armed Forces have a distinct lead in the revolution in military affairs, her efforts to defeat international terrorism and maintain regional stability for promoting economic and trade interests affecting her and her allies, is likely to guide all her future security policies. In implementation of her strategy of engagement of China, promoting democracy and human rights, America is likely to continue to adopt the policy of pluralism in security ties. America will continue to refute China's views on national defence policy, which asserts that enlargement of military blocs and strengthening of military alliances have added "factors of instability" to international security,[17] and expand her assistance and cooperation with friendly regimes in South East Asia, especially with those who consider China as their main security concern.[18]

China, Taiwan, North Korea, Islamic fundamentalism, along with her economic interests would continue to guide the American policy in the region. While the US would continue to provide arms to Taiwan and simultaneously engage China and force North Korea to suspend her nuclear weapons programme, Washington would assist countries like Philippines, Singapore and Malaysia, who are facing problems of Islamic fundamentalism and terrorism. Relations with South Korea, Japan and Australia would continue to improve, while those with Vietnam would take time to show tangible results. There is no likelihood of reduction in the US forces based in the region; on the contrary, the military to military cooperation would increase.

Despite improvement in trade and diplomatic relations, America still feels that China poses a major threat to Asia, as it faces an uncertain and perhaps an unstable future, as she tries to balance economic reforms with its "political dictatorship".[19] Hence, America has to adopt a policy of deterring and prevailing in a conflict with Beijing in Asia. In future, American strategic (including anti-terrorist), economic and trade interests in South East Asia could clash with those of China especially over Taiwan, Japan, South Korea and the East Asia region.

To meet these challenges, besides engaging China in trade and diplomacy, America would continue to position her Armed Forces in the region and co-opt friendly countries into the missile defence shield. Washington could also be expected to increase military aid and co-operation with the non-communist countries of the region, so as to enable them to face their security challenges on their own, to the extent possible. However, following the principle of Guam Doctrine, Washington is likely to avoid employment of her troops in local or regional disputes, in a land battle.

American policy of "pre-emption and pre-emptive" attacks has already caused concern to a few countries of the region. To counter it, besides strengthening their own capabilities and forging an alliance, they may even seek assistance from other powers, like China.

China. The economy of China is likely to grow at eight to ten per cent (though few analysts feel that these figures are inflated) and her demand for oil would be doubled by the year 2020, placing heavy reliance on imports from the Middle East, CAS and exploration from the South China Sea. The defence expenditure would continue to grow by at least 13 per cent to 15 per cent, allowing adequate scope for modernisation.

While stress would continue to be laid on the strategic missile force, the Navy and the Air Force would also get a larger share of funds. The Chinese Navy had started as a force adequate for defending the coast and now has the ability of defending outlying islands. With delivery of two Russian-built Sovremenny class destroyers fitted with Sunburn cruise missiles(range 120 km), the Chinese-Russian military cooperation is likely to be further strengthened. On order are SU 27 fighters, Mi-17 helicopters, Kilo class submarines, anti-air and ship-to-ship missiles, MBTs and aircraft engines,which will give the PLA the capability to fight in high tech environment.[20]

With her increased demand for oil, the South China Sea would assume greater importance. For exerting her muscle and for exerting her sovereign rights even 400 n m away from the mainland, by 2020 the Navy is likely to acquire the capability of a Blue Water Navy, capable of projecting strategic sea power. Thus, the PLAN would most likely acquire at least two aircraft carriers. Besides long-range fighters and interceptors (of SU 30 type), the PLAAF would also acquire air-to-air refuelling and additional airlift capability, which would enable Beijing to meet any off-shore contingencies. However, China's main attention is likely to continue towards her eastern and northern sea board (facing Taiwan and Japan) rather than South China Sea, as Beijing would appreciate that individually and even collectively, the countries of South East Asia pose no serious challenge to her claims.

Along with the demonstrated policy of Beijing in exerting her sovereignty in the South China Sea, this potential capability of the PLA is likely to further influence modernisation and expansion of the armed forces of most of the countries of South East Asia. It would also bring countries of the region into closer co-operation with America, as well as force them to increase their military resilience.

The aggressive economic policy of China towards her neighbours of South East Asia will increase the influence and leverage that Beijing has on the domestic policies and politics of these countries. For the next two decades this will be a matter of grave concern. The affected countries would try to face these concerns collectively and singly, by increasing their economic strength and through cooperative diplomatic forums, like the ASEAN and the ARF. In the long term, China may try to lead the region against the threat of US's "pre-emptive" doctrine and offer an alternative to regional countries, furthering her image as a strong power, in a multi-polar world.

Russia. The importance of sea lanes through the South China Sea is immense for Russia also, as all her trade and oil for Far East Russian region of Vladivostok passes through them. While economic resurgence is likely, Moscow's interests would be more towards Europe than South East Asia. The importance of oil reserves, both of Russia and the CAS (which are equal to those of Saudi Arabia) would influence economic and security ties. However, Russia would seek avenues and arrangements to supply defence equipment to China and other countries of the region. While she may extend diplomatic, economic and military support, she is not likely to commit her troops or establish bases in South East Asia.

Japan. Since the end of World War II, the US has ensured security of Japan in exchange for bases that allow her to project power across the Pacific Ocean, an essential congruence of strategic interest upon which the alliance has rested. However, since the end of the Cold War, while American strategic options have widened, those of Japan have narrowed down, reducing Tokyo's leverage. The two main security issues affecting Japan's security are China's threat to Taiwan and the nuclear North Korea's attitude towards South Korea and the region.[21] While Tokyo may be forced to spend more on her Self Defence Forces (SDF), her reliance on the security umbrella of America would continue. Quite a few people of Japan feel that their country must improve its defence capabilities to keep pace with the latest technical innovations and changing circumstances at home and abroad, so that the country is not caught off guard. Fear of foreign guerrillas and commandos taking advantage of IT revolution and nuclear know-how for terrorism, has strengthened such thought.

Commencing April 2001, the new five-year defence programme aims to meet the new challenges, though Tokyo is not likely to fully follow Washington's call to end her self-imposed restrictions on defence, but continue to rely on her bilateral military alliance. Though security of the sea-lanes through the South China Sea would continue to receive her attention, Japan's main concern would remain towards her northern sea board, facing China and North Korea. The Japanese Navy could play a more active role in protecting the sea lanes of the South China Sea, through which her oil and trade passes. Increase in economic and diplomatic relations and influence of America may also result in countries of South East Asia overcoming their inhibitions of World War II, resulting in higher level of military cooperation and inter-action with the SDF. However, security wise, Japan's attention is likely to remain towards North China Sea.

In the defence budget of 2001-2002, out of an outlay of 25.16 trillion yen, four trillion yen has been set aside for new weapons and another 150 million yen for disaster relief. This would enable procurement of two 13,5000 ton escort ships (with three helicopters each), new smaller but lighter tanks, newer transport planes and anti-submarine patrol craft. The addition of four in-flight refuelling aircraft (or tankers) would enhance flying distance by 1000 km or six hours flying time. Plans have also been formulated to buy long range missile defence system, long range transport aircrafts and large helicopters. Analysed along with the existing Aegis air defence destroyers and Tokyo's readiness to join the US sponsored Nuclear Missile Defence shield (NMD), both China and North Korea feel that besides her defensive capabilities, these weapon systems would greatly enhance Japan's offensive reach.[22] The SDF also plans to strengthen her computers and information systems, and pay special attention to fighting cyber-terrorism and biological warfare. However, as a policy, nuclear weapons would continue to be shunned.[23]

Pacifism is slowly fading away from Japan's Defence policy.

Post 11 September, while Japan was keen to revise rules regarding deployment of her SDF to support coalition efforts against terrorism and did send few logistic support ships to Pakistan for supporting US troops, her neighbours like China and North Korea were not only wary of Tokyo's moves but also issued a warning to Japan not to send her forces into the Indian Ocean, as it violated the Japanese constitution. Though Tokyo went ahead with her decision and objected to Beijing's interference in her internal matters, increase in the capability of Japan's SDF and changes in her defence policy are likely to have a strong reaction from China and North Korea.[24]

Australia is likely to remain a strong supporter of US policies in the region, and will further enhance her naval and air power. She would try to increase her influence in East Timor and improve relations with Indonesia. While economic ties with the ASEAN countries could improve further, like Japan, Australia's main focus would remain towards East China Sea and the Pacific Ocean.

References

1. *Far Eastern Economic Review*, 10 February 2000.
2. *Far Eastern Economic Review*, 21 November 2002.
3. *Web site New Strait Times Singapore*, 15 December 2002. Later investigations into the Bali Explosion also indicated that Riduan (Humbali) Isamuddin allegedly the head of Jemeah Islami (JI) in Southeast Asia was also connected with the explosion. Today, he is the most wanted man by the American's as he also had links with Al Qaida in Afghanistan. Times International, 25 November 2002.
4. ASEAN Data Base – 2000, issued by ASEAN Secretariat, Jakarta.

5. *Military Balance* 2000-2001.
6. *Far Eastern Economic Review*, October 2002.
7. *Far Eastern Economic Review*, March 2002.
8. Kim Conoby in *Far Eastern Economic Review*, 19 December 2002.
9. *Asian Defence Journal*, September 2002.
10. *Asian Defence Journal*, No. 3 and 7, 2001.
11. *Asian Defence Journal*, No. 5 and 8, 2001. *Far Eastern Economic Review*, 15 August 2001.
12. *Asian Defence Journal*, No. 7, 2001.
13. Website of Government of Singapore, Total Defence Plan 2002.
14. Asia-Pacific Center for Security Studies, an academic institution of US Pacific Command has the charter to "study regional security and preventive defence in the Asia-Pacific Region".
15. The US Security Strategy for the Far East Asia-Pacific Region, 1998, as modified after 11 September. Also, speech by Secretary of Defence, 21 July 1997, and web site Defence Link Publications-Far East Asia.
16. Largest unified command in the US defence structure, it stretches from the American west coast to the east coast of Africa, and from the Arctic to the Antarctic. Its area of responsibility includes the Pacific, Northeast Asia, Southeast Asia, South Asia and the Indian Ocean, encompassing 43 countries. Having a total strength of nearly 300,000 (about 1/5 of total of US Armed Forces), it has nearly 100,000 troops in a forward deployment posture in Asia-Pacific region, in countries like Japan and South Korea.
17. White paper on China's National Defence, July 1998, incorporated in US Defence Policy statement.
18. Statement by US Defence Secretary of 25 July 2001, The *Asian Age* of 26 July 2001.
19. Robert Lim, "The Northeastern Asian Power Equation", *Hindu*, 4 April 2002.
20. Bates Gill, "China's Newest Warships", *Far Eastern Economic Review*, 27 July 2000.
21. Charles Bickers, "Extending Tokyo's Reach", *Far Eastern Economic Review*, 18 January 2001.

22. Vice Admiral (Retired) Iqbal F Quadi, "Japan's Changing Perceptions on Defence".
23. "Japan Anti-Terror Support will fuel neighbour's fear". website of South Asia Monitor, December 2001.
24. *Asian Defence Journal*, June 2001.

7

India and the Region—Past and Future

It would be seen that India has had relations with the region since 500 BC, when Ashoka sent his messengers with the teachings of Lord Buddha. Since then, over the centuries, Buddhism, Hinduism and Islam have spread to the region and taken deep roots. While the influence of Indian civilisation declined after 1500 AD, even today it permeates and influences the art, literature, religion and politics of countries stretching from Myanmar to Vietnam and from Laos to Indonesia. Though later many countries of South East Asia did come under colonial rule, traces and imprints of Indian civilisation still run through the fabric of the region, which made G Coedes describe the region as "Farther India, Greater India and the Indianised States of South East Asia".[1] Similarly, the Indian diaspora has lived in these countries since ages and when compared to the Chinese, has adapted well to local environment. They participate actively in political, social and economic fields, and occupy white-collar positions of dignity.

India's Reactions to Events in South East Asia - 1945 to 1992

As mentioned earlier, in the 20th century up to World War II, the British hegemony dominated and ruled over South and South East Asia encompassing the Indian Ocean and the South China Sea, barring the Dutch in East Indies and the French in Indo-China. While China was a weak power, Japan had an ambition to dominate the region, which she did from the 1920s and in 1942 came close to the Indian Ocean. As proved during the battles of Coral Sea and Midway in 1942, despite attack on Pearl Harbour, Tokyo did not have enough resources for the Pacific Ocean. Though the Japanese did attack the British Navy in Ceylon, it was more to protect their flanks of Singapore, Malaya and Burma, rather than venture into the Indian Ocean. The 1940s saw decolonisation of South East Asia, first India, then Burma and Indonesia becoming independent.[2]

As regards India's relations with South East Asia, besides historical and cultural ties, as a leader of anti-colonial revolution in South Asia and supporter of independence movements, India championed the cause of Indonesia's independence at the Asian Relations Conference at Delhi in 1946, which saw close bonds being developed between Nehru and Sukarno. After 1948, India sponsored Indonesia and China's entry into the UN, and developed good bilateral relations with Malaysia, Singapore, Myanmar and Thailand. During the conference on Indonesia held at New Delhi in 1949, Philippine President mooted the idea of Asianisation of the region, on the pattern of the grouping taking place in the Pacific, to act as a bulwark against the spread of Communism. Though no military commitment was made, the grouping was aimed to encourage political, cultural and economic cooperation among South East Asia and

Pacific region. The idea was again floated on 26 May 1950 during the non-communist conference organised by Australia, which was attended by Ceylon, India, Pakistan, Indonesia and Thailand. Though it was stated that this permanent regional organisation was not directed against any country, India declined to support the proposal.

The 1955 Afro-Asian Conference at Bandung was a landmark in India's approach to South East Asia. By now the Korean War saw the world in two power blocs, the USA and the Soviet Union. India by that time was emerging as a champion of the non-aligned countries. SEATO and CENTO were also formed. These groupings were suspected by the non-aligned group as a tool of the US to interfere in internal affairs of Asian countries, and became a major point of discussion at the Bandung Conference. Pakistan, a member of CENTO, was also invited to Bandung. Though she initially hesitated and suspected that the conference might turn into an anti-US meet, she attended the conference but spoke against supporting China's entry into the UN. China, on the other hand, adopted a conciliatory approach towards her neighbours, based on Panchsheel. While some of the 29 countries attending the conference did float the idea of united action to forestall all threats and laid stress on regional approach to problems of South and South East Asia, few countries, including Pakistan, opposed it. Besides a clash between India and Pakistan on foreign policy issues, the relations between Nehru and Sukarno also deteriorated after the Bandung Conference. This became evident in1961 during the first Non-Aligned meet at Belgrade, where both leaders expressed opposite views on what constituted a threat.[3]

India did not support the West during the Korean and the Indo-China Wars, but she did chair the

Neutral Nations Repatriation Commission in Korea and sent a medical team, under the directions of the UN. She also chaired the International Control Commission on Indo-China, but following the policy of non-alignment. New Delhi kept away from all military pacts and alliances and avoided the Cold War groupings. India viewed the American presence in the region as a destabilising factor of power bloc rivalry and tried to develop good bilateral relations with the region, based on historical and cultural ties. In 1954, India opposed the Manila Treaty and establishment of SEATO. However, in 1957, New Delhi did not object to the Anglo-Malayan Defence Agreement, as it was aimed at fighting insurgency and confrontation by an independent country. Though India was wary of the British and American military and economic expansion in the region, she was more concerned about the threat from Pakistan and China, and had very little energy to spare for the region. India was concerned about the Indian Ocean and the Straits of Malacca, which provided a passage to the Pacific, but had no resources to influence the region. As the fleets of the US, the UK and the Soviet Union sailed through in two directions, the super powers established bases in South East Asia and the Indian Ocean, like Diego Garcia.

In the meanwhile, due to the personal equation between Nehru and Abdul Rahman, Bapa Malaysia (Father of the Nation on the lines of Mahatma Gandhi), India had established close bilateral relations with Malaysia. Kuala Lumpur sought New Delhi's assistance for writing the Constitution and setting up the Malaysian Navy. Dato Hussain Onn, the Prime Minister had served in India in the Indian Army (Kumaon Regiment) during the Second World War and had great personal regard for General T N Raina, the Chief of Army Staff of the Indian Army, during the late 1970s. Thus, the military to military relations between the two countries continued to improve. Diplomatically, India was seen as a torch bearer of non-alignment and anti-colonialism, leading the way for a modern nation. As India supported Malaysia during Jakarta's *Kanfrantasi* with Malaysia in the Borneo region, relations between India and Indonesia dipped low. This resulted in Indonesia giving support to China and Pakistan during the 1962 and 1965 Wars, and even offering military hardware to Rawalpindi. However, Malaysia stood by India and supported her in the UN, which greatly annoyed Pakistan, who labelled Malaysia as a "Muslim supporting a Kafir". Pakistan even broke diplomatic relations with Malaysia temporarily, but the Indo-Malaysian ties were so strong that the Malaysian High Commission in Karachi even supplied food to Indian diplomats stranded in Karachi, which further infuriated the Pakistanis.

Between 1965 and 1970, India turned more towards the Soviet Union for diplomatic and military support, leading to the signing of the 1971 Indo-Soviet Treaty of Friendship and Co-operation and New Delhi supported the Soviet policy in Vietnam. These events were interpreted by the West and few countries of South East Asia as India's leaning towards the Soviet Bloc. The period also saw India adopting an inward looking economic policy and a slow growth of economy, which did not attract the growing market economies of South East Asia. Instead, the US, China, Japan, the EU and South Korea invested in the region, thus gaining a greater share in their external trade. Though in their hearts individual countries admired India's victory in East Pakistan as a great military achievement, few countries fell to anti-India propaganda labelling New Delhi as an expansionist power, which may support local insurgencies sprouting in their areas. Deliberately, few countries even failed to comprehend India's compulsions for creating a situation for return of nearly 10 million refugees and the atrocities committed by Pakistan Army on their own kith and kin, in East Pakistan.

India's support to Vietnam during her 1978 invasion of Cambodia, denouncing of the Chinese invasion of Vietnam in 1979 and her silence on Soviet intervention in Afghanistan in the same year, also portrayed India as a country under Soviet influence. Hence, while countries of South East Asia developed closer ties with western powers led by the USA, their bilateral relations with India did not grow, but remained cordial and correct.

In the 1980s, some countries also projected New Delhi's military intervention in Sri Lanka and the Maldives, and the acquisition of the second aircraft carrier and a nuclear submarine for training her naval personal, as an exertion of regional power status by India. Though bilateral relations in the fields of trade, commerce and military co-operation continued, India's share of FDIs and trade with the region remained marginal.[4]

In the 1980s and 1990s, India had adequate food stocks. Economic liberalisation policies adopted in early 1990s led to high economic growth and emergence of a bigger middle class, which made India more relevant and attractive to South East Asia for trade. Though insurgency and terrorism showed their ugly face in the 1990s in Jammu and Kashmir, the country by and large remained stable, trouble free and peaceful.

Look East Policy

It was in September 1992 in Singapore, that Prime Minister P V Narasimha Rao articulated a "Look East Policy" for India. He announced India's desire to develop stronger relations with her South East Asian neighbours, emphasising greater cooperation, trade and cultural ties. While admitting that during the Cold War India had ignored her South Eastern neighbours, he felt that there was a need to re-engage them more energetically. Since then, successive Prime Ministers, especially Shri I K Gujral and Shri A B Vajpayee have laid stress on developing durable and vibrant relations between India and South East Asia. However, it is felt that much more could have been done.[5]

Since 1992, there has been a distinct improvement in India's relations with South East Asian countries and those of Asia Pacific region. As a result of economic reforms, Indian markets became more open and attractive to foreign investors, while the political stability and stable economy created a "feel good" factor, which made India once again focus towards South East Asia. Simultaneously, the end of the Cold War and withdrawal of the Soviet Union from Afghanistan also changed ASEAN's attitude towards India, and they started to look towards New Delhi in a more benign way. This resulted in India becoming a sectoral dialogue partner of ASEAN in 1992. After becoming a full Dialogue Partner of ASEAN in 1995, India for the first time participated in the Post Ministerial Conference of ASEAN in Jakarta, in 1996 and in ARF, where security and political concerns of Asia Pacific region were deliberated.

With the visits of the Thai Princess to Andaman and Nicobar Islands, and by India's Vice President to Thailand, bilateral relations between India and Thailand showed improvement.

Singapore organised the first ever Global Indian Entrepreneurs Conference in June 1996, in which Indian businessmen from around the world participated. From 3 to 13 March 1996, the Indian and Singapore Navies conducted a week long anti-submarine warfare exercise, off the coast of Visakhapatnam.

In 1994, Dr Mahathir bin Mohamad, Prime Minister of Malaysia was conferred with Jawaharlal Nehru Award for International Understanding, which he received during a state visit to Delhi, in August 1996. India and Malaysia jointly identified ports, power and highways as the three areas where Malaysian expertise could be used in India.

During 1997, the Sultan of Brunei paid an official visit to India and, though trade between the two countries continued to be limited, areas for further expansion were deliberated upon.

Accompanied by a big trade delegation, President Ramos of Philippines paid a state visit to India in March 1997. During the seminars and discussions, new avenues for expanding economic ties between the two countries were explored.

Indonesia agreed to India's proposal to set-up a telemetry tracking ground station at Baik (Kalimantan) for continuous monitoring of India's Geo-synchronous Satellite Launch Vehicle (GSLV), while India agreed to provide assistance to Indonesia in the field of space science. Besides cultural and trade relations, agreements for promoting closer understanding and cooperation in culture and education were also signed. Admiral Sushil Kumar, the Indian Naval Chief also paid an official visit to Jakarta.

The third meeting of the Joint Working Group between India and Vietnam was held in Delhi in March 1997,where cooperation in the field of agriculture was discussed. New Delhi also extended another credit of Rs. 90 crore on soft terms to Hanoi, for purchase of capital goods from India. To enhance mutual cooperation, the Indian Naval Chief visited Vietnam in May 1996.

Relations with Laos remained warm and cordial, with India pledging to provide medicines worth Rs 15 Lakh, as flood relief. Besides the visit of the Deputy Prime Minister on a pilgrimage to Bodh Gaya in December 1996, India and Cambodia signed agreements for enhancing cooperation in the fields of trade, economics, science and technology.

India's relations with Australia and New Zealand continued to be warm and friendly, with the Indian Naval Chief visiting New Zealand. India also opened a mission in Port Moresby, Papua New Guinea in April 1996, established diplomatic relations with Micronesia in November 1996, and decided to do so shortly with Marshal Islands. Though concerned at the events in Fiji, India stood against the racially biased constitution but did not interfere in the internal matters of the country.

Unfortunately, India did not take any initiative to assist Indonesia or other countries of the region, which suffered from the Economic Crisis of 1997. While it may have been due to New Delhi's political uncertainty or comparatively lesser economic capacity, it was essential for India to show genuine concern and take concrete measures to assist and at least offer aid to Indonesia. This could have been in the form of guarantees to foreign institutions, enhancing imports, offering long term loans at low rates and encouraging India's exports to the affected countries. Thus, India missed an opportunity to genuinely pursue her Look East Policy, which needs to be guarded in future.

ASEAN responded positively to India's efforts, by first making her a sectoral partner, and later, in 1996, invited New Delhi to join the ARF. On 5 November 2002, the first India-ASEAN summit level meeting was held in Cambodia on the pattern of ASEAN +3 (with China, Japan and South Korea), details of which are covered later.

Events Between 2002-2003

On 24 November 2002, the ASEAN Plus 4 Summit (ASEAN, India, South Korea, Japan and China) was held in Cambodia. Though it was aimed to welcome India, initially the proceedings were dominated by China. Beijing agreed to join the framework of setting the world's largest free-trade zone, by 2010. She also signed a declaration on cooperation on non-traditional security issues including terrorism, cyber crime and smuggling of people. Besides concluding an agricultural pact, China also scored a breakthrough on how to behave in the South China Sea, the likely flash point in the region. Thus, the 4 November declaration gave a face saving space to ASEAN and China. However, it did not include a code of conduct and is unlikely to have any practical impact on reduction of tension in the South China Sea, as it does not take into consideration the claims of Taiwan and the four other ASEAN states currently embroiled in a tangle, and Vietnam, which has seen two armed clashes with China over Paracel Islands, presently under the Chinese control.

While ASEAN has been trying to persuade China to agree to a code of conduct in the South China Sea, which would include a restriction on construction of new military outposts in the sea (as done by Beijing in the mid 1990s on Mischief Reef off Philippines), all they were able to get was a political declaration. China also flatly rejected ASEAN's efforts to include Paracel Islands in the declaration. In fact, this issue divided ASEAN, because while Malaysia argued that the code of conduct covers only the Spratly Islands which are claimed in whole or part by six countries, Vietnam insisted that Paracel should also be included. Avoiding mention of the geographical limits, even the suggestion of Philippines regarding imposition of a ban on erecting and constructing new structures was deleted, and a vague line "prohibition against inhabiting presently uninhabited locations" was accepted.

According to some analysts, while the Summit may have sent a message to the West that there is no likelihood of conflict in South China Sea and thus South East Asia may attract more trade, investment and aid, the basic conflict over claims of sovereignty in the South China Sea still remain.[6]

Addressing the Second Indo-ASEAN Business Summit on 4 September 2003, Prime Minister Vajpayee stressed the need for ASEAN and India to join hands for protecting the rights of their farmers at the WTO Conference, at Cancum (Mexico). He also sought their cooperation for forging an alliance on common issues like investment, competitive policy,trade facilitation and transparency in government procurement. He expressed hope that trade between India and ASEAN, which is presently US$10 billion, could grow to US$ 15 billion by 2005 and US$ 30 billion, by 2007. Vajpayee observed that trade between India and ASEAN is far below the actual potential, considering that the region has a combined population of 1.5 billion and a GDP of US $ 1.5 trillion, and has an advantage of geographical proximity. Commenting on the share of foreign trade share of ASEAN with India, he mentioned that though it has shown a modest rise from six per cent in 1991 to nine per cent in 2002, the share of India in ASEAN's foreign trade has remained at a negligible one per cent. He emphasised that apparently, latent strengths in India and ASEAN have not fully been tapped, which should be the thrust for the future. He offered India's expertise in space technology for natural resource mapping and hydrology and flood forecasting, as well as for launching satellites for remote sensing and communication purposes. He also initiated the idea of a rail link connecting Delhi with Hanoi, through Myanmar, Thailand and Cambodia. He felt that the project will further boost the economies of the region and bring the people closer.

Addressing the same conference, the Foreign Minister Shri Yashwant Sinha, had stated that India's 'Look East' policy was now entering the second phase. While phase one was primarily focused on ASEAN and trade and investment linkages, phase two extends from Australia to China and East Asia, with ASEAN being its core. Now, the focus will also shift from "exclusive economic issues to economic and security issues including joint efforts to protect sea lanes, coordination by arrangements for FTAs and establishing of industrial economic linkages between the countries of the region and India".

India has offered ASEAN grouping cooperation in five distinct areas (IT –enabled services, financial services sector, pharmaceutical and telecommunication industries and infrastructure), and signed three significant accords (a framework agreement towards a free trade area by 2011, a joint declaration against terrorism and, accession to ASEAN Treaty of Amity and Cooperation—TAC).

Vajpayee had also suggested formation of an Asian Economic Community, which besides ASEAN and India, could also include China, South Korea and Japan. India has also announced opening of Indian skies to airlines of ASEAN member countries, to fly to eighteen tourist destinations in India.

A blue print for establishing Free Trade Zone (based on early harvest programme) between ASEAN plus 4 (Japan, China, South Korea and India) was also suggested, to start from 1 November 2004. To allow competitive imports to India, lowering of tarriffs have also been announced. Special concessions on 111 items to four developing countries of ASEAN (Cambodia, Laos, Myanmar and Vietnam-CLMV) by 2006, unilaterally, have been offered while they could reciprocate by 2009. With the balance six ASEAN countries, the exchange of tarrifs on 105 commonly agreed items could take place within three years on reciprocal basis, and a full Free Trade Agreement implemented by 2011. Details of India's Trade with the region are given at Appendicies L and M.

India has also offered to assist ASEAN in formulating her "Vision 2020", in Cambodia. An agreement for economic cooperation has also been signed, which draws a roadmap for creating the Free Trade Zone, both for goods and services, and free flow of investment. Besides signing a joint declaration against terrorism, Shri Vajpayee also offered India's help in fighting HIV/AIDS, by providing medicines at cheaper rates.

Present Status

India views ARF as "an experiment for fashioning a new pluralistic, cooperative security order in tune with the diversity of Asia-Pacific region and in consonance with transition away from a world characterised by poles built around military alliances",[7] and is ready to contribute to it. Though the ARF covers a broader region, it is India's belief that it is built around the nucleus of ASEAN and is ASEAN driven – hence of importance to India and South East Asia.

In 1995 ASEAN had declared South East Asia as a Nuclear Weapons Free Zone (SEANWAFZ). Thus, after Pokhran II, they expressed grave concerns about India and Pakistan's nuclear explosions, but at the same time admonished world's nuclear powers for their arsenals. As at that time India's entry into ARF as a full dialogue partner was under consideration, Indian diplomats were able to convince ASEAN that her nuclear experiments did not pose any threat to the region.[8]

As far as Pakistan is concerned, while she has made attempts to join the ASEAN, and lately the ARF, the member countries are concerned that Islamabad would not refrain from raising bilateral issues against India specially of Kashmir, in these forums. Thus, she would disturb the principle of not raising bilateral issues and consensus on all matters, and vitiate the atmosphere of the forum. ASEAN has also appreciated that as Shimla Agreement and Lahore Declaration provide adequate scope for resolving bilateral issues, Pakistan has not honoured them. Instead, she has been sponsoring terrorism, militancy and insurgencies in India. Thus, despite support from some ASEAN member countries, so far Pakistan's efforts to join the groupings has not succeeded.

Till the 1990s India was more focussed towards Kashmir and her border disputes with Pakistan and China, and was not showing much interest in the formation of military alliances and groupings in South East Asia. She, however, continued to develop bilateral relations, which showed moderate growth in trade and economic relations. In the defence field, though India continued to offer seats for students from Indonesia, Malaysia, Singapore and Thailand and ships of Indian Navy exchanged courtesy visits with these countries, no substantial defence sales or joint training was conducted, as till 1990s South East Asia continued to be oriented towards the West. This has changed since late 1990s, and more so after 11 September which has not only brought countries of the region closer, but also given a new impetus to US-India relations, including in the field of military cooperation.

INDIA AND OTHER REGIONAL FORUMS

Besides ASEAN, India has also positively responded to other regional economic development initiatives; among them the Kunming Initiative by Beijing, Mekong-Ganga Cooperation by Delhi and Greater Mekong Sub-regional Initiatives need mention. Launched by the two major powers of Asia to reach the same countries, their aim is cooperation in projects of mutually advantageous economic and infrastructure development and energy security.

Mekong-Ganga Cooperation (MGC)

Launched on 10 November 2000 in Vientiane (capital of Laos), the Mekong- Ganga Cooperation is aimed at increasing trade and tourism between six countries (India, Myanmar, Thailand, Laos, Cambodia and Vietnam) by developing an East-West trans-Asian trade highway. This is expected to boost the economies of the areas falling in the Mekong Delta.

The project was started after BIMST-EC (Economic Cooperation between Bangladesh, India, Myanmar, Thailand and Sri Lanka-another regional grouping formed in June 1997). Initially, it was named as Ganga-Mekong Swarnbhoomi project, which was objected to by some countries. Thus, the name was changed to Mekong-Ganga Initiative. This is India's most significant co-operative movement launched in the region. By developing transportation and trade links, it aims to give new impetus of growth to regional economies in the otherwise backwards areas, without changing the identities or characters of the local environment.

The project also includes construction of the Asian Highway. When completed, the Highway would also link Delhi and Calcutta via Moreh (Manipur) with Tamu, Kalemyo, Mandalay, Yangon (all in Myanmar), Chang Mai and Bangkok (in Thailand), Kaula Lumpur (Malaysia), Singapore, Phnom Penh (Cambodia), Vientiane (Laos) and Ho Chi Minh City(Vietnam). India has already taken the first step in constructing the Tamu - Kalemyo road, and has also developed a network of roads going from Calcutta towards Bangladesh.

China's Kunming Initiative

Through this initiative, China seeks to link her province of Yunan with Myanmar, India's North-eastern states and Thailand, in an economic grid. With China already having strong economic and military links with Myanmar, any attempts by New Delhi to woo Yangon could be seen with a yellow eye. Thus, the initiative launched with much fanfare, has not taken any forward movement.

Greater Mekong Sub region (GMS)

This sub regional cooperation has the support of Asian Development Bank, and besides the five South East Asian states, extends to Yunan province of China. It has identified eight key sectors for development, namely transport, energy, telecommunications, tourism, environment, human resource development, trade and investment. Though India is not directly involved in this project, she is likely to contribute towards its construction.

INDIA'S INITIATIVES WITH OTHER COUNTRIES

Review of Events Between 1998 to 2003

While the 1998 Pokhran Tests by India and

subsequent Chagai tests by Pakistan were not supported by any South East Asian country, they refrained from directly criticising them. In fact, India was granted membership of the ARF even after the Pokhran tests, which showed that New Delhi's security concerns were well appreciated by the ASEAN members.

India's efforts to develop cordial relations with Pakistan by initiating the Lahore process and inviting General Musharraf to Agra even after the Kargil War, were greatly appreciated as genuine efforts to reduce tension in South Asia and as mature diplomatic moves. India not only refrained from making any comments on the events in East Timor it being an internal issue of Indonesia, but also declined to join the UN Peacekeeping Force. This policy was seen as a support to Indonesia.

The trend of improvement of relations with ASEAN and the Pacific region continued in 2000-2002, with India holding the first comprehensive security dialogue with Japan in June 2001, where the proposal of joint exercises between the armed forces and Coast Guards of two countries was also formalised. A similar dialogue was held between India and Australia in August 2001, in which serving officers of the two armed forces also participated for the first time. Visits by the Thai Prime Minister to India, participation by India's Vice President in the G 15 Summit, visits by Prime Minister Vajpayee to Japan, by Shri Jaswant Singh (who at that time was holding dual charge of Foreign and Defence ministries) to Australia, New Zealand, Vietnam, Thailand and Myanmar, went a long way to show India's interest in the region. Besides SAARC, India also continued to participate actively in BIMSTEC, Kunmin and Mekong-Ganga initiatives, all of which are aimed at improving communications and economies of the member states.

Post 11 September, India's condemnation of terrorism is in consonance with the policy of South East Asian countries. New Delhi also offered whole hearted support to the UN sanctioned American led operations against the Taliban in Afghanistan. This was also appreciated by most of the countries of the region, which were also endorsing the offensive.

As regards defence co-operation, besides assistance in courses and limited arms sale, the role model could be seen from Exercise Milan[9] being conducted regularly by the Indian Navy. Similarly, the International Fleet Review organised by the Indian Navy in Mumbai in September 2001 with the theme of "Building Bridges of Friendship" attracted ships and contingents from 19 countries, including those of Singapore, Japan and Australia. Besides showing the power of the Indian Armed Forces, such events also build-up confidence amongst neighbours, which could act as a building block for stronger bonds of friendship and co-operation.

Pakistan

In mid-April 2003, Prime Minister A B Vajpayee again renewed India's offer of seeking "decisive" peace with Pakistan. Pakistan responded favourably, resulting in exchange of high commissioners, resumption of bus services and, allowing of visas for people-to-people contacts. However, as Pakistan continued to train and send terrorists to create violence in Jammu and Kashmir, no talks at ministerial or Prime Minister's level took place.

Response to Operation Iraqi Freedom

Despite pressure from America, India did not endorse the American led intervention in Iraq, nor did she agree to send military contingent for maintaining peace, as the operations were not authorised by the UN.

China

India and China are not only making efforts to move closer in trade and diplomatic matters, but even the Sikkim issue is being resolved. While India accepted Tibet as part of China, Beijing agreed to open the trade route through Sikkim, for trade with India and deleted it from her maps on the web site. The Chinese Prime Minister, Mr Wen Jiabo reaffirmed this to Vajpayee at Bali on the sidelines of ASEAN Summit, on 8 October 2003.

Both countries also agreed to speed up talks to resolve the boundry issue. A meeting was held between the Principle Secretary and National Security Advisor of India and the Vice Minister of China on 23 October 2003, in Delhi.

Indonesia

President Wahidi visited India in February 2000, and Prime Minister Vajpayee reciprocated the visit in January 2001. In the field of defence, a co-operation agreement was signed on 11 January 2001, but so far it has not borne fruit. Ms Megawati also visited India in June 2002, and while relations between the two countries are cordial, specific differences over Islamic fundamentalism and terrorism remain. Though four trade and commerce agreements were signed during her visit, these are yet to show results. Since 1951, the two countries have signed nearly twenty bilateral agreements covering spheres of trade, commerce and defence, but they have not been very successful.

Both, India and Indonesia, have agreed to expand co-operation for fighting terrorism and for improving trade. While India showed interest in undertaking rail construction projects in Indonesia, she was invited to invest in existing and new palm oil plantations.

India also offered to train Indonesian students in IT related subjects.

Thailand

Shri Vajpayee visited Thailand from 9 to 12 October 2003. Here also, he signed an agreement to double bilateral trade to US$ two billion, in the next two years. An Indo-Thailand free trade area will also be formed, over the next seven years and both countries have agreed to remove import duty from 84 items, with effect from March 2004. Besides this, he signed four other agreements, covering cooperation in agriculture and promotion of tourism, and complimenting India's "Look East" policy coinciding with Thailand's "Look West" policy. New Delhi also offered to sell defence equipment to Bangkok, while the latter asked for safe passage for her fishing vessels passing through India's Extended Economic Zone, to African ports. A review of proposals made by India at the ASEAN meet at Bali was also carried out, and Thailand allowed Indian air charters to fly freely not only to Bangkok, but to other Thai destinations as well. A review of the road project linking India-Myanmar-Thailand was also undertaken. Feasibility of enhancing mutual cooperation through regional initiatives like BIMST-EC (in which Bangladesh, Sri Lanka, Myanmar are partners of India) and the Mekong-Ganga project, were also discussed.

Both countries also agreed to intensify security co-operation and make joint efforts in their fight against terrorism, drug trafficking and narcotics. They also agreed to carry out joint naval patrolling, to fight piracy.

Singapore

Mr Goh Chok Tong, Prime Minister of Singapore, while addressing the summit of East Asian economists in Singapore on 12 October 2003, strongly supported India's long term vision of Asian Economic Community (ASEAN+ 4) proposed by Vajpayee at Bali. He opinioned that besides Japan and China, India could be the "third Node of Growth" that could be integrated into the East Asian economy. He felt that by 2025, India will become at least a lower-middle income economy, while parts like Bangalore and Mumbai will be in upper-middle class income bracket.

Mr Teo Chee Hean, Defence Minister of Singapore visited India from 13 October 2003, for four days. A Memorandum of Understanding was signed between the two countries, envisaging enhanced co-operation in training and in prevention of piracy on high seas in the Andaman Sea. It is expected that besides the Singapore Navy, which has been carrying out joint exercises with India since last twenty years, the co-operation will also be extended to Army and Air Force. The two sides have also agreed to hold regular discussions on security matters affecting them.

USA

Post 11 September attacks and having suffered from a terrorist attack in Yemen, the US Navy has sought assistance from the Indian Navy while sailing through the Straits of Malacca. Joint exercises between the armed forces of the two countries, dialogue on nuclear issues, visits by Service chiefs and inter-action at think-tank levels have also increased. These have further cemented the ties between Washington and New Delhi, and are likely to improve further.

India denounced the US led Operation Iraqi Freedom, as it did not have the mandate from the UN. She also declined to send a military contingent for peace keeping to Iraq, under American control. Though her stance was not liked by America, they appreciated New Delhi's principled stand on the issue.

Co-operation in defence field improved. A team of US troops carried out joint training with the Indian Army in Ladakh, while the two Navies participated in Exercise Malabar, off the eastern coast.

Though America's thrust on fighting and eradicating terrorism world-over remained unchanged, her soft approach towards General Musharraf and Pakistan (which continued to stoke militancy in Jammu and Kashmir) continued to irritate Indian leaders.

Nepal, Bhutan and Sri Lanka

In April 2003, India gave two helicopters and military equipment worth Rs two crore to Nepal in her operations against the Maoist insurgents. India also stepped up surveillance of the Indo-Nepal border, to guard against their members from seeking refuge and sanctuaries in India.

The King of Bhutan paid a state visit to India in September 2003, to foster the existing bilateral relations.

The President of Sri Lanka also visited India in September 2003, and was happy at India's support to her country in resolving the LTTE issue.

Myanmar

Relations between India and Myanmar have seen many ups and downs, especially since the military took over power in Yangon. A Treaty of Friendship was signed in 1951, a boundary agreement in 1967 and the maritime boundary fixed in 1986. Due to the porous land border, an agreement for mutual co-operation for preventing illicit trafficking in narcotics, drugs, and arms was concluded on 30 March 1993. A Memorandum of Understanding for Science and Technology and for cultural cooperation was also signed on 25 June 2001. In the field of agriculture, India offered a credit of US$ 10 m in 1999 and $ 15 m in 2000. Development of the old World War II road that linked Moreh (in Manipur) with Tamu and Kalemyo (both in Myanmar) was undertaken in February 2001, followed by an MOU for its maintenance. These are all positive developments.

The Vice President, Naval Chief and the Army Chief of Myanmar visited India, while India's Foreign and Finance Ministers and two Services Chiefs returned their visits. The meeting of BIMSTEC initiative on 1 December 2001 was also a step in the right direction.

Mr U Win, the Foreign Minister of Myanmar visited India, on 20 January 2003. He suggested that as SAARC had made no progress due to Pakistan blocking the free trade zone, the BIMSTEC initiative needed to be pursued more vigorously, by holding a summit in 2004. Myanmar also informed India that the Chinese plan to link her Yunan province in South-West China with the Bay of Bengal through the Irrawadi corridor was still in discussion stage. In any case, Myanmar would ensure that the projects undertaken with Chinese assistance do not pose any security problem for India. India's Oil and Natural Gas Commission is already exploring for oil in Myanmar in the Bay of Bengal, and has now been invited to do so on land also.[10] Mr U Win Aung also emphasised the need to expedite the proposal of India-Myanmar-Thailand road, and sought assistance for building a deep sea port at Dalwe in southern Myanmar, which would help

Indian and Thai ships to refuel, instead of waiting to cross the Straits of Malacca. Describing India as a more understanding neighbour, he re-assured India that while Myanmar has many armed groups in the country fighting the government, the country will not allow any groups to launch a rebellion from Myanmar into another country.

Vietnam

Bilateral trade and economic co-operation between the two countries increased. Leading a high level delegation,Vice President Nguyen Thi Binh accompanied by representatives of ministries of agriculture, foreign trade, industry, transportation and petroleum visited India in March 2001. The question of Mekong-Ganga Project, co-operation by ONGC (which has already invested US$ 380 m in a pipeline in Southern Vietnam) and the feasibility of Chennai refinery processing the Vietnamese crude, which is of heavy grade, were also deliberated upon. In tourism, the proposal of "pilgrim tourists" to Buddhist sites in India and Vietnam,was also discussed. During his tour of South East Asian countries, India's Foreign Minister paid a return visit to Vietnam the same year. In March 2000, George Fernandes, the then Defence Minister visited Vietnam and signed an MoU on defence co-operation. India offered joint naval training and assistance in combating piracy, while Vietnam agreed to train Indian Army officers in guerrilla warfare. India also agreed to repair and overhaul Russian aircraft of the Vietnamese Air Force, and to set-up industry to manufacture small and medium weapons.[11]

Japan

Relations have been on an upswing since 1990s. Though after Pokhran II Japan suspended economic aid to India, by early 1999 both countries agreed that they will not let the nuclear issue dominate their overall ties. Besides high level visits and agreements to hold regular defence dialogues, Tokyo has been suggesting a strategic "triangulation with India in the west and Japan in the east of China, which could keep any Chinese belligerence in check", America being the third partner, which has not been accepted by India.

The sudden urge for a strategic partnership has been based on four reasons, as under-

(a) Petroleum security for Japan's oil flow from Persian Gulf through sea-lanes of Indian Ocean dominated by India.

(b) India's democratic status is ideal for working on international issues like environment, energy, UN reforms, and improving functioning of World Trade Organisation.

(c) Economic advantages of India's 200 million strong middle-class.

(d) India's high technology base.

Australia

After the cooling of relations post Pokhran II, the relations improved in 2001. A Defence delegation from Australia visited India for high-level talks, and for evolving a strategic partnership. Post 11 September, the relations have further improved, specially in tackling international terrorism.

ASEAN

Addressing the First India-ASEAN Business Summit at New Delhi on 11 October 2002, Prime Minister Vajpayee emphasised that besides cultural

and historical ties with the region, India wants future relations to be based on trade and economic partnership. Though ASEAN has made some progress towards integration of internal trade through ASEAN Free Trade Zone, scope still exists for India to join-in, as New Delhi has already announced reduction of peak tariff rates to East Asia levels, by 2005. India also sees a Regional Trade and Investment Area as a near-term objective of India-ASEAN economic relations.[12]

ASEAN Plus One Summits-November 2002 and October 2003

Though economic and trade linkages between India and ASEAN are inadequate, no trade agreement to improve these in the near future have been signed. Following China's announcement on 4 November 2002, of establishing a Free Trade Zone with ASEAN within the next ten years, India has also announced similar concessions. While the Prime Minister stated that India and China had become competitors in South East Asia, the Foreign Minister accompanying him stated that India's "Look East" Policy had nothing to do with China.[13]

At the meet of 2002, China announced formation of a free-trade area with ASEAN, which would be the biggest in the world with nearly 1.7 b people. Beijing also declared that duties between China and ASEAN will be reduced to zero, by the year 2010, and permitted ASEAN to sell cars assembled in their plants, in China. Thus, it is likely that China and Japan will continue to dominate the trade and economic scene in South East Asia, in the coming 25 years.

During the meet of 2003, India proposed setting up of free trade zone with ASEAN countries by 2010, while agreeing to reduce tariff on certain items by as early as 2006. Thus, India's intention of doing greater trade and developing stronger ties with ASEAN was reflected in these proposals.[14] Presently, ASEAN's share of India's exports is only 7.8 per cent. There are number of items which Indian can trade with the region, to enhance economic ties (See Appendicies N, Q, and R)

From the above it would be evident that while all countries of the region endeavour to improve economic, trade and diplomatic relations with China, the long-term uncertainty of the Middle Kingdom is a reason to create a framework, which could contain any future Chinese adventurism. Though India may not share this perception, she should be willing to co-operate with all countries in trade, economic and defence fields. Thus, while bilateral relations between India and South East Asian countries have continued to grow, there is greater scope to improve them further.

It would also be evident that threat of terrorism, deprivation and backwardness continues to pose security challenges to the countries of the region. While some countries may be economically strong, others face near poverty conditions.

India's principled stand on American led Operation Iraqi Freedom, comprehensive proposals made at the ASEAN Summit at Bali and extension of assistance to neighbouring countries, are proof of her non-hegomonistic policy and desire to help countries of South East Asia. Much more needs to be done by India, to strengthen her "Look East" policy.

Challenges for India

India has had close cultural and economic links with the countries of South East Asia, but these ties have undergone many ups and downs, especially since the end of World War II. In the last 50 years or so, the threat perceived by individual countries of South East Asia and the Region have also undergone a sea change, leading to defence arrangements and economic groupings like ASEAN.

ASEAN as an economic grouping has gained importance, as has the ARF. India being a regional and international player cannot afford to be left out or neglect the region. It is vital that she develops strong, dependable and lasting ties and capabilities with individual countries as well as with the region to influence crisis situations, yet not pose a threat to them. For this, India needs to formulate a comprehensive " Vision 2035 for South East Asia", in consultation with the countries of the region. To identify the type of assistance that needs to be offered, it is essential to have a brief overview of each country of the region.

Some eminent persons of South East Asia feel that besides resolving Kashmir dispute with Pakistan, for enhancing and strengthening her relations with the region India needs to overcome a few important hurdles and initiate steps as under-

(a) Enhance and accord greater diplomatic, trade and economic priority to the region.

(b) Post 11 September; enhance security cooperation against terrorism, including sharing of information, support and suppression of funds to such groups.

(c) Work towards curbing international crime, such as illegal trade in small arms, drugs, piracy and illegal migrants.

Thus, besides assuring greater priority to the region, India should also work towards removing their security concerns. While India may not fall within the geographical sphere of South East Asia, her security and economic interests demand that the region remains stable. Though India has in the past assisted few countries of the region in developing their defence potential, post Cold War and specially after 11 September, much greater scope exists to enhance such co-operation further.

India's Future Strategy

As we grow in international stature, our defence strategies should natuaraly reflect our political, economic and security concerns, extending well beyond the geographical confines of South Asia".[15]

Besides the proxy war from Pakistan on her western borders, the greatest challenge that India faces in the region is from Chinese trade and economic policies, and the financial prowess of Japan. However, India has a great advantage too, in that she is not considered a challenge to any individual country or a grouping, and does not pose any security threat. It has no territorial dispute with ASEAN members, has an advanced technological base and a large developing economy.

Considering that India has cordial relations with all countries of South East Asia and has definite edge in technology and scientific fields, India could offer such assistance that would enhance the security of the individual countries and the region. As peace and stability in the region is vital for India's trade, economic and security interests, the key areas of assistance and spheres of co-operation should be jointly identified. These could include the following spheres-

(a) Trade and Investment, by reducing bottlenecks and granting preferential trade regulations.

(b) Science and Technology, in which India is a leader. Besides agriculture, animal husbandry and horticulture, assistance could also be offered in medicine, technical, information and communication technology.

(c) Development of human resource, including advance education, in the field of medicine, engineering and management.

(d) Transport and infrastructure, by undertaking major communication projects (like Singapore-Kunming rail link project), ports, roads, air links, development of Mekong delta, energy generation and distribution.

(e) Tourism, jointly with respective countries and with ASEAN as a group.

(f) Assistance in military field, including weapons and equipment, training facilities and exchange of ideas and co-operation in counter terrorism and anti-smuggling operations.

(g) People-to-people contacts, between academics, intellectuals, artists, sports persons, representatives of trade and industry, and defence persons.

As regards Indian economy, it is likely to grow at least at the the rate of five per cent to six per cent, allowing a defence allocation of 3.5 per cent to 4.5 per cent of the GDP. The situation in Jammu and Kashmir would have been brought under adequate control, like that prevailing in Nagaland at present, releasing bulk of the Indian Army from the counter insurgency role. The Navy would have acquired a second aircraft carrier and a few nuclear submarines, the Air Force Su 30s Mk II and air-to-air refuelling capability, and the Army adequate conventional punch of modern tanks and guns, including T 90 tanks. The security management of the country would have improved and strategic planning undertaken, realistically on a long-term basis.

Thus, the threat from Pakistan would have been negated while that from China adequately neutralised, which would allow resources for creation of a strategic capability in the form of marine and airborne forces of adequate size. India's economic strength and military capability would be well in place to give her the status of a strong regional power, both towards the Indian Ocean as well as in the South China Sea.

The strategic partnership and understanding with America, Russia, France, Germany, the UK and Australia would be further strengthened. The relations with the countries of South East Asia and friendly neighbouring countries would also grow, with emphasis on wider security "co-operation and understanding" rather than on "alliances and groupings". This would result in grater interaction in training and export of weapons and equipment, leading to modernisation of the armed forces of the recipient countries.

Having analysed the likely security concerns of the respective countries, it is now possible to evolve India's 'Look East' policy for a period upto the year 2035.

References

1. G. Coedes, *The Indiansied States of Southeast Asia* (Honolulu: East-West Center Press, 1968).
2. Frederic Grare and Amitabh Mattoo (eds.), *India and ASEAN : The Politics of India's Look East Policy* (New Delhi: Manohar, 2001).
3. Reviews by Ms Man Mohini Kaul on The ASEAN Region in India's Foreign Policy by Kripa Sridharan (Aldershot, U.K.: Dartmouth Publishing Company, 1996); *India and Southeast Asia: Challenges and Opportunities* edited by Baladas Ghoshal (New Delhi Konark Publishers, 1996); and the *Future of the ARF* edited by Koo How San (Nanyang Technological University, Singapore :

Institute of Defence and Strategic Studies, 1999). Refer web http://www.india-seminar.com/2000/487.htm

4. ASEAN Data Base-2000, issued by ASEAN Secretariat, Jakarta.
5. *Far Eastern Economic Review*, December 2002 and Ministry of External Affairs Website.
6. *Far Eastern Economic Review*, December 2002.
7. Website bharatrakshak.com, issue 3-3, 10 July 2002.
8. Barry Wain, "China and Asean taking charge," *Far Eastern Economic Review*, www.feer.com, November 4, 2002. Also see *Far Eastern Economic Review*, 14 November 2002.
9. In these exercises, ships and commanders of friendly Indian Ocean littoral states spend a week in India. Besides sports and social events, seminars and discussions on strategic and professional subjects are also conducted. The latest exercise was conducted in February 2003 at Vishakhapatnam, where five South East Asian countries were represented. *Hindustan Times*, 05 February 2003.
10. *The Hindu*, 22 January 03.
11. *Strategic Digest* of IDSA, November 2002.
12. *Ibid.*
13. Refer *Far Eastern Economic Review*, December 2002.
14. ASEAN Cartels, article by B Jhunjhunwala in the *Statesman* of 28 October 2003.
15. *Hindustan Times*, New Delhi, of 2 November 2003.

8

Proposed "Look East" Policy for India-2035

Present Policy

While the present policy of "Look East" is based on economic, cultural, trade and security concerns, it does not have a long-term perspective or vision. Also, an impression has been created that projects and initiatives are being announced at the spur of the moment, and not being implemented with speed and vigour, in a systematic manner.

India needs to do more than merely attempt to match China or Japan, through consultations with individual countries of South East Asia, as well as with ASEAN as a grouping. Hence, a need exists to evolve an Action Plan for India's Look East policy.

Aim

India's Look East policy should aim "to create such inherent strength and potential in each country of South East Asia and the region, so as to enable her to develop resilience to withstand internal and external threats to her security."

Suggested Action Plan

At the outset, India should adopt a "consultative and co-operative approach," rather than extend a helping hand when either a crisis arises or when it suits New Delhi. Irrespective of the type of government or political party in power, the policy should be consistent. All types of assistance and aid should be categorised as Immediate (year 2005 to 2010) Mid Term (2011 to 2025) and Long Term (2026 to 2035), and projects planned and executed accordingly.

Initially, India should earmark an allocation of US $ 10 billion for all development under the scheme, for the next 10 years. Out of this, while 1/3 should be channelled through ASEAN, the balance should be utilised for bilateral assistance. This fund should cover the cost of all material, services and support, and not on purchases from any other countries, but India or the host.

To encourage Indian businessmen and industrialists venturing into projects in these countries, they should be compensated for the first ten years, from this fund. No proposals for cash grants or purchases outside India should be accepted, and bilateral trade by commodity with the host country should be encouraged. The projects should be reviewed periodically and additional funds could be allotted depending upon their successes.

To achieve the above objectives, in consultation with respective individual countries, India should evolve and formulate a well-synergiesd plan and offer support and assistance in the specific areas. The implementation of the policy should be monitored by a special integrated cell in the Ministry of External Affairs, where serving or retired officers from the Armed Forces and an economist could be co-opted, as term members for at least three years.

The policy should concentrate on four main spheres of co-operation – diplomatic, economic, military and cultural, in that order of priority, with specific thrust areas, as mentioned in succeeding paragraphs. All assistance should be routed through India's diplomatic missions in the recipient countries, and all personnel deputed for development projects placed under their control.

Identification of Assistance Required

This should be done in consultation with the recipient countries, for which two conferences should be organised at Delhi, in September 2005. The ten countries of South East Asia could be placed in two groups based on their economic and development status, as perceived from feasibility of extending aid. For instance Vietnam, Laos, Cambodia, Myanmar and Indonesia could be in Group I, and the balance in Group II.

Before conducting Exercise PUNAR MILAN (lasting co-operation and friendship), each country should be requested to indicate the area of co-operation and the type of assistance required by her. After an in-house analysis, these should be discussed over three days with delegations from respective countries (comprising of a diplomat, economist and defence representative) in the conference. The agreed projects should be approved within three months and their implementation should commence by 1 January 2006.

Diplomatic Priorities

The aim should be to dispel India's image as a big brother which threatens her neighbours, by that of *"an old and a reliable friend, who is dependable in all adversities."* India should not be seen to be competing with either China , Japan or any other country. Thrust should be to project India's *"genuine desire in improving the inherent strength and resilience of each individual country, as perceived by her,"* and of ASEAN as a grouping. Identification of areas of support in foreign forums like the UN, WTO, ARF and for conflict resolution through peaceful means should be emphasised. Development of cultural ties, sharing of intelligence on terrorism, drug trafficking and gun running, illegal immigration, extradition treaties and areas of common and mutual interests should be taken up.

To build lasting and enduring friendship and relations, heads of states and governments of the South East Asian countries and those of India should exchange visits, at least bi-annually, and certainly once in three years. Heads of states of South East Asian countries should also be invited as the chief guest for the Republic Day, at least once in three years. Besides these, annual inter-action at the ministerial and other levels, including sports and cultural, should also take place.

India has a vast resource base and expertise in agriculture, horticulture, animal husbandry, forestry, medicine, education, family planning, information technology, finance, human resource, engineering, disaster management and business management, which could be offered. Selected teams of dedicated persons from these fields could be offered, under time bound non-profit programmes, for establishing practical training institutions in the recipient country.

As regards education, besides offering seats in India, the feasibility of establishing high quality Indian educational institutions and professional institutes like the IITs, engineering, medical, dental and IT colleges, could be examined. Depending upon demand, the feasibility of establishing special institutions exclusively for countries of the region in India, with a small mix of highly talented Indian students, could also be examined.

The teams being sent abroad should be given adequate incentives of pay and allowances from the funds earmarked, put through a comprehensive one-month orientation course to include motivation, knowledge of the country, spoken local language other than English, basic military training and knowledge of first aid. They should be enrolled in the Territorial Army, so that they come under the Act for discipline purposes. Their tenure should be of two years, with only ten days emergency home leave at government expense. Those spending leave in the host country and gaining proficiency in local language, should be suitably compensated and rewarded.

Besides using facilities existing in the host country or being provided by them, all other equipment and stores should be purchased in India and shipped to them, being debited to the development fund.[1] The Composite Teams should be headed by an ex Defence officer not below the rank of Brigadier, and all members should be selected for their knowledge, dedication and flare for outdoor and challenging tasks. Special insurance cover against professional hazards and adequate non-family compensation should be given, so that the individual is able to fully devote his or her attention to the project in hand. Their approach should reflect on *"India's genuine desire to assist in strengthening and uplifting the country"*, and not on showing off her advanced technological status.

Indian media also has a major role to play in this effort. *At present, except for the Statesman, no Indian daily has an exclusive coverage of the region, even in English language.* Similarly, only functions organised by the diplomatic missions in Delhi get coverage on

TV. Feasibility of including a weekly or fortnightly supplement in print media and allotment of time on electronic media, could be examined. Each country in turn could offer India reciprocal facilities.

Economic and Trade Aspects

With immediate effect, India should grant special concessions and extend most favoured nation tariffs for enhancing bi-lateral trade with these countries, targeting at least five per cent growth per year.[2] Special incentives, grants and dispensations should be offered to small scale and middle level entrepreneurs of India for taking on turn key projects in manufacturing and services sectors, so that India's positive co-operation in nation building is visible to the masses of the recipient country. As all projects of even private sector would be routed through the host government, *transparency and honesty* should become key words.

While monetary controls and policies of AFTA, WTO and MFN would have to be taken into consideration, India's aid and assistance should aim to create new and additional employment avenues, both in India and the country being assisted.

For advanced and developed countries like Singapore, Malaysia, Brunei and Thailand, special assistance by private and public sector institutions and companies in IT, financial management, medicine and health and in the fields of space and nuclear science could be offered.

At present, few countries of South East Asia participate in the Annual Trade Fair in Delhi, each year. Feasibility of establishing a permanent exhibition of their products could be examined. Alternatively, a special exhibition of South East Asian countries could be organised annually, in few selected cities of India.

Joint development projects in infrastructure, like roads, canals, bridges, tube wells, oil exploration, hydroelectricity, transportation, nuclear and conventional power plants and housing should be encouraged. These projects should use local labour and material, to the extent possible.

Military Sphere

As the security of the Straits of Malacca is paramount for the region, India should offer a fleet of naval boats, helicopters and trained manpower from either the Indian Navy or the Coast Guard, to form a nucleus for forming a Protection Force. This Force should be placed under ARF, and the Indian contingent should be willing to serve under even a coalition officer, if need be. Joint patrolling in the Straits of Malacca[3] is already being carried out. India's Coast Guard could also be co-opted in anti piracy and anti highjacking operations even on high seas, like the rescue of Japanese cargo ship Rainbow in 2000.

In other fields, once commonality of interests and compatibility of weapons and equipment has been identified, then sales of spares, support and repair infrastructure and technology training facilities could be offered, after obtaining end user approval from the original manufacturers. Emphasis should be on training technicians from the host country and then transferring the whole plant. Offered on deferred payment or adjusted against the special fund, this would also promote sales of Indian manufactured weapons and equipment. Feasibility of organising a floating defence exhibition of Indian weapons and equipment on board an Indian naval ship visiting friendly ports, could also be examined.

New Delhi has already announced setting aside a sum of Rs 250 crore for boosting exports of arms to friendly countries like Myanmar, Indonesia, Nepal, Malaysia, Thailand, Bhutan and Sri Lanka.[4] By exporting weapons at competitive prices, India could hope to make inroads into these countries and counter China, which has been offering concessional rates for upto 10 years. As India manufactures small arms, ammunition, patrol boats, light helicopters, components of aircraft, light field guns, jeeps and trucks which are very reliable and competitive in price, a good scope and opportunity exists for assisting these countries. Feasibility of undertaking joint ventures for developing and manufacture of weapons, spares and equipment also exist. India has very good expertise in repairs, manufacturing and maintenance and her facilities are of international standards. For compatible equipment (like for MiG-29 aircraft), these facilities could be offered.

Special training facilities and infrastructure could be made available to defence forces of friendly South East Asian countries. More seminars should be organised by security think-tanks, to discuss regional security issues. Besides serving and retired defence officers, other specialists from South East Asian countries should also be invited for these discussions. Military commanders at appropriate levels should also be invited to attend exercises of the Indian Armed Forces, and joint exercises encouraged.

Terrorism, including cyber terrorism are new fields in which India has good expertise, which could be shared. Similarly, special teams of retired personal from the Corps of Engineers could be organised for mine-lifting tasks in Laos and Cambodia, thus saving limbs and life, as also bringing additional area under cultivation.

Likely Gains for India

While tangible results which can be accounted in figures may not be easy to identify, India's status as a reliable partner which is genuinely interested in uplift of the region would stand out. Thus, without application or show of force, India would gain the status of a strong regional power. This would also counter China's expanding interest in the region, winning India many friends. India would also gain support of these countries in the world forums, especially for her candidature as a permanent member of the U N Security Council. By showing genuine concern for Indonesia, New Delhi would indirectly counter Islamabad's influence in the OIC and counter Pakistan's propaganda against India's stand on Jammu and Kashmir.

By sending dedicated teams of Indian experts from varied fields and disciplines, India would open new employment opportunities for Indian youth as well as for her senior, experienced personnel. Also, by co-opting the locals of the recipient country, new employment avenues would be generated in the host countries as well, thus enhancing their economy. Emphasis on use of only Indian made goods and machinery would also result in financial advantage to the manufacturing and services sectors, and give them expertise and confidence of competing with other countries. Barter trade would also ensure greater variety of goods being available to Indian consumers, at competitive rates.

Participation in local projects would greatly enhance the prestige of Indian diaspora in the host countries, create a sense of pride and enhance patriotism amongst them. The exemplary social behaviour of the teams would also raise India's reputation and status in the host countries. Such features will cumulatively make India a strong regional power, on which the recipient country and the region can depend, for development and security.

India's exports, both of materials and services, will not only boost local economies but also give impetus to Indian industry. Competition from Japan and China as well as from local markets will force better quality control and transparency in dealings, winning India more hearts and status.

Impact of India's "Look East" Policy

India's assistance to the developing countries of South East Asia is not likely to clash with the interests of America or any other Western partner, like Japan or the UK. In fact, by augmenting the resilience of countries of the region, India will be doing exactly what America has been aiming at, without any expansionist or hegemonistic motives.

However, China is likely to feel threatened, as besides her economic ties, security strength of these countries is likely to give them adequate power to confront China in the South China Sea. India's growing status in the ASEAN and the ARF is also likely to give her a greater voice in these forums, to guard interests of smaller powers. This will further curtail China's unilateralism, but is not likely to bring her in an open clash with India.

Military co-operation between India and the Region will also bring in stability and possibility of a co-ordinated action against any outside power threatening a country, which may call upon India's support. This will also see reduction in terrorism and Islamic fundamentalism, a menace which is likely to worry the region for some years to come.

References

1. *Hindustan Times*, 28 August 2002.
2. *Ibid.*
3. *Ibid.*
4. On 5 August 2002, the Defence Minister announced setting aside Rs 250 Crore for such a scheme. *Indian Express*, 6 August 2002.

9
Conclusion

Since 500 BC, India has had cultural and social ties with countries of South East Asia, traces of which are evident even today. While post-Independence India gave a lead to the region in decolonisation and forged stronger ties with a few, these relations have undergone many turbulences. Due to her continuing concern with Pakistan and China, India's policy towards the region has not been consistent or progressive, nor was it implemented effectively.

The region is of strategic importance to India, as countries on the rim of the South China Sea also control the sea lanes between the Indian Ocean and the Pacific through the South China Sea, through which India's trade is carried. Also, Myanmar has a land border of 1400 km with India, which offers a land bridge between India and the landmass of South East Asia. The region also has a population of 140 million, few developed and developing economies, which offers great potential for stronger trade and economic relations. Besides the Chinese, the Indian diaspora has the largest presence in these countries, and unlike the Chinese, they identify with the host countries. Yet today, India does not enjoy her rightful place and status in some of the countries of South East Asia. This is due to her inconsistent "Look East" policy.

In the last fifty years or so, the region has endured internal and external wars and colonialism. It also became an arena of Cold War confrontation, with both the Communist and the Non-Communist blocs eyeing for military bases and areas of influences. The Korean War and the Vietnam War severely impinged on the economic development of the region and caused extensive devastation, greatly retarding economic progress of the three Indo-China states. Since 1980s and more so after the end of the Cold War in 1990s,while the threat of an external war has receded and internal dissentions are generally under control in most countries except Indonesia and Philippines, new security challenges have engulfed the region. Concern for human rights, hunger, poverty, unemployment, economic deprivation, migration of population and environmental matters disturb peace and continue to weaken certain countries of the region.

Except for the three Indo-China states, countries of the region were always concerned about being engulfed by communism, initially from the Soviets and then the Chinese, specially during and after the Vietnam War. Even today, this is the major security concern which though not stated, continues to influence their defence thinking. The growing power of China, coupled with Beijing's claims over most of the South China Sea have often resulted in armed clashes, a threat which continues to loom large and has the potential of engulfing the region. From the point of trade and oil transportation, the sea lanes of the South China Sea are of great importance not only to the region, but also for East Asia, Australia, China, Japan, America and India. The disputed areas of Paracel and Spratly Islands also contain large reserves of minerals, oil and gas. Spread of gun-running, piracy, narco-terrorism, Islamic fundamentalism, international terrorism, economic slow down and financial crises, are also real dangers, which could destabilise the region.

Post Cold War, the prevailing peace had enabled the non-communist countries of the region to improve their economic status. This feel good factor, coupled with the threat in being from China, resulted in increased defence spending for modernisation. However, the financial crunch of 1997 retarded most of these plans, but they are likely to be revived as soon as the economy improves.

While the collapse of the Soviet Union has resulted in the USA emerging as the only global power, both, militarily and economically, gigantic progress has been made by China in economic and military spheres in Asia. While western countries have more or less resolved their differences and the European Union is a strong economic grouping, countries of South East Asia, which had formed ASEAN with similar aims, are yet to achieve their aims, fully. Thus, a few countries continue to remain under-developed and face problems of human security as well. However, ASEAN members have decided to underscore their bilateral disputes and differences, and hope to face China collectively, through diplomatic dialogue through the ARF, trade and economic ties.

Though India has often provided military assistance to few countries of the region and her trade has shown some improvement, her pre-occupation with China and Pakistan has not allowed her to evolve a holistic, long term and an all-encompassing "Look East Policy". India needs to adopt a consultative, dynamic and co-operative policy for next quarter of a century, so that each country of the region builds up strength and resilience to face her security challenges, which are peculiar to each country. Spanning diplomatic, economic and military fields, the emphasis of the policy should be on "*assistance and co-operation*" rather that "*alliance and defence pacts"*. Besides allocating an initial sum of U$ 10 billion for development projects and aid under mutually agreed programme of Exercise Punar Milan, India should ensure that the projects are implemented with dedication, in a time bound manner. These teams of dedicated Indians should become torch–bearers of India's genuine desire to assist host countries of South East Asia, in enhancing their self reliance, in all spheres. The goodwill so generated will make India an important regional player, and a trusted partner of all times.

Today, India's geographic location, growing economic strength and military power allow her to adopt an independent foreign policy, even in the inter-dependent world. Her record of qualitative support to countries of the region and of being a non-interfering and a non-expansionist country gives her special position to adopt a new "Look East" policy towards her neighbours of South East Asia. Thus, India can achieve her rightful status as a strong regional power, respected by all her neighbours, for extending a helping hand.

New Delhi has been announcing initiatives and extending cooperation to South East Asian countries from time to time, but these do not seem to be based on a holistic long term–plan. Thus, there is a need to evolve, adopt and implement a well conceived long term policy, which should be of mutual benefit. The aid and assistance should follow an Action Plan, which can be monitored and modified, from time to time.

India's "Look East Policy" should not only project her genuine desire of building friendship by a trusted and dependable friend, but by one who does not interfere in internal matters, yet is keen to see a prosperous and strong nation.

APPENDICES

Appendix A

COMPARATIVE SOCIAL DATA-ASEAN COUNTRIES-2002

Country	*Area sq kms*	*Population Lacs*	*Languages*	*Religions % wise*	*Literacy %*	*Life Expectancy Years*
Brunei	5,770	3.3	M, E, C	Mu 67, Bu 13, Ch 10	88.2	71
Myanmar	678,500	417	Bur, Ethnic	Bu 89, Chr 4, An 1, Others 2	83	56
Philippines	300,000	81	Philipino, E	RC 83, Prot 9, M 5, Bu 3	94.6	64
Cambodia	69,899	112	Khamer	Bu 95, Others 5	95	54
Indonesia	741,099	224	Bhasa, E, D	Mu 88, Ch 8, Bu & rest 4	83	61
Laos	91,428	54	Lao, F, & E	Bu 60, Animist & rest 40	57	51
Malaysia	121,317	217	M ,C, E & T	Mu 53, Ch 35, H & rest 12	90	68
Singapore	647	10.7	C,M,T &E	Bu, Mu, Ch, H, S & Taoist	91.1	71
Thailand	514,000	61	Thai,English	Bu 95, Mu 3, Christians 5, H1	83	65
Vietnam	329,560	787	V, C, F & Khamer	Bu, Ch, Mu	93.7	66
INDIA	3287,590	1.01 bn			65	63
CHINA	9596,960	1.2 bn		81	75	

Abbreviations Used

Languages-M-Malay, E-English, C-Chinese, Bu-Burmese, Bhasa-Indonesian Malay, D-Dutch, F-French, T-Tamil, V-Vietnamese.

Religions-Mu-Muslims, Bu-Buddhists, Ch-Chinese, Chr-Christians, An-anamists, RC-Roman Catholic, Prot-Protestants, H-Hindus, S-Sikhs, b-billion.

Source-ASEAN Year Book 2002 and Statesman Year Book 2002.

Appendix B

COMPARATIVE DATA OF ASEAN COUNTRIES (ECONOMIC STATUS)

Country	*GDP (In US $)*	*Lab%*	*Industry*	*Expo*	*Imports*
Brunei	17,400	G 48, Ind 50, Fish&Agri-2	Oil Explo	Oil/Gas	Mach, Tpt, Food
Cambodia	710	Agri 80	Garments	Tin, Rub, Rice, Fish, Gems, Wood	Cigs, Gold, Mach, Tpt
Indonesia	2800	Agri 45, Tour 1	Pet/N Gas	Oil/Gas, Mining, Chem Rubber, Textiles	Mach ,Tpt, Chem, Tex, Timber, Food items
Laos	1300	Agri 80	Mining	Tin,Gympsum	Hydro Power, Mining
Myanmar	1200	Agri 65, Ind 10, Ser 25	Agri, Tex	Teak,Pulses Mach, Tin	Tpt,Med
Malasia	12,900	Agri/Forest 10 Ser 15, log	Rubber, Palm Oil, Tin, Pet, Logging	Pet, Oil	Mach, Chem
Philippines	3600	Agri-39 Ser & Gov 9	Pet,Tex,Pharma Elec,Tpt	Elect assy, wood	Raw mat, fuel
Singapore	27,800	Fin,Buis/others-38 Manu-21, Careers 21	Elec,Oil drilling Finance, Manuf	Mach&Eqp	Food, Chem, Mech, Med. Fuel.
Thailand	6400	Agri 51, Ind15,ser 31	Tourism,Garments, Elec assy, Timber	Cpmtr,Rice,	
Vietnam	1850	Agri and Ser	Food,Gar,Chem Rubber	Crude,Marine	Mach,Tpt
INDIA	1800	Advantages-Green and White revolutions, IT, Chem, Ind. Diaspora, affinity, no fear of domination, cultural and religious ties.			
CHINA	3800				

Country	Arable%	Agri Products	Natural Resources	Environmental Hazards
Brunei	1	Rice	Fruits, Pet, Oil	Smoke/Haze
Cambodia	13	Rice, Rub	Tim, Hydro	Logging
Indonesia	50	Rice, Coffee, Palm Oil	Pet, Tin, Gas	Forest Fires
Laos	3	Veg, Poultry	Tim, Hydro	UXB, Soil
Myanmar	15	Paddy, Oil Seeds	Pet, Tin	Ind Pollution
Malaysia	3	Veg, Palm	Pet, Tin, Timber	Pollution
Phillipines	19	Fruits, Poultry	Pet, Tin	Pollution
Singapore	2	Fruits, Poultry	Fish	Drinking Water Haze
Thailand	NK	Rice	Gas, Hydro	Tree Felling
Vietnam	17	Rice	Forest, Pet, Cement, Oil, Coal	Nil

Abbreviations–Agri-agriculture, Chem-chemicals, Env-environmental issues, Expo-exports, G-Government, Hydro-hydroelectricity potential, Ind-industry, IT-Information Technologies, Lab-labour, Mach-machine tools. Mat-material, Med-medicines, NR-natural resources, Pet-petroleum Products, Rub-rubber, Ser-services, Tex-textiles, Tour-tourism, tpt-transport, UXB-un exploded bombs, Veg-vegitable,

Appendix C

GROWTH RATE OF ASEAN COUNTRIES 1991-98

Country	*91*	*92*	*93*	*94*	*95*	*96*	*97*	*98*	*02/03*
Brunei	4.0	-1.1	0.5	1.8	3.0	3.5	--	--	3.0
Cambodia	7.6	7.0	4.1	4.0	7.6	7.0	1.0	0	3.6
Indonesia	8.9	7.2	7.3	7.5	8.2	8.0	4.7	-13.7	3.7
Laos	4.0	7.0	5.9	8.2	7.1	6.9	6.5	5.0	5.7
Malaysia	8.6	7.8	8.4	9.3	9.4	8.6	7.7	-6.8	4.1
Myanmar	-0.7	9.7	5.9	6.8	7.2	6.4	4.0	1.1	5.3
Philippines	-0.6	0.3	2.1	4.4	4.7	5.9	5.2	-0.5	4.4
Singapore	7.3	6.2	10.4	10.5	8.9	7.5	8.0	1.5	2.2
Thailand	8.1	8.2	8.5	8.6	8.8	5.5	-0.4	-0.8	5.3
Vietnam	6.0	8.7	8.1	8.8	9.5	9.3	8.8	3.5	7.0
INDIA								3	
CHINA								9	

Authy- IMF,www.state.gov;d fat.gov.gov,au;aseansec.org

@ Reference Yearbook 2005, Penguin Books, India.

Table 2.2 Gross Domestic Product per capita in US Dollar

Country	*1996*	*1997*	*1998*	*1999*	*2000*	*2001*	*2002*
Brunei	17,096	16,227	11,961	12,670	12,751	12,121	12,070
Cambodia	317	320	265	295	291	283	296
Indonesia	1,167	1,128	488	693	731	688	820
Lao, PDR	396	360	259	285		328	333
Malaysia	4,766	4,672	3,257	3,485	3,881	3,698	3,924
Myanmar	109	100	144	189	210	162	175*
Phillipines	1,184	1,157	896	1,018	980	924	959
Singapore	25,127	25,147	20,892	20,611	22,757	20,553	20,823
Thailand	3,134	2,656	1,900	2,046	2,029	1,887	2,050
Vietnam	337	361	361	374	403	415	439
ASEAN**	**1,505**	**1,429**	**947**	**1,079**	**1,128**	**1,058**	**1,153**

Source: ASEAN Finance and Macroeconmic Surveillance Unit (FMSU) Database.

* Fiscal Year beginning in April and ending in March of the following.

** As a proxy, combined GDP of ASEAN is computed as the sum of the GDP of ASEAN Member Countries, and the GDP per capita as GDP/ number of population.

ASEAN Statistics Unit.

Appendix D

GLOBAL FLOW OF F D I TO ASEAN, CHINA AND INDIA 1987 TO 1998 (IN US $ MILLIONS)

	87/92	*93*	*94*	*95*	*96*	*97*	*98*
ASEAN	9541	15994	19681	21643	25980	27813	21400
Brunei	1	14	6	13 a	11a	5a	4a
Cambodia	-	54	69	151	294	204	140a
Indonesia	999	2004	2109	4346	6194	4673	(356)
Laos	4	36	59	88	128	86	45
Malaysia	2387	5006	4342	4178	5078	5106	3727 a
Myanmar	96	149	91	115	38 a	124 a	40 a
Philippines	518	1283	1591	1478	1517	1222	1713
Singapore	3674	4686	8550	7206	7884	9710	7218
Thailand	1656	1805	1364	2068	2336	3733	6969
Vietnam	206 a	1002	1500	2000	2500	2950	1900
ASEAN share of global FDI for developing nations of the world-							
	27%	20%	19%	20%	19%	16%	13%
ASEAN share to Asian region							
	49%	29%	31%	32%	32%	29%	25%
China	4652	27515	33787	35849	40180	44236	45460
INDIA	58	550	973	2144	2464	3351	2258

Note-Auth-ASEAN Secretariat Database 2000/2001.

a- indicates annual average from 1989 to 1992.

Appendix E

F D I TO ASEAN AND INDIA FROM SELECTED COUNTRIES

	1990	1995	1998
By Japan to			
ASEAN	5995	5326 100 million	5156 (in yen)
India	44	125	329
China	511	4319	1363
By USA to			
ASEAN	1986	3421	3379 (in US $ million)
India	74 (approx)	181	25 (data incomplete)
China	30	261	1490
By EU to			
ASEAN	892	1685	3519
India	53	254	740
China	112	739	933

Authority-ASEAN Secretariat Data base 2000/2001.

Appendix F

COMPARATIVE DATA – ARMED FORCES OF SOUTH EAST ASIAN COUNTRIES

Country	*Size sq km*	*Pop*	*GDP In US $/local currency (in US $)*	*Def Exp*	*Armed Forces*	*Army*	*Navy*	*AF*	*Remarks*
Brunei	5,765	3,34,000	6.1b/per	8100	267m	5,900	3,900	900	Bn Gorkhas
Cambodia	1,81,035	1,14,50,000	3.2b/730	128 m	1,40,000	90,000	3,000	2,000	Prov Forces,45,000
Indonesia	19,19,443	21,62,13,000	160b/4000	1,268 m	2,97,000	2,30,000	40,000	27,000	
Laos	2,36,800	5,564,000	1.7b/2800	19.7m	29,100	25,600•	600*	3,500	
Malaysia	1,27,330	2,20,92,000	88b/12,900	1.9b	1,00,500	80,000	12,500	8,000	
Myanmar	6,76,577	4,53,81,000	37b/1400	1.7b	4,44,000	3,25,000	10,000	9,000	
Philippines	1,15,830	7,73,18,000	3.3b/3400	1.1b	1,07,000	67,000	24,000	16,000	
Thailand	5,13,115	6,15,86,000	123b/8500	1.7b	3,06,000	1,90,000	68,000	48,000	
Singapore	659.9	36,91,000	97b/26,000	4.3b	60,500	50,000	4,500	6,000	
Vietnam	3,23,338	8,09,76,000	31b/1300	1.8b	4,84,000	4,12,000	42,000	30,000	
India	3,165,596	1,029,548,000	471b/1900	15.6b	12,63,000	11,00,000	53,000	11,000	
China	95,74,000	1,29,32,39,000	794b/4300	17b	23,10,000	1,60,000	2,50,000	4,20,000	1 lac Strat Msl Force
Japan	3,77,819	12,70,14,000	4.7tr/24,600	45.6b	2,39,800	1,48,000	44,200	45,000	

Note-

1. Strength of Armed Forces does not include reserves.
2. Authority -Mil Balance 2002. Data pertains to year 2000/2001.
3. Land Areas-The Statesman's Year Book, 2000

Abbreviations- AF-Air Force, Armd-Armed, b-billions, Def Exp-defence expenditure, * Marines. m-millions, Pop-population, sq km-square kilometres, Strat Msl Force-Strategic Missile Force, tr-trillions,

Appendix G

GROWTH OF MILITARY STRENGTH OF SOUTH EAST ASIAN COUNTRIES-1990/91 TO 2001/2002

Country	*Def Exp*	*Total Armed Forces*	*Army*	*Navy*	*Air Force*	*Major Weapons and Equipment*
Brunei	229 m	4250/275,000	3400	550	300	AFV, Ptl & Msl crafts, Heptrs (all UK)
	348 m	5,900/334,000	3900	900	1100	Scorpion, Ptl & Coastal Combat crafts,Bell 212
Cambodia	917.84 m	112,000/ 8,344,000	55,000	1000	500	Tks-T55/54, Ptl Crafts, Mig 21
	128 m	1,40,000/ 11,45,000	90,000	3000	2000	T 59s,Sov & PCR Ptl Crafts,Mig 21
Indonesia	1.57bn	278000/ 182,269,000	212,000	42,000	24,000	AMX/PT,Subs(Ger),Frigates(UK)F5
	1.5bn	297,000/ 216,213,000	230,000	40,000	27,000	AFVs(UK)Corvettes(Ger),Hawks(UK)
Laos	18.94 m	52,600/ 4,183,000	52,600	600	2000	T54/55,Sov & PCR Ptl Crafts, Mig 21
	19.7 m	29,100/5,564,000	25,000	600	3500	T85, Ptl Crafts, Mig 21,Mi 8 heptrs
Malaysia	1.7bn	127,000/ 17,730,200	105,000	10,500	124,00	AFV(UK),Frigates(UK),Ptl Crafts (Sw) F5
	2.8 bn	100,500/ 22,092,000	80,000	12,500	8000	T90s, Subs(5),Hawks(UK),F18(USA)

Country	Def Exp	Total Armed Forces	Army	Navy	Air Force	Major Weapons and Equipment
Myanmar	1,060 m	280,000/ 41,469,800	259,000	12000	9000	Comet,Corvettes(US), PRC F 7
	2.1bn	444,000/ 45,381,000	325,000	10000	9000	MBT100(PRC),Msl Crafts(PRC),F7
Philippines	968.40 m	106,500/ 62,875,400	68,000	23,000	15,500	AFV(UK),Ptl Crafts(US)F5(US)
	1.3 bn	107,000/ 77,318,000	67,000	24,000	16,000	AFV(US), Frigate(US)F5,55 Bell armed hepts.
Singapore	2.12 bn	55,000/ 2,719,00	45,000	4,500	6,000	AFV(Fr &US),Corvettes & Msl Boats,F5
	4.8 bn	60,500/391,000	50,000	4,500	6,000	MBT 80(UK),Subs(Ger),F16(US)
Thailand	2.4 bn	283,000/ 57,481,000	190,000	50,000	43,000	MBT,Frigates,F5A,F16(mostly US)
	2.0 bn	306,000/ 61,586,000	190,000	68,000	48,000	MBT(PRC/US),Aircraft Carrier (UK), F16
Vietnam	2.32 bn	1,041,000/ 70,217,000	900,000	31,000	10,000	T34/54/55,Frigate & Msl crafts, SU 17/21(Sov)
	1.0 bn	484,000/ 80,976,000	412,000	42,000	30,000	T62,Subs(2-Yugo),Su 22,Su 27

Country	Def Exp	Total Armed Forces	Army	Navy	Air Force	Major Weapons and Equipment
India	8.96 bn	1.265 lac/ 858960200	1,100,000	55,000	110,000	T55/72,two Carriers, 17 Subs, Jaguar, Mig 21/23/29/Mirages
	15.9 bn	1.263 lac/ 1,029,548,000	No change	53,000	No change	T72/Arjun, one Carrier, 16 Subs, Su 30
China	7.56 bn	3.03lc/ 1,132,072,600	2,300,000	260,000	470,000	T80s,1 SSBN, 92 subs, J5, J7 & J8,H6 bombers
	8.2 bn	2.3lac/ 1,293,239,000	1,60,000	250,000	420,000	T88/98,69 subs,1 SSBN, J8, Su 27
Strat Msl Forces		90,000				ICBM 8, SUB-1
		100,000				ICBM 20,IRBM 130/150,SLBM/ SRBM

Note-

1. Figures in line one represent the status in year 1990/91, while in the second line that in 2001/2002.
2. Figures of strength of armed forces include that of reserves and Para Military Forces where applicable, and the total population is given after their strength.
3. Only major weapons and equipments have been shown. While some of these may have been discarded by 2001/02, in most cases line two represents new and proposed inductions.
4. Defence Budget has been indicated in US $.
5. Authority-The Military Balance 1991/92 and 2001/02.
6. Abbreviations used- AFV-Armoured Fighting Vehicles (includes tanks), bn-billion, Cr-Craft, Def Exp-defence expenditure, ICBM-Inter Continental Balistic Missiles, IR-Intermediate Range, Msl-Missiles, PRC-Peoples Republic of China, SL-Surface Launched, Sov-Soviet, Strat Msl-Strategic Missiles, Subs-submarines, Yugo-Yugoslavia,

Appendix H

GROWTH OF NAVAL POWER OF SOUTH EAST ASIAN COUNTRIES-1991-2001

Country	*Size*	*Ships/Crafts*	*Def Strategy*	*Remarks*
Brunei				
1991	550	3 msl and 3 ptl cr	Coastal protection	
1995	700	-do-		
2001	900	-do-		--
Cambodia				
1991	1000	10 cr	Patrol and coastal combat	
1995	2000	12		
2001	3000	12		Naval Infantry 1500
Indonesia				
1991	42,000	Subs 2, F 17,43 cr	Defence of archipelago	Incl 1000 Air Arm and 12,000 Marines
1995	40,500	Subs 2, F 13, 44 cr		
2001	40,000	Subs F 17, 36 cr		
Laos				
1991	600	40 crafts	River Patrolling	
1995	500	52		
2001	600	16		
Malaysia				
1991	10,500	F 4, Msl cr 8, 39 others	Def East & West Malaysia	Six heptr Naval Air Arm
1995	12,000	F 4, Msl cr 8, 29 others		
2001	12,500	F 4, Msl cr 8, 41 others		

Country	Size	Ships/Crafts	Def Strategy	Remarks
Myanmar				
1991	12000	46 combat & 44 ptl cr	Def coastline & ptl rivers	One bn Naval Inf - 800
1995	- do -	56		
2001	10,000	68		
Philippines				
1991	23,000	F 1, Ptl & Coastal Cbt cr - 37,	Coastal and isl def	8,500 Marines, 5 ac naval arm. Reliance on US Navy
1995	- do -	Ptl & Coastal Combat cr - 47		
2001	24,000	- do - - 58		
Singapore				
1991	4,500	Corvettes 6,Ptl cr - 20	Coastal def	Amphibious capability 200
1995	2,900	- do - - 22		
2001	4,500	Sub 1, Ptl & Cbt cr-24		Two subs on trial, one awaiting collection
Thailand				
1991	50,000	F 6, Ptl cr - 53	Def	Naval Air Force 900 (26 cbt and 8 armd hepts)
1995	66,000	F 10, - do -- 62		- do - 1150
2001	68,000	Aircraft Carrier 1,F 12,Cbt cr - 88		- do - 1700, 18,000-20,000 Marines
Vietnam				
1991	31,000	F 7, Ptl Cbt cr - 64	Def coast & Isl	Naval Inf-21,000
1995	42,000	- do - - 57		- do - 30,000
2001	- do-	Subs 2, F 6, Ptl Cbt cr - 56		- do - 26,000

Country	Size	Ships/Crafts	Def Strategy	Remarks
China				
1991	2,60,000	Sub-92, D 19, F 37	Def N, E & W sb	Naval AF 25,000, Marines 6000
1995	- do -	Subs 52,1 SSBN,D 18,F 32	- do -	- do - - do - 5000
2001	2,50,000	Subs 67,1 SSBN, D 21, F 41		- do - 26,000, - do - 10,000
India				
1991	55,000	Subs 17, Carriers 2, Cbt ships 26	E& W Fleets	Fleet Air Arm 5,000, Marines 1000
1995	- do -	Subs 13, Carriers 2, Cbt ships 41		- do -
2001	53,000	Subs 16, Carriers 1, Cbt ships 27		- do -
Japan				
1991	44000	Subs 13, D 6, F 60	Self Def Force	Including 12,000 Air arm.
1995	43,700	Subs 18, D 8, F 55		- do -
2001	44,200	Subs 16, D 42, F 12		- do - 9,800

Note: -

1. Authy-Military Balance (a) 1991/92, (b) 1995/96 and (c) 2001/2002.
2. Besides Singapore, Malaysia is also keen to acquire submarines from the West.
3. India – negotiating for a second carrier with Russia. China – acquired carrier hull for experimental purposes.
4. Abbreviation - Cbt cr-combat crafts. cr-crafts. D –destroyer. F –Frigates. heptr-helicopters. incl-includes/including. Inf-Infantry. Isl-Islands. msl-missile. N.S.E.W-North. South. East and West. Ptl-Patrol. sb-Sea Board. Subs-submarines.

Appendix J

GROWTH OF AIR POWER OF SOUTH EAST ASIAN COUNTRIES

Country	*Combat ac*	*Type*	*Remarks*
Indonesia	108	A-4, F-16, Hawk, F5	All strike a c, no spares since 1999, range twice Mig 21
Malaysia	71	Hawk, F-18, Mig 29	Mig 29-AD, bal strike, radius of action 300 nm, adequate for isl def
Myanmar	113	F7, Mig 29, A5-m(Mig 17)	Mig 29-AD, Bal ltd range
Philippines	44	F5 A (one sqn)	Range 150 nm, barely adequate for Isl def
Singapore	150	F 16 (A,B,C,D)A-4,Tanker(4)	Range 350 nm+ tanker
Thailand	153	F5A, F 16(A,B,C)	

Authority-Military Balance, 2001-2002.

Abbreviations used- + indicates range enhanced by air to air refuelling by the tanker aircraft, A,B,C,D-represent various models, ac-aircrafts, ac-aircrafts, AD-Air Defence, Bal-balance, def-defence, Isl-Island/s, ltd-limited, m-miles, nm-nautical miles, sqn-squadron.

Appendix K

PROFILE OF AIR POWER OF SOUTH EAST ASIAN COUNTRIES

Country	*Combat ac*	*Type*	*Remarks*
Indonesia	108	A-4,F-16,Hawk, F5	All strike ac, no spares since 1999, range twice Mig 21
Malaysia	71	Hawk,F-18, Mig 29	Mig 29-AD, bal strike, radius of action 300m, adequate for Isl def
Myanmar	113	F7,Mig 29, A5-m(Mig 17)	Mig 29-AD, Bal ltd range
Philippines	44	F5 A (one sqn)	Range 150 m, barely adequate to cover Isl territories.
Singapore	150	F 16(A,B,C,D)A-4,Tanker(4)	Range 350 nm+tanker
Thailand	153	F5A, F 16(A,B,C)	
Vietnam	189	Su 22M(7), Su 27(AD)	Mig 21(ltd range)

Country	*Combat ac*	*Type*	*Remarks*
Other Countries of the Region			
China	4000+	mostly Mig 19s & 21s	Presently ltd range, pay load, endurance and lt air to air refueling.By 2010, approx 1000 Sus. Ltd airfds in Tibet and 200 km inland opposite Taiwan. No integration.
	J 500	Mig 21s	By 2010, equalant to IAF, adequate for two fronts (Taiwan and India)
India	750	39+1/2 sqn. Mig 21, Su 30 (multirole), Mig 27	By 2010, 800 acs, 6-7 sqns Su 30s and Mig 29s, Mirage and Jaguars. Mig 23, Mirage, Jaguar, ROI 4000 km, ae refuling.
Taiwan	480	Mirage 2000-V,F5, F 16	
South Korea	555	F16, F4 (Phantom), F 5	
Australia	140	F111, F18, Long Range tankers	
Japan	300	F 16, F 15	
Pakistan	353	Mig 21(equalants), Mirage III & IV,F 16.	By 2010, J 10, few Mig 21 & Super 7(in collaboration with China) and a few Mirage 2000 V.

Support India can provide-1. Spares and armaments. 2 Training facilities 3. Air fields. 4. Maintenance and spares support.

Authority-Military Balance 2001-2002.

Abbreviations used - + enhanced range with air-to air tanker refuelling, ac-aircrafts, AD-air defence, ae-aerial, approx-approximately, Bal-Balance, Isl-Islands, ltd-limited, nm-nautical miles, sq-squadrons.

Appendix L

DIRECTION OF TRADE OF INDIA-EXPORTS (IN CRORES)

YEAR	1960/61	1970/71	1980/81	1990/91	2000/2001
OCED	425/66.1%	760/50.1%	3126/46.6%	9146/57.3%	107241/52.7%
OPEC	26/4.1%	99/6.4%	745/11.1%	16910/5.6%	22223/10.9%
East Europe	45/7%	323/21%	1486/22.1%	4894/17.9%	4964/24%
Other LDCs	95/14.8%	305/19.8%	1286/19.2%	40906/16.8%	54282/26.7%
ASIA	**45/6.9%**	**166/10.8%**	**900/13.4%**	**33391/14.3%**	**43566/21.4%**
Others	**51/8%**	**39/2.7%**	**68/1%**	**5390/**	**14861/7.3%**
TOTAL	**642**	**1535**	**6711**	**159561**	**203571**

DIRECTION OF TRADE OF INDIA -IMPORTS (IN CRORES)

OCED	875/78%	1042/63.8%	5740/45.7%	23310/43%	92090/39.9%
OPEC	52/4.6%	126/7.7%	3488/27.8%	7041/22.5%	11885/5.1%
East Europe	38/3.4%	220/13.5%	1296/10.3%	3377/1.6%	2968/1.3%
Other LDCs	132/11.6%	239/14.6%	1996/15.7%	7965/20.7%	40347/17.5%
ASIA	**64/5.7%**	**54/3.3%**	**1431/11.4%**	**6033/15.7%**	**33149/14.4%**
Others	**25/5.7%**	**7/0.4%**	**59/0.5%**	**1505/12.3%**	**83583/36.3%**
TOTAL	**1122**	**1634**	**12549**	**43198**	**23,0873**

Note-

1. OCED-Includes EU, N America, Canada, USA, Australia and Japan.
   OPEC-Includes Iran, Iraq and Saudi Arabia.
   East Europe-Includes Russia.
   Other LDCs-Include Africa, Asia, Latin America and Carribean countries.
2. **Commodities exported** -Oil meals, gems and jewellery, eletronic goods, cotton and fabrics, machinery and instruments, primary and semi-finished iron and steel, drugs and pharmaceuticals, meat, etc.
3. **Commodities imported**-Coal/coke/briquettes, vegitable oils, electronic goods, organic chemicals, machinery except electrical machinery, wood and wood products and non-ferrous metals.
4. **Impact of Financial Crisis 1997/98** (Indonesia, Malaysia,Philippines and Thailand).

(a) While imports registered growth of 15%($ 5165 m), exports declined by 14%($ 2895).

(b) During 1998/99, trade declined by 1.3% to $ 6690 m. Exports declined by 33%, while imports went up by 1.31%.

(c) In 2000/2001,trade declined by 4.4% to $ 8580.11 m, Though exports went up by 24.37% to $3384.19 m (Authority India Book 2000).

Authority- Economic Survey of India, 2000-2001, Ministry of Finance, Economic Division (Pages S-89 and 90).

APPENDIX M

INDIA'S BUISNESS VENTURES AND INVESTMENTS IN SOUTH EAST ASIA-1994-99

(VALUE IN US$)

	1994	***95***	***96***	***97***	***98***	***99***
First line Indicates number of Indian Projects planned for each country, followed by its value. For comparison, C indicated Chinese projects and J of Japan, for the same period. FDI-indicates Foreign Direct Investment.						
Brunei	Nil	0	0	0	0	0
	China (C) 0	0	0	.0	0	0
	Japan (J) 0	0	0	0	0	0
Cambodia	0	-	-	-	-	1/340,
	C -3/13785,400	13/3349	29/24637	31/34832,	39/5798	115/34,591
	J	0	-	2/1,207	4/2,873	
(Opened for FDI only in 1994)						
	1990	1995	1998	Total 1990-98		
Indonesia	2/41,000	1/2600	2/9,810	12/48,600		
	C	0	3/7,000	2/1,400	31/185,770	
	J	45/1,446,670	106/3,496,159	38/935,540	529/21,576,600	

Laos PDR	J		1/350		
	C	]	Nil	16/22,043	
	J	]		7/5,992	
Malaysia	3/324,640	5/23,655	6/20,500	36/465,540	
	C	8/25,263	5/9,445	4/19,098	39/543,509
	J	105/1,411,457	136/1,159,329	132/2,498,496	1,085/12,044,585
Myanmar	0	0	0	0	
	C	2/22,300	6/26,521		
	J	0	0	2/2,538	8/38,247
Philippines	4/195	6/541	4/9,060	47/25,342	
	C	1/195	1/3,691	0	3 / 483
	J	46/187,234	38/241,182	19/40,337	219/1,711,843
Thailand	Not known	0	5/5,743	41/911,057	
	C		6/13,560	36/656,969	
	J		175/1,652,708	1169/13,965,340	
Singapore	0	0	0	1/200	
	C	0	0	0	0
	J	0	1/NK	7/NK	11/NK

Vietnam	0	1/7,000	2/486	4/29,486
	C	5/7,340	3/7,100	40/62,199
	J			

COMPARATIVE INVESTMENT FLOW TO MANUFACTURING SECTOR IN PROJECTS IN SOUTH EAST ASIA THROUGH FOREIGN INVESTMENT, COUNTRY WISE - FROM 1990 TO 1998 (IN US $)

Country	*Total Projects*	*Total Investment*
INDIA	143	1,480,851,850
JAPAN	3,222	57,693,322,012
CHINA	280	1632,917,943
PAKISTAN	3	41,480,435

Note-

Auth-ASEAN Secretariat: ASEAN Database, 2000.

Appendix N

INDIA'S EXPORTS TO FOREIGN COUNTRIES

Region	*1998/99*	*1999/2000*	*2000/01*	*2001/02*	*% share*
EU	8,946.62	26,9325	10,410.76	9,845.93	22,4655
N America	7,672,60	23,0972	9,961.59	9,098.20	20,7594
NE Asia	4,597.18	13,8391	6,282.16	5,822.48	13,2852
WANA	4,214.79	12,6880	5,613.58	5,822.48	13,1834
ASEAN	**1,624.27**	**4,8896**	**2,905.93**	**3,445.74**	**7,8621**
S Asia	1,692.02	5,0936	1,954.41	2,050.39	4,6784
W Africa	580.71	1,7481	778.23	1,048.77	2,3930
Latin America	661.30	1,8402	1,018.91	960.31	2,1911
Other CIS	751.16	2,2613	980.92	903.59	2.0617
WE Countries	579.30	1,7439	879.65	728.02	1.6611
E Africa	529.04	1,5926	560.73	557.06	1.2730
E Asia	466.19	1.4034	501.38	518.06	1.1821
S Africa	476.82	1.4354	405.87	463.13	1.0567
E Europe	222.20	0.6689	229.73	268.26	0.6121
C Africa	71.09	0.2140	77.51	91.21	0.2081
CARs	61.97	0.1866	88.33	68.78	0.1569
Baltic	18.39	0.0553	1,889.94	2161.80	4.9326
Total Exports	**33,218.72**	**36,822.49**	**44,560.29**	**43,826.91**	

Exchange rate-200/01-1 US$=Rs 45.6844, 2001/02-1US $= 47.6917. All values in US $ Million. Authority-Web site of India Trade Promotion Organisation, N Delhi, 27 October 2003.

Appendix Q

INDIA'S EXPORTS TO COUNTRIES OF SOUTH EAST ASIA

Country	*1998/89*	*1999/2000*	*2000/01*	*2001/02*	*% Growth*
Brunei	3.26	1.30	3.31	2.86	-13.67
Indonesia	185.27	325.58	399.75	533.71	33.51
Lao PD RP	1.24	1.39	6.24	3.16 -	49.34
Malaysia	321.69	447.09	608.15	773.70	27.22
Mayanmar	30.12	34.10	52.71	60.89	15.52
Philippines	118.74	143.53	202.61	247.79	20.30
Singapore	517.53	672.71	877.11	972.31	10.85
Thailand	321.00	449.59	530.12	633.14	19.43
Vietnam	125.43	154.37	225.90	218.17	-3.42
Total	**1,624.27**	**2,229.65**	**2,905.93**	**3,445.74**	**18.58**

Authority-Website of India Trade Promotion Organisation, New Delhi, of 27 October 2003. All values in US$ millions.

Appendix R

SCOPE OF ENHANCING IMPORTS AND EXPORTS BETWEEN INDIA AND SOUTH EAST ASIAN COUNTRIES

Country	*Imports*	*Exports*
Brunei	Machinery and eqpt, goods, Food and chem	Crude oil, LNG, Pet products
Cambodia	Cigs, Gold, constr material, pet, machinery,motor veh	Timber, garments, rubber, rice, fish
Indonesia	Machinery & eqpt, chem.,food stuff	Oil and Gas, plywood, textiles, rubber
Laos	Machine & eqpt,veh,fuel,	Wood products, garments, elect, coffee, tin
Malaysia	Machines & eqpt, chem.,food,fuel & lub,natural gas	Pet and LNG,chem.,palm oil, wood, rubber, timber, electricity
Myanmar	Machines & eqpt, Vehs, constr material,food	Pulses & beans, fishery items, rice, teak wood
Philippines	Raw material & intermediate & capital goods, fuel	Electronics, garments,coconut products.
Singapore	Machinery & eqpt, mineral fuel, chem.,food	Electronics, chem., services
Thailand	Capita,consumer & intermediate goods,raw material	Gas, computer parts, rice, textiles, gas
Vietnam	Machinery & eqpt, pet ,fertizers ,raw cotton,chem.	Crude oil,marine products, rice, coffee, rubber, tea, garments, shoes
India	**Crude Oil & LNG, gems, fertilizers,chem.**	**Machine and eqpt, vehs, Textiles, leather, gems, engr goods, chem.**
China	Crude oil, machine & eqpt,plastics,chem.,iron	Textiles, mach and eqpt(low tech),textiles and clothes, footware, sports

Note-

Details of trade and commerce taken from web site Atlas Asia.com and the Statesmen Year Book, 2002.

Abbreviations used- Chem.-chemicals. Cigs-cigarettes. constr-construction. elect-electronics. engr-engineering. Eqpt-equipment. LNG-liquid natural gas. lub-lubricants. Pet-petroleum. veh-vehicles.

Index

A

Abbas, 41
Abdul Rahman, 186
Abdullah Puteh, Aceh Governor, 38
Abdullah Radawi, 55
Abu Bakar Bashir, 51, 159
- Jemeah Islamiah Leader, 41
- Trial, 42-44

Abu Sayyaf, 68-69, 143, 145, 172
Aceh, 36, 37, 39-40, 44
Achenese, 36
Acquino, Corazon Cory, 66
Advanced Countries, 155
- Brunei, Malaysia, Singapore, 155

Advanced Military Range Air-To-Air Missiles, (AMRAAMS), 64
Afghanistan, 25, 111, 120, 124, 138, 140, 188-89, 200
- and Iraq, 45
- War, 43

African Ports, 202
Afro-Asian Conference (Bandung), 1955, 21, 103, 185
AFTA (Asian Free Trade Agreement), 107, 110, 220
Al Qaeda, 11, 40-43, 45, 49-51, 68-69, 145, 154, 172
Ali Ghuffar, 41
Alonda Rainbow, Japanese Ship, 100
Ambon, 44
America(n), 35, 39, 41, 45, 51, 54, 64-65, 68, 85, 103, 106, 109, 111, 113, 120-21, 123, 125-28, 131-32, 136-43, 145, 161, 165, 169-71, 173, 177-78, 200, 207, 213
- and China, 152
- and Vietnam, 79
- Embargo, 159
- Embassy, 32
- Forces, 153
- Intervention in Iraq, 71
- Led Operation in Iraq, 125
- Led War in Iraq, 49

American Operation in Afghanistan and Iraq, 133
- Policy, 139, 144, 174-75
- Policy towards Indonesia, 46
- Relations with China, 111
- Tourists, 162
- Trade Relations with Taiwan, 111
- Troops of Cobra Services,

164
- Troops, 25, 70, 172-73

American—Singapore, 43
American—South Vietnam, 83
American-Spanish War, 1858, 66
Amrozi Nurhesyn, 41, 43
Andaman and Nicobar Islands, 56
Andaman Sea, 18, 27, 46, 49, 61, 100, 167, 203
Angkorian Temples, 83
Anglo-Malayan Agreement, 24
Anglo-Malaysian Defence Agreement, 186
Anti-Chinese
- Clashes, 26
- Riots, 35

Anti-Insurgency Operations, 26
Anti-Ship Missiles, 58
Anti-Terrorism Law, 41
Anti-Terrorist Operations, 11, 54
ANZUK, 25
APEC (Asia Pacific Economic Coop.), 108, 112-13, 137
Arab Traders, 19
Architecture, 83
Armed Communist Insurgencies, 105
Armed Forces, 14, 16, 22, 32-33, 38, 44-45, 49, 55, 58, 117, 119, 124, 131, 160-61, 163, 166-170, 173
Arroya, Pres., 69-70
Arunachal Pradesh, 56
ASEAN (Association of S E Asian Nations), 11, 17, 27, 31-32, 53-55, 60-61, 64-65, 72-73, 78-79, 82, 85, 87, 101, 104-15, 120, 123, 153, 155, 157, 162-63, 165, 168, 171-72, 176, 189, 191-99, 207-12, 215-16, 218, 224, 229
- and China, 192
- and Indonesia, 193
- Countries, 41, 152, 158, 179, 208
- Developed Countries, 112
- Foreign Trade, 193
- Free Trade Zone, 208
- Grouping Coop., 194
- in Jakarta, 189
- Industrial Coop. Scheme (AICS), 109
- Investment Area (AIA), 109
- Member Countries, 167, 194-95
- Philosophy, 51
- Regional Forum (ARF), 100, 106-07, 110-11, 114, 120, 152, 169, 172, 176, 189, 191, 195-96, 199, 210, 218, 221, 224, 229
- Standards, 170
- Summit (Bali), 42, 201, 209

Ashoka, 18, 183
Ashoka's Rule, 17
Asia and Africa, 29
ASIA bond, 115
Asia Pacific Region, 189, 195
Asian
- Conference, 21, 30
- Countries, 134
- Development Bank, 36, 198
- Economic Community, 203
- Relations Conference, 184

Asianisation, 23
Asia-Pacific Region, 112, 135-36, 139-40

Asiatic Organisation, 23
Aung San Suu Kyi, 60-61
Australia, 17, 23, 25, 31-32, 45, 87, 117, 133-34, 136, 139, 155, 172, 174, 179, 185, 191, 194, 199-200, 207, 213
- and Israel, 71
- Led UN Force, 111

Australia—ANZUK, 150
Australia—Myanmar, 199
Australian Territories, 155
Australia—Papua New Guinea, 134
Ayanthaya, 50
Azadigam Oil Fields Japan, 132

B

Bali, 33, 41, 105-06, 110, 123, 143, 163, 201, 203
- Bomb Blasts, 42, 68-69, 138, 160
- Bombing, 51, 109
- Culprits, 41
- Terrorists, 162
- Trials, 41

Ballistic Missile Technology, 120
Banda Aceh, Acehnese Cap., 37
Bandung, 103
Bandung Conference, 25, 103, 185
Bangkok, 113
Bangkok Declaration, 104
Bangladesh, 60, 198
Bases at-, 25
- Cambodia's Ranh Bay, 25
- Vladivostok, 25

Bathurst Island, 133
Battles of Coral Sea, 21
Bay of Bengal, 18, 46, 56, 167, 205
Belgrade, 25
Bengal Traders, 19
Bengal, Gujarat, Malabar Coast, 17
Bhasha Indonesia, Off. Language, 33
Bhutan, 204
Bidwai, 68
BIMSTEC, 197, 199, 202, 205
Black Hawk, 164
Blue Water Navy, 121, 124, 176
Bodh Gaya, 191
Bomb Blasts, 42
Bomb Explosions in Thailand, 163
Borneo, 22, 31, 44, 65
Borneo Region, 187
Britain and America, 24, 186
British
- Empire, 19
- Navy at Ceylon, 21, 184
- Troops, 30

Brunei, 28, 52, 71-73, 93, 97, 105, 156, 169, 173, 190
Brussels, 29
Buddha in Bangkok, 18
Buddhism, 17, 62, 77, 183
Buddhist Statues, 18
Buddhist, 47, 81, 57, 84, 129
- Sites, 206

Burma, 17, 21, 184
Burma-Australia, 19
Burma-Ceylon, 21
Burma-Vietnam, 18
Burmese Refugees, 153
Bush, George W, Pres. USA, 42, 46, 49, 64, 136, 138, 142
Bhutani, SK, 8

C

Caka Period, 28
Cambodia, 17-18, 23, 29, 39, 48-50, 75-77, 79, 82-83, 85, 115, 144, 151, 188, 191-92, 194, 195
Cambodia and Vietnam, 79
Cancun, 193
Cann Ranh Bay, 78
Capones Island, 99
Ceasefire, 35
Cebu Island, 66
CENTO, 24-25, 103, 185
Central Asian States (CAS), 158, 170, 175, 177
Ceylon, 185
Chagai Tests by Pakistan, 199
Champa (North Vietnam), 29, 75
Changi Naval Station, 172
Changmai Province, 153
Chavalit, Yongchaiyud, PM, 163
Cheng He, Admiral, 18-19, 52
Chi Minh, 75
China, 11, 14, 17, 18, 22-24, 26, 35, 45-46, 51, 56, 60-61, 63, 65, 71, 74-75, 77-83, 85, 97-99, 101, 103-07, 109-10, 112-14, 120-24, 127-28, 131, 139, 144, 151-52, 157-58, 163, 166, 168, 171-75, 178-79, 187, 192, 194, 207-09, 213, 215, 217, 222-24, 228-29
- and Indonesia, 93
- and Japan, 35
- and Korea, 20
- and North Korea, 79, 142
- and Philippines, 99
- and Russia, 59, 126-27, 144
- and Vietnam, 84, 98
- Economic Policy of-, 176
- Economy, 175
- Japan and India, 32
- Laos and Cambodia, 25
- Modernization, 175
- Taiwan and Vietnam, 95
- Trade with-, 168

China's
- Economic Buildup, 152
- Entry in UN, 184
- Expansionism, 151
- Growing Economy and Military Power, 114
- Kunming, 198
- Maritime Ambition, 124
- Military, 106
- Threat to Taiwan, 177

China-India, 56
China-Soviet Nexus, 24
China-Taiwan Clash, 131
Chinese, 18, 33, 59, 76
- Aggression, 22, 25
- and Malays Islamic Fundamentalists, 54
- Armed Forces, 119
- Army, 121
- Claims, 107
- Community, 31
- Group, 119
- Invasion (Vietnam), 188
- Law, 97
- Muslim Separatists, 124
- Navy, 175
- Occupation of Atoll, 99
- Patrol Boats, 58
- Russian Military Coop., 175
- Strategies, 120

- Trade and Economic Policy, 211
- Traders, 20

Chinese-US Relations, 121
Chola Rulers, 18
Christianity, 62
Christians and Muslims, 57
CIA, 50
Civil War, 14
Claim Lines, 95, 97
Clinton, 170
Coal—Uranium, 119
Coast Guard, 221
Cold War, 23, 25-27, 76, 78, 106, 112, 119, 131, 135-36, 139, 142, 149, 177, 186, 189, 211, 228-29
Communal Riots, 44
Communication Technologies, 15
Communism, 24, 26, 103, 105, 184
- in China, 21

Communist
- and Non-Communist Bloc, 228
- Insurgency, 55
- Parties, 26
- Party of Indonesia, 30-31
- Party of Malaya, 26
- Party of Philippines, 69
- Pathet Lao, 80

Confidence Building Measures, (CBM), 107, 172
Coromandal, 17
Cuba and Philippines, 66
Cyber Crime, 192
Cyber Warfare, 14, 155

D

Da Lac Reef, 98
Dalwe, Deep Sea Port, 205
Dang Kirk Mountains, 84
Darao City, Bomb Blast at-, 68
Dato Hussain Onn, 186
Dayak Tribesman, 44
Death Sentence, 41
Decision Making, 110
Defence and Security Pacts, 16
Defence Arrangements, 150
Deforestation, 47
Democratic Republic of Vietnam, 75
Devare, ST, 8
Developed Countries, 110, 155
- Thailand and Philippines, 155

Developing Countries, 155
- Laos and Cambodia, 155

Developing Economy, 211
Diego Garcia, American Base in Indian Ocean, 25, 64
Diplomatic Missions, 8
- Australia, 8
- China, 8
- Indonesia, 8
- Malaysia, 8
- Myanmar, 8
- Philippines, 8
- Singapore, 8
- Thailand, 8
- Vietnam, 8

Domino Theory, 105
Drug Trafficking, 13-14, 48-49, 51, 54, 202
Drug Warlords, 48

Drugs and Narcotics, 14
Drugs, 48, 153
Dulles, John Foster, Pres. US, 24
Dutch, 20-21, 29-30, 33, 39, 52
- and British, 72
- in East Indies, 184

E

East
- Asia—India, 228
- Asian Economy, 203
- China Sea, 117
- India Company, 29
- Java, 30
- Malaysia, 104
- Pakistan, 14, 187-88
- Timor, 28, 40, 86-87, 111, 135, 160-61, 172, 179
- Referendum, 32
- Portuguese Colony, 30-33

East-Australian Countries, 93
Economic Aid to-, 25
- Cambodia, 25
- Laos, 25
- North Korea, 25
- Vietnam, 25

Economic
- Aid, 36
- and Military Strength, 169
- and Political Reforms, 32
- and Security Environment, 91
- Crisis, 1997, 31, 35, 108, 158-59, 191
- Development, 117, 170
- Extension Zones, 73-74
- Growth, 16, 104-05
- Reforms, 35, 189

Economic Sanctions, 106
- Zones, 108

Economy, 14, 31, 35, 45, 71, 85, 105, 114-15, 119, 133, 160, 166, 169-70
Education, 50
Educational Policies, 168
EEZ (Exclusive Economic Zone), 44, 65, 73, 93, 97, 117
Elections, 37, 50, 84-87, 121
Electronic Technology of Warships, 121
Embassies of- in Bangkok, 49
- USA and Singapore in Indonesia, 42

Embassies of-, 42
- Afghanistan, 49
- Israel, 49
- Singapore, 49
- UK, 49
- USA, 49

Endriartono Sutarto, Genl., 39
Energy Resources, 15
English—Telugu (L), 53
Estrada, Joseph, 70
Ethnic
- Chinese, 52
- Conflicts, 13

Ethnic Groups, 28
- Achen, 28
- Ambones in Molucas, 28
- Balinese (Slaws), 28
- Bataks, 28
- Dayaks (Kalimantan), 28
- Irianese (West Papua), 28
- Javanese, 28
- Madres (Madura), 28
- Minangkabans, 28

- Sumatra, 28

Ethnic
- Rioting, 54
- Violence, 160

European Union, 60, 78, 107, 110, 112-13
Exercise Cobra Gold, 49, 140, 172
Exercise Malabar, 204
Exercise PUNAR MILAN, 217
Expansionist China, 55
Expansionist Policies, 117, 158
Exports and Imports, 14, 84
Exports, 34

F

Famines, 13
Far East Russian Region, 177
Fargo, Thomas, Admiral, 140
Fathur Rohman al Ghozi, Indonesian Bomb Expert, 69
FDI (Foreign Direct Investment), 14, 34, 46, 135, 155-56, 159, 188
Ferdinand Magellan, Portuguese Sailor, 65
Ferdinand Marlos, 66
Fernandes, George, 206
Fiji, 191
Financial Crisis, 1997, 115
Five Power Defence Agreement, 63
France, 20-21, 24, 135, 213
Free Aceh Movement (GAM), 36-38
Free Trade Agreement (FTA), 64, 123
Free Trade
- Area, 208
- Pact, 143
- Zone, 194-95, 208

Freedom Movement in Malaya and Indonesia, 22
French in Indo-China, 184
French Indo-China in Vietnam, 80
French Rule, 83
French/American, 75
French-Indo-China, 23
French-Laotian Treaty, 80
FTA (Free Trade Agreement), 194-95
Fundamentalism, 55, 167
- and Terrorism, 15

Fundamentalist Groups, 153

G

GAM, 36-40
Gas and Oil—Palm Products, 34
Gas Producing Countries, 35
- Australia, 35
- Malaysia, 35
- Qatar, 35
- Russia, 35

Genocide, 83
Germany, 136, 213
Ghoshal, B, 8
Gia-Linay Rulers, 75
Global
- Economy, 14, 107
- Environment, 13-14
- Indian Entrepreneur Conference, 189
- Interlinking of Economies, 15
- Market, 14
- Trade and Economic Issues, 16
- Warming, 14

Goh Chok Tong, PM, Singapore,

64, 110, 141, 203
Golex, National Security Adviser to Arraya, 70
Gonzalves, E, 8
Greater Mekong Sub-regional Grouping, 108
Green House Gases, 14
GSLU, 190
Guam Doctrine, 175
Guizhou, 59
Gujral, IK, 189
Gujrati Muslims, 19
Gulf of Siam, 19
Gulf of Thailand, 18, 46, 48, 74, 82, 170-71
Gulf of Tinkin, 74
Gulf War, 120, 142, 151
Gun Running, 51, 55

H

Habibie, 32
Hainau Island, 121
Hambali, Sea Raider, 69
Han Dynasty, 97
Hanoi, 75, 78-79, 98, 105, 150, 170, 194
Hatto (Dr.), 29-30
Hawke, Bob, Australia PM, 112
Henry Dunant Centre Geneva, 38
Hezbul Dawah Al Islamiah, 69
High Commissions, 7
- Malaysia, 7
- Singapore, 7

Hindu Buddhist, 33
- Kingdoms, 29
- Settlements, 19
- Traditions, 19

Hindu Culture, 27
Hindu Islamic Traditions, 19
Hinduism, 17, 28, 62, 183
Hmang Army, 82
Ho Chi Minh, 80
Hong Kong, 34, 98, 120
Howard, John, PM, 133
Hu Jintao, Pres., 121
Human Relations Violations, 121
Human Rights, 14-15, 39, 79, 141, 152, 171, 228
- Legislation, 44
- Violations, 14, 32, 40, 45, 85

Human Security, 13
Humbali, Terrorist, 43
Hun Sen, PM, 85-86

I

Idris, Terrorist Leader, 43
Illegal Immigrants, 155
Immigration, 134
India and
- China, 201
- Chinese Trade Route, 83

Indonesia, 202
- Japan, 114
- Myanmar, 11
- Pakistan Nuclear Explosions, 195
- Persia, 29

India's
- Exports, 209
- Extended Economic Zone, 202

Independence Movement, 21
- North East Borders, 56
- Relations, 8
- Trade, 195

India-Asian Economic Relations, 208
Indian
- and Pacific Oceans, 20-21
- Armed Forces, 200
- Army in Ladakh, 204
- Army, 186, 206, 212
- Civilization, 183
- Community, 21
- Labour to Burma and Malaya, 20
- Markets, 189
- Migrants (Gujarat), 28
- Navy, 100, 203, 221
- Ocean, 7, 17-21, 27, 32, 46, 56, 61, 91, 139, 179, 184, 186, 213, 227
- Planners, 25
- Tamils, 19

India—Nepal, 108
India—Thailand, 23
Indira Col, Island in Nicobar, 40
Indo-Aryan Migrants, 28
Indo-ASEAN Business Summit, 191, 193
Indo-China States, 79, 82, 156, 228
Indo-China, 20-21, 149, 186
Indo-China War, 173, 185
Indo-Chinese
- Federation, 75
- States, 77
- Union, 75

Indo-Nepal Border, 204
Indonesia, 11, 18, 21-23, 26-28, 30, 33, 35-37, 40-41, 43-45, 51-52, 60, 91, 93, 97, 104, 106, 109, 110-11, 138-39, 141, 144, 149, 152, 155-56, 158-60, 172, 179, 184-87, 190, 196, 201, 223
- Admission to UN, 22
- and China, 52, 87, 140
- Army, 40
- Citizens, 41
- Military, 37-38, 46

Indonesian
- Archipelago, 17
- Armed Forces, 44, 172
- Armed Volunteers, 30
- Army, 31, 86-87, 160
- Islamic Terrorist Group, 40
- Muslims, 42

Indo-Pakistan War, 25
Indo-Soviet Treaty—Coop., 187
Indo-Thai Free Trade Area, 202
Industrial Infrastructure, 25
Industries, 33, 84, 129
Influx of Refugees, 14
Information Technology, 14-15, 202, 220
Insurgency, 14-15, 26, 68, 76, 169, 196
Internal
- Anarchy, 66
- Rising, 66
- Wars, 72

International
- Community, 31, 86
- Control Commission, 76, 186
- Monetary Fund, (IMF), 35, 60
- Security, 173
- Trade, 15

Islamic Fundamentalism, 45
- Law, 141

Iran—India, 144

Iraq, 55, 131-32, 141-42
- Crisis, 126
- War, 120, 127

Iraq and Afghanistan, 144
Iraqi Freedom, US Led Operation, 55
Irrawadi Corridor, 205
Irrawady, 59, 61
Islam, 62
Islamic
- Extremism, 166
- Fundamentalism, 45-46, 143, 154, 174, 228
- Fundamentalist Groups, 32
- Fundamentalists, 51, 65, 111, 114, 152, 160, 166, 169
- Radical Groups, 69
- Radicals, 41
- Separatists, 54
- Terrorism, 49, 54

Island of Borneo, 51

J

Jakarta, 28, 35-37, 40-41, 43-45, 86, 138, 154-55, 160, 162, 187, 190
Jamaeh Islamiah, 68-69
Jammu and Kashmir, 22, 188, 204, 212, 223
Japan, 17, 20, 25, 37, 52, 66, 75, 93, 117, 119, 123, 128, 129-33, 136, 139, 144, 149, 152, 164, 172, 177-78, 184, 187, 191, 194, 200, 206, 215, 217, 224
- and China, 203
- and South Korea, 25, 127, 144
- Defence Policy, 179
- Self-Defence Forces, 132

Japan's
- Constitution, 177
- Imports, 132
- Security Policy, 132
- Security, 177

Japanese, 11, 30, 184
- Forces, 20
- Navy, 20, 178

Japan—Singapore, 141
Jaswant Singh, 199
Java, 18-19, 29
Java (East), 35
Java Dwipa (Java), 28
Java-Bali Region, 18
Java—Sulavasis, 27
Jawaharlal Nehru
- Award, 190

Jayavarman II, 83
Jehadi Fundamentalists, 45
Jemeah Islamiah, 41-43, 49-50, 154
Jiang Zemin, Pres., 61
Jihad, 42
Jihadis and Ummah, 54
Johnson Reef (Spratly), 98
Johore Baru Port, 154
Joint Development Projects, 221
Judiciary, 41
Junta Military, 70

K

Kalimantan, 44
Kamsuri, Abdul Manaf, Lt. Col., 54
Kashmir, 196
Kaula Lumpur, 165, 186
Keran and Wan Armies, 153

Khalid Shaik Mohammad, 50, 68
Khanth Ho, 98
Khin Nyunt, LG, 60
Khmer Rouge, 76, 83-84
Khmer Rule, 83
Kikesh Fish Area, 73
King Norodom Sihanouk, 83-84, 86
King Rama VII, 47
Kingdom of Funan, 83
KMT, 21
Kohima, 11
Korea, 17, 149
Korean War, 1949-51, 24, 185, 228
Koreas, 152
Kosovo, 124
Kota Islands, 99
Kotah Aceh, 39
Kra Isthmus, 8, 19
Kublai Khan, Mongol Hordes, 29, 80
Kuomintang Regime, 21
Kutai, 28

L

Lahore, 199
Lahore Declaration, 196
Land Borders, 120
Land Mine Treaty, 69
Land Routes, 11, 18
Languages, 77
Lao People's Democratic Republic, 80
Laos (Lao), 79-82
Laos and Cambodia, 26, 46, 49, 74, 105, 107, 110, 155-56, 170, 173, 183, 222
Laos, 17, 23, 85, 166, 195
- Exports, 81
- Imports, 81
- Main Languages, 81
- Security Concerns, 81
- Socio-Economic Status, 81

Law of the Sea Conference, 95
Limbay River, 74
Lisbon Government, 31
Literacy, 156
Literacy Rate, 33, 72, 84
Littoral Region, 19
Littoral States, 18
Lombok and Makassar Straits, 91
Look East Policy, 12, 191, 194, 202, 208, 215, 224, 229-30
Lord Buddha, 183
LTTE, 204
Luzan Island, 65

M

Madrasas, 50
Madurese Migrants, 44
Mahathir, Mohammad, PM Malaysia, 54-55, 141, 145, 190
Majapahit Rule, 29
Malacca Port, 18, 52
Malacca, Islamic Kingdom, 29
Malacca—North Borneo, 20
Malaka (Malacca), 19
Malaku, 27
Malay, 72
- Official Language, 72
- Peninsula, 19
- Rivers, 52

Malaya – Hong Kong, 21

Malaya and Singapore, 25
Malaya, 11, 17, 22, 24, 26, 29, 39, 41, 52-53, 103-04, 110, 184
Malaysia, 25-26, 28, 31, 40, 45, 48-49, 51-55, 62-64, 68, 71, 73, 104, 106, 109, 111, 134, 139, 141, 144-45, 149, 154-58, 164-65, 172, 174, 184,186-87, 190, 196
- and Brunei, 74
- and Indonesia, 134, 143
- and Philippines, 100
- and Singapore Waters, 100
- and Singapore, 46
- and Thailand Border, 55
- and Thailand, 74
- Armed Forces, 164
- Bhasha Malaysia, Offi. Language, 53
- Economy, 54
- Exports, 53
- Literacy Rate, 53
- Security Concerns, 55
- Size and Economic Progress, 51
- Socio-Economic Status and Trade, 53
- Trade and Terrorism, 53

Malaysia—Bangkok, 51
Malaysia—China, 95
Malaysia—Indonesia, 150
Malaysian Navy, 186
Malaysia—Singapore, 150
Maldives, 188
Mandanao, 104
Manila, 65-66, 69-70, 97, 99, 172
Manila Treaty, 24, 186
Manipur, 56
Maoist Insurgents, 204
Marco Polo, 29
Maritime Expeditions, 18
Maritime Frontiers, 120
Market Economy, 58, 78
Marriot Hotel Blasts, 51
Marshal Islands, 191
Martial Law, 66
Medan, 43
Megawati, Sukarnoputri, 32-33, 36, 38, 40, 42, 45, 87, 145, 201
Mekong Delta, 78, 82, 84, 197
Mekong-Ganga Coop., 197, 199
Mekong-Ganga Project, 202, 206
MERCRRSOR, 107
Methamphetamine Tablets, 48
Mexico, Spanish Colony, 66
Middle East and Saudi Arabia, 50
Migration, 14-15
Militancy, 49
Militant Groups, 31
Militants, 55
Military and Economic Support, 137
Military Bases, 106, 150
Military Junta of Myanmar, 48
Military Junta, 60
Mine Laying, 82
Ming Dynasty, 19, 97
Ministry of External Affairs, 8, 216
Minority Community, 61
Mischief Reef, 71, 99, 124
Mizoram, 56
Modernisation, 159-61, 166, 169-70, 172
Modernisation and Industrialisation, 15
Molucca Islands, 33, 44

Mongoloid Migrant of Asia, 28
Moro and Islamic Liberation Movement, 43
Moro Insurgency, 69
Moro National Liberation Front (MLLF), 68-69
Multi-Fibre Agreement, 60
Multi-Party Communist System, 84
Multi-Sectorial Market Economy, 77
Mindanao Island, 65, 68
Mundanao Rebels, 69
Muslim
- Lashkar-Jihadi Extremism, 44
- Population, 68
- Terrorists, 54
- and Buddhists, 67

Mutual Defence Policy, 71
Myanmar Army, 48
Myanmar, 17, 46, 48-49, 56-61, 79, 87, 105, 107, 110, 153, 156-57, 163, 166-67, 173, 184, 194-95, 204-06, 227
- Army, 61
- Exports, 57
- Land Borders, 56
- Literacy Rate, 57
- Main Industries, 67
- Main Language-Burmese, 57
- Military Planners of-, 166
- Natural Resources, 57
- Refugees, 61
- Sea Border, 56
- Security Concerns, 58
- Socio-Economic Status, 57
- Textile Exports to America, 60

Myanmar—Cambodia, 144
Myanmar—Sri Lanka, 22
Mynamar—Vietnam, 183

N

Nagaland, 56, 212
Najib Raza, 55
Nanggaro Aceh Darussalam, 38
Narasimha Rao, PV, PM India, 188
Narathiwar Region, 50
Narcotics, 48, 202
National Defence College, 8
National Security Strategy, 136
NATO, 23, 25, 71
Natural
- Gas, 93
- Fields, 97
- Island, China, 28, 93
- Resources, 119

Naval Bases, 167
Navang Penanan, Thai Nationalist, 49
Ne Win, General, 58
Nehru and Sukarno, 25, 222
Nehru, Pandit, 29-30, 103, 184-86
Nepal, 169, 204
Netherlands, 30
Neutral Nations Repatriation Commission (Korea), 23, 186
New Defence Policy Board, 71
New Delhi's Military Intervention, 188
New Zealand, 25, 191
Nicobar Islands, 40, 189
Non-Alignment, 16, 23-25, 103,

187
- Countries, 185
- Meet at Belgrade, 185
- Movement, 22
- Policy, 23

Non-Communist Bloc, 23
Non-Governmental Organisations, 13
North and South Korea, 75
North Borneo, 26
North China Sea, 75
North East Asia, 56, 106
North Korea, 11, 23, 25, 117, 123, 125-28, 131-32, 141, 143-45, 149, 152, 159, 172, 174, 178-79
- Nuclearisation, 122

North Vietnam, 149
NPT, 136
Nuclear
- and Missile Regimes, 121
- Programme, 127
- Proliferation, 128
- Research Reactor, 59
- Threats, 15
- Weapons Programme, 174
- Weapons, 11, 126, 128, 159, 172

Nusa Tenggare, 27

O

Oil and Gas Revenues, 72
Omar Ali Safuddin Sultan, 72
ONGC, 205
Operation
- Enduring Freedom (USA), 11, 131, 158
- Iraqi Freedom, 11, 113, 139, 145, 200, 204

Osama Bin Laden, 145
- Terrorist Leaders, 50

P

Pacific, 17-18, 27
- and Indian Ocean, 75
- Ocean, 21, 117, 132, 177, 179, 184
- Region, 25
- Rim Countries, 112
- Security, 45
- Union, 23

Pakistan, 22, 25, 166, 179, 185, 187, 196, 199, 204, 213, 223
- and China, 186-87, 227, 229
- and India, 55
- Army, 188
- ISI, 40

Palawan Island, 65
Palawan Province, 97
Panama Canal, 93
Panchsheel, 22, 103, 185
Pan-Islamic State, 41-42
Papua New Guinea, 30, 123, 191
Paracel and Spratly Islands, 74
Paracel Island, 95, 101, 192
Parameshwara, Prince, 19
Paratas Island, 98-99
Paris Agreement, 76
Parthasarathy, G, 8
Pearl Harbour, 184
People's Party of Hun Sen, 86
Persian Gulf, 25, 141, 207
Pervez Musharraf, 199, 204
Philippines, 20-21, 24, 26, 29, 41, 43, 51, 65-71, 91, 103-04, 109-11, 136, 139, 141, 143-

44, 154-57, 169, 172, 176, 184, 192
Army, 68
• and Vietnam, 99
• Environmental Threats, 67
• Main Exports, 67
• Main Industries, 67
• Main Produce, 67
• Navy, 99
• Security Concerns, 68
• Socio-Economic Status, 67
Phnom Penh, 83
Piracy, 15, 51, 55, 72, 202
Piracy and Hijacking, 100
PLA (People's Liberation Army), 77-78, 120, 151, 169
PLAAF, 176
PLAN, 176
Plutonium, 11
Poaching, 47
Pokhran II, 206-07
Pol Pot, 76
Pol Pot Regime, 85, 111
Police, 41
Policy of Pluralism, 173
Political System, 13
Pollution, 13
Pope John Paul II, 68
Port Morashy, 191
Port of Johore Baru, 63
Portugal, 86
Portuguese, 20-21, 29, 52
Powell, Colin, 160, 170
Pre-Emptive Operation, 159
Prince Aji, 28
Prince Wijaya, 29

Q

Quirino, Pres. Philippines, 23

R

Racial Polarization, 166
Rahman, Tengku Abdul, Father of Modern Indonesia, 22
Raina, TN, 186
Raja Hayam Wuruk, 29
Raja of Indonesia, 30, 38
Raja Udayana of Bali, 29
Ram, N, 8
Ramos of Philippines, 190
Rangathan, CV, 8
Red River Delta, 78
Regional
• Economic System, 58
• Groupings, 103
• Information Secretariat, 8
Religion and Espionage, 121
Religious Fundamentalism, 14-15, 162
Republic of Vietnam, 75
Republic of-, 137
• Australia, 137
• Japan, 137
• Korea, 137
• New Zealand, 137
• Philippines, 137
• Taiwan, 137
Re-Unification of Vietnam, 76
Revolution in Military Affairs (RMA), 120
Ridnan Isamuddin Hambali, 50, 69
River Mekong, 79
River Port of Bhamo, 59
RMA, 142

Roh, Pres., 128
Royes, Angelo, 70
Russia, 17, 59, 119-20, 131-32, 161, 170, 176-77, 213
Russia, Japan, 106
Russian and Americans, 20
Russia—Vietnam, 117

S

SAARC, 108, 199, 205
Sabah and Sarawak, 104
Saddam, 68
Saddam Regime, 141
Saigon, 76, 80
Sarawak and Sabah Provinces, 51-52
Sarawara, 71
Satellite Telephones, 38
Science and Technology, 8, 120, 205, 212
Scud Missiles, 143
Sculptures in-, 18
- Laos, 18
- Myanmar, 18
- Vietnam, 18

SEA, 58, 77, 84, 91, 95, 98, 124, 135, 137-38, 140, 142, 145, 152-54, 156, 174, 176-77, 183-89, 196, 198-200, 208-11, 213, 215, 217, 227, 230
- Convention (UN), 95
- Countries, 100, 113, 152, 156, 172, 218, 220, 222
- Nuclear Weapons Free Zone, (SEANWAFZ), 195

Sea of Japan, 125, 132
Sea Routes, 7
Sea Trade, 100, 104, 106, 113, 116-17, 120
SEATO, 24-25, 103-04, 150, 185, 186
Secessionist Movement, 160
Sectorian Violence, 160
Security, 14-15, 21, 88, 105, 107, 119, 129-32, 156-58, 171, 173, 178, 194, 205, 213, 215
- Alliance, 135
- Challenges, 230
- Concept of-, 13
- Concerns, 72, 85, 106, 129, 172
- Conventional, 49
- Environment, 11, 114
- Forces, 159, 171
- Implications of-, 7
- Internal, 35
- Management, 212
- National, 14-16
- Regional, 163
- Threats, 7, 14, 155, 169
- Ties, 177

Self Defence Forces (SDF), 177-79
Seol, 112
Shan and Kachin Rebels, 48
Shan and Karen Guerrillas, 48
Shan State Army, 48, 153
Siagon, 83
Siberia, 132
Sichuan, 59
Sikkim Issue, 201
Sikri, Rajiv, 8
Singapore, 11, 19-20, 24-26, 28, 40, 51-54, 62-65, 91, 103-04, 110-11, 114-15, 136, 139, 141, 143, 145, 149, 154-58, 160, 167, 172, 174, 184, 188-89, 196, 200, 202

Z

Zinni, Genl, 37

Zone of Peace, Freedom and Neutrality (ZOPFAN), 105